FROM A PAINTING BY MATTHEW H. JOUETT.

COLONEL JOHN ALLEN.

Historic Families of Kentucky.

WITH SPECIAL REFERENCE TO STOCKS IMMEDIATELY
DERIVED FROM THE VALLEY OF VIRGINIA; TRACING
IN DETAIL THEIR VARIOUS GENEALOGICAL CONNEX-
IONS AND ILLUSTRATING FROM HISTORIC SOURCES
THEIR INFLUENCE UPON THE POLITICAL AND SOCIAL
DEVELOPMENT OF KENTUCKY AND THE STATES OF
THE SOUTH AND WEST.

BY

THOMAS MARSHALL GREEN.

GENEALOGICAL PUBLISHING CO., INC.
BALTIMORE   1975

Originally Published
Cincinnati, 1889

Reprinted
Genealogical Publishing Co., Inc.
(Regional Publishing Company, Affiliate)
Baltimore, 1959

Baltimore, 1964

Baltimore, 1966

Baltimore, 1975

Library of Congress Catalogue Card Number 64-8604
International Standard Book Number 0-8063-7958-8

Made in the United States of America

PREFATORY.

In his interesting "Sketches of North Carolina," it is stated by Rev. W. H. Foote, that the political principle asserted by the Scotch-Irish settlers in that State, in what is known as the "Mecklenburg Declaration of Independence," of the right to choose their own civil rulers, was the legitimate outgrowth of the religious principle for which their ancestors had fought in both Ireland and Scotland—that of their right to choose their own religious teachers. After affirming that "The famous book, *Lex Rex*, by Rev. Samuel Rutherford, was full of principles that lead to Republican action," and that the Protestant emigrants to America from the North of Ireland had learned the rudiments of republicanism in the latter country, the same author emphasizes the assertion that "these great principles they brought with them to America."

In writing these pages the object has been, not to tickle vanity by reviving recollections of empty titles, or imaginary dignities, or of dissipated wealth; but, in a plain and simple manner, to trace from their origin in this country a number of Kentucky families of Scottish extraction, whose ancestors, after having been seated in Ireland for several generations, emigrated to America early in the eighteenth century and became the pioneers of the Valley of Virginia, to the communities settled in which they gave their own distinguishing characteristics. A later generation of these same families of the Valley were also among the early pioneers of Kentucky, and here, too, impressed the qualities transmitted to them upon the people of the Commonwealth they helped to found. Connected with them in the process of intermarriage are many families of a different origin and from other parts of Virginia. Apart from the bare genealogical details of dates and intermarriages, the writer has derived a personal gratification in relating the public services of many of the persons mentioned in all the struggles of the country for independence and existence; and in dwelling upon the marked and beneficent influence they have exerted, individually and as families, upon the material progress, the educational and religious advancement, and the political action of the Commonwealth, as well as upon the martial spirit exhibited by them and their descendants upon the battle-fields of the country.

Among the families, some account of whom is attempted briefly to be given, are those of: Alexander, Allen, Anderson, Andrews, Ball, Barbour, Bell, Benton, Birney, Blair, Bowman, Brashear, Breckinridge, Brown, Buford, Bullitt, Burden, Butler, Campbell, Carlisle, Carrington, Carson, Caruthers, Carthrae, Chrisman, Christian, Clarke, Clay, Crittenden, Cummings, Dickson, Drake, Duke, Fontaine, Frogg, Hall, Harbeson, Hardin, Harvey, Harvie, Hawkins, Helm, Innes, Irvine, Gordon, Jones, Keith, Kirk, Le Grand, Lewis, Logan, Luke, Lyle, Madison, Marshall, McAlpine, McClure, McClarty, McClung, McDowell, McKnight, McPheeters, Metcalfe, Miller, Moffett, Monroe, Montgomery, Moore, Murray, Neil, Newton, Patton, Parker, Paxton, Pepper, Pickett, Preston, Price, Randolph, Reade, Reed, Reid, Smith, Starling, Stuart, Strother, Taylor, Thornton, Todd, Venable, Warner, Washington, Woodson, Wallace. Besides these the names of many other families omitted in this list occur in the narrative.

Maysville, Ky., *December*, 1888.

HISTORIC FAMILIES OF KENTUCKY.

THE McDOWELLS.

Of all the fierce and warlike septs that ranged themselves beside the Campbells, under the leadership of the
chiefs of that name, in the struggles so replete with deeds
of crime and heroism, of oppression and stubborn resistance, which had their fruit in the overthrow of the right
line of the Stuarts, there was none more respectable, nor
one which more perfectly illustrated the best qualities of
their race than the sons of Dowall. Sprung from Dougall,
the son of Ronald, the son of the great and famous Som-
erled, they had, from the misty ages, marched and fought
under the cloudberry bush, as the badge of their clan, and
had marshaled under the banner of the ancient Lords of
Lorn, the chiefs of their race. The form of McDowell
was adopted by those of the McDougal clan who held lands
in Galloway, to which they, the Black Gaels, had given its
name. The latter branch became allied by blood and intermarriages with the Campbells. Presbyterians of the strictest sect, and deeply imbued with that love of civil and religious freedom which has ever characterized the followers
of John Knox, they found their natural leaders in the
house of Argyle. In what degree related to the chiefs of
the name was the McDowell who left behind him the hills
of his native Argyleshire, to settle with others of his name
and kindred and religion in the North of Ireland, during
the Protectorate of Cromwell, can not be accurately stated;
he was, so far as can be gleaned from vague traditions,
one of the most reputable of the colonists who there
founded the race known as the " Scotch-Irish," the characteristics of which have since been so splendidly attested

1   (1)

by its heroes, scholars, orators, theologians and statesmen all over the world. This Scotch colonist, McDowell, had, among other children, a son named Ephraim, which, of itself, indicates that he was a child of the Covenant. It was fitting that Ephraim McDowell should become, at the early age of sixteen years, one of the Scotch-Irish Presbyterians who flew to the defense of heroic Londonderry, on the approach of McDonnell of Antrim, on the 9th of December, 1688, and that he should be one of the band who closed the gates against the native Irishry, intent on blood and rapine. During the long siege that followed, the memory of which will ever bid defiance to the effacing hand of time, and in which the devoted preacher, George Walker, and the brave Murray, at the head of their undisciplined fellow-citizens—farmers, shopkeepers, mechanics and apprentices—but Protestants, *Presbyterians*—successfully repelled the assaults of Rosen, Marmont, Persignan and Hamilton—the McDowell was conspicuous for endurance and bravery in a band where all were brave as the most heroic Greek who fell at Thermopylæ. The maiden name of the woman who became the worthy helpmeet of the Londonderry soldier boy was Margaret Irvine, his own full first cousin. She was a member of an honorable Scotch family who settled in Ireland at the same time as their kinspeople, the McDowells. The names of Irvin, Irvine, Irving, Irwin and Erwin are identical—those bearing the name thus variously spelled being branches from the same tree. The name was and is one of note in Scotland, where those who bore it had intermarried with the most prominent families of the kingdom, breeding races of soldiers, statesmen, orators and divines.

EPHRAIM McDOWELL,

who fought at Boyne river, as well as at Londonderry, was already an elderly man, when, with his two sons, John and James, his daughters, Mary and Margaret, and numerous kinsmen and co-religionists, he emigrated to America to build for himself and his a new home. In his interesting "Sketches of Virginia," Foote states that he was accompanied to Virginia by his wife, and that his son John was a widower when he left Ireland; but, as in the deposition of Mrs. Mary E. Greenlee, the daughter of Ephraim, her father, her brother John, her husband, and herself, are designated as composing the party emigrating to Virginia from Pennsylvania, and no mention is anywhere made of her mother, Mr. Foote is probably in error; and the uniform tradition of the family is more likely to be correct—that the wife of Ephraim McDowell died in Ireland, and that John McDowell had never been married until he came to America. The exact date of his arrival in Pennsylvania is not known. The journal of Charles Clinton—the founder of the historic family of that name in New York—gives an account of his voyage from the county of Longford, in the good ship "George and Ann," in company with the "John of Dublin," having many McDowells aboard as his fellow passengers. The "George and Ann" set sail on the 9th of May, 1729. On the 8th of June, a child of James McDowell died, and was thrown overboard; several other children of the same afterward died; also a John McDowell, and the sister, brother and wife of Andrew McDowell. The ship reached land, on the coast of Pennsylvania, on the 4th day of September, 1729. Whether or not the conjecture that Ephraim McDowell was a passenger with his kindred on board this ship at that time is correct, it is certain that about the same time he and his family, and numerous other McDowells, Irvines, Campbells, McElroys, and Mitchells, came over together, and settled in the same Pennsylvania county.

In Pennsylvania, Ephraim McDowell remained several years. There his son, John, was married to Magdalena Wood, whose mother was a Campbell, and, as tradition has it, of the noble family of Argyle. There Samuel, the eldest son of John and Magdalena McDowell, was born, in 1735. There, too, probably, Mary, the daughter of Ephraim, met, was beloved by, and married James Greenlee, a Presbyterian Irishman, of English descent, and said to have been remotely descended from the Argyle Camp-

bells. Some years before, a near relative of Ephraim Mc-
Dowell, by name

JOHN LEWIS,

had left Ireland, a fugitive; Sir Mungo Campbell, an op-
pressive landlord, had attempted in a lawless and brutal
manner to evict him from premises of which he held a
freehold lease, had slain before his eyes an invalid brother,
and, with one of his cruel henchmen, had died the death
of the unrighteous beneath the strong hand of Lewis.
First seeking refuge in Portugal, where lived a brother of
his wife, he was by him advised to find a safer asylum in
the great central valley of Pennsylvania, whither were
then flocking many of the Protestants of Ulster. His first
resting place was at Lancaster, where he was in time
joined by his sons, Samuel, Thomas, and Andrew, and by
his noble wife, Margaret Lynn. The latter was a native
of Ireland. Her ancestors, the chiefs of their clan, derived their patronymic from the beautiful Loch, on whose
banks in Scotland nestled their homes, and in the mountains, reflected by the translucent waters of which, they
hunted. He landed in Pennsylvania the same year that
brought the McDowells to America—1729. Leaving his
family among their kindred and countrymen in Pennsylvania, and thence turning his footsteps southward, in
Williamsburg, then the seat of government and learning
in Virginia, he listened with wondering admiration to the
description of the fertility and picturesque beauty of the
country lying west of the great mountains, as given by
Salling. This adventurer had been captured by the Indians of the Upper Tennessee; had hunted with them
around the salt and sulphur springs of Kentucky; and,
captured again from the Cherokees by the Illinois Indians,
had with the latter penetrated the prairies of Kaskaskias,
and thence roved to the Gulf of Mexico. His poetic fancy
set aglow by the account of the clear streams, fertile soil,
luxuriant herbage, and wood-crowned hills of the valley
immediately beyond the Blue Mountains, Lewis determined there to seek a home for himself and a fortune for
his posterity; and John Lewis, John Salling, and John

Mackey set out together on a voyage of discovery in this new land of Canaan. His expectations more than realized, in the summer of 1732, Lewis removed his family from Lancaster to a body of land he had selected a few miles from the present city of Staunton, in the midst of the large tract afterward patented by Governor Gooch to Wm. Beverly, two of the Randolphs, and John Robinson, and called "The Beverly Manor." He named his place Bellefont, from an immense spring whose crystal waters gushed from the side of the eminence on which he built the stone fort so long and grimly held by the stout Irishman and his warrior sons. Shortly afterward, he obtained the grant of 100,000 acres, which he located principally on the waters of the Greenbrier river. That John Lewis and Ephraim McDowell were related, and had been friends in Ireland, appears from the deposition of Mrs. Mary Greenlee, the daughter of the latter, in 1806, in the suit of Joseph Burden *v.* Alex. Cueton and others. The degree of the kinship is not stated; but, from the similarity of Christian names in the two families, and other circumstances, it is believed their mothers were sisters. The mother of John Lewis was a Miss Calhoun. In most of the references to him it has been said that his father was the son of a French Huguenot, who fled to Ireland after the revocation of the Edict of Nantes; an error that is none the less singular from the fact that John Lewis himself, the grandson of the alleged refugee, was born in Ireland, of an Irish mother, in 1678, fully eight years before the revocation. Lewis is not a French name, but is as distinctively Welsh as Llewellyn—from whom their descent is more likely than from any Frenchman—or Howell, or Griffith. Of those bearing the name now in Ireland, there is not a family that does not directly trace itself to a Welsh origin. In Cromwell's time, Welshmen of the name were among the Protestant settlers in Ulster, and from these the soldier race of the valley unquestionably came. More certainly than their name itself, their immense size, herculean strength, martial bearing, dauntless courage, thin, fair skins, and every physical, mental and moral characteristic, attest their mingled Pictish

and Celtic origin. In the "Chronicles of Border Warfare," by Alexander S. Withers, published in 1831, and
now out of print, it is stated that Jane Lynn, the sister
of Margaret, the heroic wife of John Lewis, married in
Ireland John Paul, son of Hugh Paul, the Bishop of Not-
tingham; by whom she had three children: John, who
became a Roman Catholic priest, and died on the eastern
shore of Maryland; Audley, who was for ten years an officer in the British army, in the colonial service; and
Polly, who married the brave George Matthews, distinguished as a soldier in all the Indian wars and in the Revolution, and afterward governor of Georgia. John Paul,
the husband of Jane Lynn, was a partizan of the Stuarts,
and fell in the siege of Dalrymple castle, in 1745. Jane,
his widow, married John Stuart. The latter was an intimate friend of Robert Dinwiddie, and, with many other
adventurers, accompanied Dinwiddie to America, where he
was made governor of Virginia, bringing with him the
three step-children above named. By John Stuart, Jane
Lynn had issue, the celebrated Colonel John Stuart, of
Greenbrier, and Betsy, who became the wife of Colonel
Richard Woods of Albemarle, whose daughter is also said
to have been the wife of George Matthews. Colonel John
Stuart, of Greenbrier, distinguished himself at Point Pleasant, as a captain under his cousin, General Andrew Lewis.

BURDEN'S GRANT.

James McDowell, the second son of the Londonderry
soldier, had planted corn and made a settlement on the
South river, in the Beverly manor, in the spring of 1737,
and thither the remaining members of the family determined to proceed and pitch their tents. Accordingly, in
the fall of that year, Ephraim and John McDowell and
James and Mary Greenlee left Pennsylvania, traversed the
lower valley of the Shenandoah, intending to locate not
far from John Lewis, and had reached Sewell's creek,
where they went into camp. The fires had been lighted,
and arrangements made for the evening meal, when a
weary stranger, coming up, solicited their hospitality. It

was Benjamin Burden (or Borden, as the name is spelt by those of the family who clung to New Jersey, and gave its designation to Bordentown), an Englishman, who had recently come over as the agent of Lord Fairfax, the proprietor of the Northern Neck. Meeting, at Williamstown, with John Lewis, in 1736, he had accepted the cordial invitation of the latter to visit him at Bellefont, had chased the roaming buffalo with the hospitable Irishman and his stalwart sons, and, with their assistance, had taken a buffalo calf, which, carrying as a trophy to Williamsburg, he presented to Governor Gooch. Pleased with what was then a curiosity in tide-water Virginia, and anxious, besides, to promote the extension of the frontier, and the settlement of hardy pioneers, as a means of protection and defense to the more populous lower country, Sir William issued to Burden a patent for 500,000 acres of land, or any less quantity, situated on the Shenandoah or James rivers, not interfering with previous grants, on condition that, within ten years, he should settle, on the lands so located, not less than 100 families; 1,000 acres for every family settled or cabin built, with the privilege of purchasing an additional adjacent 1,000 acres at one shilling per acre. Making himself known to the McDowells, and producing the patents as proof of his rights, he informed them that he had located 10,000 acres in the forks of the James river, to which he could not find his way, and stated he would give 1,000 acres to any one who would pilot him to his possessions. John McDowell was a man of education, a practical and skillful surveyor. He accepted Burden's proposition; writings were entered into to complete the agreement; and finally the whole party agreed to settle in "Burden's Grant," and to assist him in conforming to its conditions. The next day proceeding to John Lewis', and remaining there a few days until all the stipulations of the contract could be reduced to writing, they then went on until they came to the lands upon which Burden had the privilege to enter, building their cabins in what is now Rockbridge county, not far from the present town of Lexington—Ephraim and John McDowell and James Greenlee, the first three settlers in all that region. Complying with their agreement with Burden, they immediately entered into communication and opened negotiations with their kindred, friends and co-religionists in Pennsylvania, Ireland and Scotland, soon drawing around them other Scotch and Scotch-Irish families—McClungs, McCues, Mc-Cowns, McElroys, McKees, McCampbells, McPheeters, Campbells, Stuarts, Paxtons, Lyles, Irvines, Caldwells, Calhouns, Alexanders, Cloyds,—names which have since gloriously illustrated every page of Western and Southern history. In the field, at the bar, in the pulpit, in the senate, on the bench, on the hustings, every-where, by their courage, eloquence, learning and patriotism they have made themselves conspicuous, making famous their own names and building up the country with whose history and growth they are inseparably identified. Burden lived in the Grant until near the time of his death, in 1742. His daughter had married in Ireland, James Patton, a ship owner and master, a man of some property, acquired by "privateering" on the Spanish main, and of great energy and force of character; and Elizabeth, a sister of James Patton, had married John Preston, a Protestant Irishman of English descent, of large and handsome person and of good character. Having, through the McDowells, fulfilled the conditions of his "Grant," Burden induced his son-in-law, James Patton, to seek an increase of fortune in the New World; and with Patton, or shortly after him, came his brother-in-law, John Preston, with his family— his son William, and his daughters Lettice and Margaret having been born in Ireland. The emigration of the Pattons and Prestons took place April, 1740. They settled near Staunton, where Preston continued to live, and died.

Remarkable in many ways, other than the great age of more than a century to which he lived, the span of Ephraim McDowell's life covered the overthrow of the Stuarts, the rise of the House of Hanover, the establishment of the empire of Britain in India and over the seas, the wresting of New York from the Dutch, and the expulsion of the French from North America; the erection of the electorate of Brandenburg into the kingdom of Prussia; the victories of Marlborough and Eugene and of the great Frederick; the consolidation of the Russian empire under Peter and his successors; the opening of the great West by the daring pioneers, and the growth of liberalism in Great Britain, France and America. Foremost of the virtuous and hardy community, planted chiefly by his influence and exertions, he and his associates erected school-houses and churches in the Valley, even before they constructed forts. Eminently useful and practical in the character of his mind and the manner of his life, Howe records the fact that he built the first road across the Blue Ridge, to connect the Valley with the tide-water country, at once affording a mode of egress for the productions of the former, and facilities for receiving from the merchants of the latter the manufactures of the Old World. Religious, moral, intelligent and shrewd, the singular and beneficent influence he acquired among the independent and intrepid spirits by whom he was surrounded, was a natural tribute to his virtue, sagacity and unflinching devotion to the cause of civil and religious liberty he had all his life upheld. It is scarcely necessary to state of such a man, at once hospitable and provident, that he failed not to use the opportunities with which fair and generous nature had surrounded him to reap and store a fortune considered very large in those days. Retaining full possession of all his faculties to the very last, he died not until the outbreak of the Revolutionary war, and not until he had heard the praises bestowed on his grandchildren for good conduct shown at the battle of Point Pleasant.

MARY E. GREENLEE.

The oldest daughter of Ephraim McDowell was Mary E. Greenlee, a woman so remarkable for her intelligence, uncommon sense, unusual strength of character, and great physical endurance, that, as tradition reports, the superstitious of her Scotch-Irish neighbors were not without misgivings that her life was lengthened to the 104 years allotted to her, by the powers of witchcraft. Born in 1711,

she was in the camp, enduring all the trials incident to the
toilsome journey through the roadless wilderness into a
region then unpeopled and almost unknown, when Burden
approached the party; and was the first white woman ever
within the Grant. From her deposition, taken in 1806,
when she was ninety-five years old, is gleaned all that is
known concerning that early settlement. To the end of
her long life she rode, erect, on horseback over all the
country-side, giving an active personal supervision to her
business affairs, in which she was at once thrifty and prosperous. In his history of Augusta county, Mr. Peyton
dwells at undue length upon the alleged suspicions of the
ignorant that this remarkable woman was possessed of mi-
raculous powers—suspicions to which a voice was scarcely
given, and which were tributes to the brightness and vigor
of her mental faculties and the robustness of a constitution that had been strengthened by a pure and simple life,
and not arising from any apprehensions they entertained
of experiencing injury at her hands. She aided in re-
deeming the valley from the Indians; helped to fit out the
soldiers who fought in the French and Indian war; saw
the men march who conquered, and mourned over her kindred who fell, at Point Pleasant; watched the pioneers as
they started on their exploring and hunting expeditions
into Kentucky and the North-western Territory; made
clothing for the heroes of the Revolution; and rejoiced at
the news of the defeat of the British at New Orleans.
Before the death of her husband, she had borne him eight
children, whose descendants number hundreds, and are
among the most prominent and reputable citizens of Virginia and of the Carolinas. John Greenlee, her oldest
son, was the first white child born in the grant—in 1738;
he married Hannah, daughter of Elijah McClanahan, a
name famous in all the forays of the border land and
on many a hard-fought field in the Revolution. Elijah
Greenlee, one of the three sons of John and Hannah
Greenlee, born in 1772, was an eminent surgeon of the
United States army, and died in Milledgeville, Georgia.
Another son, John, removed to Kentucky, and died in this

state. The eldest son, James, born in 1769, married Mary, daughter of William Paxton and Jane Griggsby, both belonging to families which have become distinguished in Virginia and in Kentucky; the mother of Sam. Houston, the President of Texas, was a Paxton, while the Griggsbys gave to literature a brilliant light in the person of the historian, Hugh Blair Griggsby. James Greenlee and Mary Paxton had, among other children, a daughter, Hannah, who married James D. Davidson, a distinguished lawyer of Lexington, Virginia; their son, James Greenlee Davidson, died the death of a hero at Chancellorsville; their son Frederick fell gloriously at the first battle of Manassas; and Albert was killed in battle in South-western Virginia the day before the Southern cause went down at Appomattox. James Greenlee and Mary E. McDowell had a second son, also named James, born in 1740. He went first to North Carolina, but settled finally in South Carolina, where he married his first cousin, Mary Mitchell, daughter of his mother's youngest sister. This James Greenlee and Mary Mitchell had a son named John Mitchell Greenlee, who also married his full cousin, Mary Greenlee,.the only daughter of John Greenlee and Hannah McClanahan, already mentioned; and this John Mitchell Greenlee and Mary Greenlee had an only son, Colonel James Harvey Greenlee, who completed this singular interweaving of close kindred by also marrying his full first cousin, Hannah Ann Eliza Greenlee, the daughter of his father's brother. Colonel James Harvey Greenlee, a double great-grandson of Mrs. Mary E. (McDowell) Greenlee, is still living in his ancestral home at Turkey Cove, North Carolina, at the age of seventy-five years, a man of handsome fortune, and a splendid type of the intermingling of the races of the McDowells, Greenlees, McClanahans, Paxtons, and Griggsbys. Grizel Greenlee, one of the daughters of James and Mary E. (McDowell) Greenlee, first married Captain John Bowman; afterward, General Charles McDowell, a distinguished kinsman of a branch of the family which, coming to America some years after old Ephraim, followed him to Virginia, at first locating in the lower part of the valley, near Winchester, and then struck out for themselves into North Carolina, where they won and wore reputations as the grimmest of rough and ready fighters. It would be interesting to follow these Greenlees through all their branches and generations; but this is intended more as a sketch than as a genealogical table.

THE MITCHELLS.

Margaretta, the second daughter of Ephraim McDowell, married James Mitchell, also born in Ireland, and, from his name, probably one of those who came over in the "George and Ann." Removing to North, and then to South Carolina, in the latter state they prospered and accumulated large wealth. Many children were born to them, of whom one, Mary, married, as stated above, James Greenlee. Inheriting the fighting qualities of their rugged progenitor, the old Presbyterian Ephraim, they were all the staunchest of Whigs in the Revolution. Four of Margaretta's sons were officers of the line in that struggle. Two laid down their lives at Camden. A third there received the ghastly wound from which he died after agonized lingering. A fourth, Major Mitchell, was captured at Charleston. Among the respectable and reputable families of South Carolina, none are more so than the Mitchells and the descendants of Margaretta McDowell bearing other names. In Kentucky, there is but one branch of her descendants known to the writer—that of Mr. Thomas Mitchell, the former venerable cashier of the Bank of Kentucky, at Danville. One of his sons, in wedding the beautiful Mary Marshall, married back among his McDowell kindred. His only daughter, Louisa Mitchell, is the wife of Rev. Thomas Clelland, the Presbyterian minister at Springfield, Missouri —from a family which has given many ministers to the church.

JAMES McDOWELL,

the second son of Ephraim, the first of the family who went to Virginia, and raised corn in the Beverly manor, in the spring of 1737, had an active part in the defense of the valley from Indian raids. A gallant soldier in the

French and Indian wars, the official records of those campaigns show that he had won and held the rank of lieutenant in an Augusta company. He married near Williamsburg. Leaving no male issue, very little is known of
the descendants of his daughters.

CAPTAIN JOHN MCDOWELL,

the oldest son of Ephraim, was born in Ireland, where he
was educated and grew to manhood. In Pennsylvania,
probably in 1734, he married Magdalena Wood. When
he located in Burden's Grant, in 1737, he was in the prime
of a vigorous manhood. Most active in colonizing the beautiful valley with his co-religionists and clansmen and kinsmen of Scotch-Irish blood, he was a man of mark, and natural leader of spirits as self-reliant, independent, and bold
as any the world ever saw. Well instructed in the branches
of a practical English education, he was a skillful and accurate surveyor, a branch of knowledge perhaps more
useful and certainly more remunerative in the then situation of the frontier than almost any other. It was he
who, assisted by one Wood, made the first survey of the
Grant, and determined its boundaries. Intelligent, energetic, and of proved courage, when concerting measures
for their joint defense, the eyes of the community, at whose
head he stood, instinctively turned to him, as endowed with
the qualities for command. Their petition to Governor
Gooch to commission him as a captain, as the initial step
to organize for the protection of the people " of the backwoods," is recorded in Palmer's publication of Virginia
state papers, under date of 1742. A marvel of spelling, it
reminds the tardy governor of their previous application
for the legal organization of a military force to provide
against impending peril, and in respectful but forcible language, insists upon his immediate action; it enumerates
the names of men whom the petitioners had furnished the
governor, as those for whom appointments as officers were
desired, and whom the " people of the backwoods "—
" thought properist men & men that had Hart and Curidg
to hed us in ye times of —— & to defend your Countray and

your poor Sobjacks Intrist from ye voilince of ye Hai-
then,"—and at the head of these "men of Hart and Cur-
idge," stands the name of John McDowell as that of the
man they had chosen as their chieftain. The petition was
signed, among others, by Andrew and David Moore, George
Moffett, James McDowell and Matthew Lyle; its prayer
was speedily granted by Governor Gooch, whose confidence and respect had already been won by McDowell's
manly qualities. Fixing his own habitation near where
the far-famed Timber Ridge Church was afterward built,
the brief space of life left to him after his removal
to the Valley was passed in providing for the educational wants and religious yearnings of those whom
he had induced to settle in the Grant, and in organizing for their mutual defense against the Indians. The
fruits of his labor and daring he did not live to enjoy; on
Christmas day of 1742, with eight of his men, who had
accompanied him in pursuit of savages who had made an
inroad upon the settlement, he fell into an ambuscade and
was killed; all were buried in one common grave, near
Lexington. His widow afterward married Benjamin Burden, Jr., son of the grantee, who had come into the Grant
before John McDowell's death, and, for a long time, lived
at his house, but had returned to his father's before the
massacre in which McDowell fell. After the death of the
elder Burden, the younger returned into the Grant, fully
empowered, by the will of his father, to complete titles
and make deeds, and then married the widow, Magdalena
McDowell, continuing to live with her until his death, at
the place near the Timber Ridge, called the Red House,
where John McDowell had settled. The widow, Magdalena McDowell, and the junior Benjamin Burden had one
daughter, Martha, who married Benjamin Hawkins—a
name noted in Virginia, North Carolina, Kentucky, and
all the way to Texas, for the oddity of some, and the gallantry of *all* of its members. The wife of John Todd,
who fell at Blue Licks; the mother of the gallant and honorable Butlers, of Carrolton; Colonel Ben. and General
William Hawkins, of North Carolina: Colonel John Haw-

kins, who was adjutant of the Third Virginia Infantry, during the Revolution, and afterward removed to Scott county, Kentucky—father of Augustus Hawkins, of Lexington, and the maternal ancestor of the Harvies, of Frankfort; the brave Colonel Thomas T. Hawkins, of Kentucky, and General Joseph Hawkins, of Texas, were all of the same game breed. Thomas Mitchell, the old cashier at Danville, was not only descended on his father's side from James Mitchell and Margaretta McDowell—daughter of old Ephraim—but, on his mother's side, was also descended from Benjamin Hawkins and Martha Burden—the daughter of Magdalena Wood (John McDowell's widow) by her second husband. After the death of Ben. Hawkins, his widow, Martha (Burden), married Robert Harvey. Her daughter by her first husband, Magdalena Hawkins, married Matthew Harvey, a younger brother of Robert; and from this latter marriage descended Maria Hawkins Harvey, who married her relative, Wm. A. McDowell, and was the mother of Henry C. McDowell, of Lexington, of Mrs. Bland Ballard, of Louisville, and Miss Margaretta McDowell, the accomplished artist and architect. After the death of her second husband, Magdalena Wood-McDowell-Burden married a third time, Colonel Bowyer, a gentleman twenty years younger than herself. The 104 years to which she lived, gave ample time for a full repentance of this singular matrimonial adventure. Tradition states that Colonel Bowyer destroyed the marital settlement by which the wary Magdalena had essayed to secure her property to herself and children. He outlived her; thousands of acres of the sightly lands which John McDowell owned thus passed into the hands of Bowyers.

THE MOFFETTS.

Captain John McDowell and Magdalena Wood had three children—Samuel, James, and Sarah. The latter married George Moffett, probably a son of the Captain John Moffett, whose name appears among the Scotch-Irish emigrants who early settled in the "Manor" and in the "Grant." After the death of the father of George Moffett, the widow married John Trimble, grandfather of the distinguished Allen Trimble, Governor of Ohio. George Moffett bore a manly part in the French and Indian war, and in all the subsequent border warfare with the savage foe. His step-father, John Trimble, fell a victim in one of their murderous raids; several members of his family and many of the neighbors were captured and carried off. The large band of savage murderers were swiftly pursued by Captain George Moffett and his hardy company, overtaken at Kerr's creek, were attacked with vigor, and defeated with heavy loss; the despairing victims were released and returned to their friends. Among them was James Trimble, half brother of Captain Moffett, and father of Governor Allen Trimble. Their common mother was Mary Christian, daughter of Robert Christian and Mary Richardson, of Ireland. Captain Moffett was in turn ambuscaded and repulsed by the Indians at Falling creek, in Alleghany county. In the Revolution, from the beginning to the end of which he fought with honorable distinction, he held the rank of colonel. His services against the southern Indians and the Tories were valuable. At King's Mountain, the Cowpens, and Guilford Court-house, he won fresh laurels. As a friend and promoter of education, as one of the founders of the academy at Lexington, which first grew into a college and then into a university, he was not less prominent than as a soldier. Colonel George Moffett and Sarah McDowell had eleven children. Of these, the oldest, Margaretta, married her relative, Colonel Joseph McDowell, of North Carolina—a younger brother of the General Charles McDowell already mentioned as the second husband of Grizel, or Grace, Green-lee. Besides being of near blood kin to old Ephraim, these North Carolina McDowells are so interwoven with his descendants by frequent intermarriages, and are so like them in appearance and all physical, mental, and moral traits, that no sketch of the family would be complete that did not contain some account of them.

THE NORTH CAROLINA BRANCHES.

Joseph McDowell, Sr., the father of General Charles and Colonel Joe, was born in Ireland in 1715. There his gallant bearing won the heart of Margaret O'Neil, descended from ancient Irish kings, and a member of one of the proudest families of the old native Celtic race; it was the boast of the O'Neils that not one of the name, neither in battle nor in private quarrel, had ever turned his back upon a foeman. The fair Margaret's family did not look with favor upon the young McDowell. Her reputed ancestor, Con O'Neil, for rebellion was laid in the King's castle, and his broad lands in Down and Antrim confiscated. His liberty was secured by surrendering two-thirds of his estate to Hugh Montgomery and James Hamilton— both Scots, and founders, respectively, of the houses of Ards and Claneboy. The two latter colonized their possessions thus obtained with their kinsmen, clansmen, and other Scots; and from the foundations thus laid, and from subsequent migrations to Ulster, sprung the hardy race of Scotch-Irish, of whom had come the Mc-Dowell. The O'Neils continued Catholics; the McDowells were Presbyterians—Covenanters at that. The O'Neils were of lofty station—wealthy even when stripped of two-thirds of their ancient patrimony; the sons of Scotch exiles were not apt to have been rich. Love laughs not only at locksmiths, but as well at the artificial distinctions of rank and class; yet frowns born of these considerations determined the young McDowell and the brave Margaret to encounter all perils in search of what better fortune might await them on this side of the ocean. They first settled in Pennsylvania. Thence they soon removed to Winchester, Virginia, where a colony had been already planted on a patent issued to Joist Hite, a German, William Duff, of the Scotch family in Fife, to his nephew, Robert Green, a Welshman, and to others—the first settlement west of the Blue Ridge. There their sons, General Charles and Colonel Joe McDowell, were born; the former in

2

1743; the latter in 1756. The elder Joseph McDowell had all
the fighting qualities of the breed, and they were not curbed
by the fair O'Neil. He had a part in the early defense of the
border; in the French and Indian war he was a captain
from Frederick; his name and rank are mentioned in
Henning's Statutes; he was one of those who fought when
Braddock fell. His brother, afterward known as "Hunting John" McDowell, who had emigrated from Ireland
with him, had early removed from Frederick to the Catawba country of North Carolina, some time prior to 1758,
settling in that beautiful tract which he well named the
"Pleasant Garden," a designation made historic by his
own deeds of valor, and those of his descendants. Not
long thereafter, "Hunting John" was followed to the ro-
mantic but then wild frontier region by his brother, Joseph McDowell, Sr., who pitched his tent and planted
vines at the "Quaker Meadows." There the sons grew to
manhood. Opportunities were many for vindicating their
right to the honorable name they bore—for proving the
quality of the stuff of which they were made. With the
manner in which they bore any test, and met every demand upon their manhood, the proudest of the O'Neils
would have had satisfaction. The exact degree of relationship between the elder Joseph McDowell and old
Ephraim is unknown; the former was probably a nephew,
or a cousin's son of the latter. General Charles McDowell
early embarked in the patriotic struggle for independence
in 1776. Discharging his duties well, he was promoted to
the command of the military district in which the victory
of King's Mountain was won; stoutly he had held the
mountain passes; and the summer before that memorable
fight had commanded the armies of militia assembled in
that quarter against the able British leader, Ferguson.
This fact entitled him to the command of the several regiments led against Ferguson at King's Mountain by Colonels Shelby, Sevier, William Campbell, Cleveland, Williams, and himself. Why he did not command or participate in that battle, is thus explained by Shelby, in his letter published in 1823, in reply to an attack made upon

him by Wm. C. Preston, of South Carolina: " Colonel Mc-
Dowell was a brave and patriotic man, but we considered
him too advanced in life and too inactive for the command
of such an enterprise as we were then engaged in. I was
sure he would not serve under a younger officer from his
own state, and hoped that his feelings would in some degree be saved by the appointment of Colonel Campbell. In this way, and upon my suggestion, was Colonel Campbell raised to the command, *and not upon account of any superior military talents or experience he was
supposed to possess.* He had no previous acquaintance
with any of the colonels, except myself, nor had he, at
that time, acquired any experience or distinction in war,
that we knew of. Colonel McDowell, *who had the good of
his country more at heart than any title of command,* sub-
mitted to what was done; but observed that, as he could
not be permitted to command, he would be the messenger
to go to head-quarters for the general officer. He accordingly started immediately, leaving his men under his
brother, Major Joseph McDowell, and Colonel Campbell
assumed the chief command. He was, however, to be
regulated and directed by the determinations of the colonels, who were to meet in council every day." Captain
John Bowman, the brave and successful Indian fighter,
who married Grizel Greenlee, having been killed in the
battle of Ramsour's Mills, June 20, 1780, General Charles
McDowell afterward married the widow, his relative.
They had several children, among them Captain Charles
McDowell, who, as late as 1851, lived on the fine plantation he had inherited from his father, on the Catawba
river, near Morgantown. General McDowell was a senator from Burke county in the state legislature in 1778,
and held the same office from 1782 to 1788. He died in
1815. His son, Captain Charles, represented Burke in the
House of Commons in 1809, '10, '11.

The reader who has followed these pages thus far, un-
derstands that Colonel Joseph McDowell, who married
Margaretta Moffett, was a brother of General Charles Mc-
Dowell, who married Grizel Greenlee, and that both were

sons of Joseph McDowell, Sr., of the Quaker Meadows, and his wife, Margaret O'Neil. The McDowells, in all their branches, were among the earliest to fly to arms for the patriot cause in the Revolution. In February, 1776, Joseph McDowell, Jr., then only twenty years of age, marched with his elder brother's regiment, as its major, on the expedition against the Scotch Tories. In July of that year, the Cherokees burst upon the Catawba settlements, killing thirty-seven persons, and beleaguering a fort containing a hundred and twenty women and children, and defended by Colonel Charles and Major Joe McDowell, with nine other men; the Indians were forced to retire before a resistance which was as desperate as it was skillful and intelligent. In the fall of the same year Major Joe served in Charles's regiment on Rutherford's campaign against the Cherokees, winning a high reputation as a shrewd and energetic commander. In 1779, on the Stono expedition, he earned new laurels as a vigilant soldier. During all the years that passed, from the beginning to the close of the struggle, he was constantly in arms, always on the alert, ever present where hard fighting had to be done. In 1780, he had a large share in the victory over the Tories at Ramsour's Mills, where Captain Bowman, the first husband of Grizel Greenlee, was killed. Earle's Ford on the Pacolet, Musgrove's Mill and the Cowpens, all bore witness to his gallantry and heroism. At the last-named engagement, he led the North Carolina troops, conspicuous even among the heroes whose valor overcame the discipline of the British veterans. [*Draper.*] At King's Mountain, in the absence of his brother, he commanded the regiment from Burke and Rutherford counties. Stationed on the right, with Shelby and Sevier, he served under the immediate observation of those experienced and stern fighters, with such invincible pluck as to extort from both the most generous praise. His men, with those of Shelby, were first engaged hotly, and pressed on by their commanders to the closest quarters. The bayonet charge down the mountain-side, by Ferguson's regulars, was driven back by the well-directed fire from the rifles of Shelby's and McDowell's men. The victory was complete. The characteristics of the man are well described by an incident related by Sharp as occurring while on the march after the victory. When the half-starved and shivering men reached his plantation at the Quaker Meadows, beside feeding them, he rode along the lines, and telling the soldiers that the plantation belonged to him, invited them to take rails from the fences to make fires by which to warm themselves. A short month before, when the two McDowells had been forced to retreat before Ferguson, some of the latter's officers had visited their home, presided over by their aged mother, Margaret O'Neil, ransacked the house, appropriating the clothing of the two brothers, tantalizing Margaret by telling her that when caught they would kill Charles outright, and after compelling Joe to beg for his life, in order to humiliate him, they would then kill him, also, while still upon his bended knees. Fearless as she was energetic, the daughter of the O'Neils and the mother of the McDowells, so far from being intimidated or overawed, bade them be careful lest all the begging should be done by themselves. These same officers, captured at King's Mountain, were brought as prisoners to the house they had despoiled, cold, wet and hungry. The rigid sense of justice of the aged mother at first revolted at bestowing shelter and food upon those "thieving Tories," as she called them in plain Irish; but, finally, yielding to the solicitations of the brave son, of whom she was so justly proud, she fed, warmed and clothed them. In the spring of 1781, Major Joseph McDowell served in a campaign against Cornwallis. In August of the same year, and again in March, 1782, he led the expeditions that so severely chastised the Cherokees; and in the fall of the latter year he commanded the Burke county regiment, in the expedition against the same troublesome and warlike tribe which was so successfully prosecuted by General Charles McDowell. He was a member of the North Carolina House of Commons from 1780 to 1788. During the most of this time, General Charles McDowell was in the senate from the same county; and, during a part of it, their

cousin, Joseph McDowell, of the "Pleasant Garden," son
of "Hunting John," was the associate of his namesake
in the house. From 1791 to 1795, Colonel Joseph was in
the state senate; twice he was elected to Congress, serving two terms in that body, opposing with energy the
alien and sedition laws. In 1788, he was a member of the
state convention which had under consideration the federal constitution, which he opposed, and which was rejected by the convention by a vote of 184 to 84. The
statement that he removed to Woodford county, Kentucky, is erroneous. He died at his home in the Quaker
Meadows in 1801, in the forty-fifth year of his age.
Moore, in his History of North Carolina, says of him that
"he was the recognized leader of the Republican party in
the western counties, and was as eminent for his sagacious
leadership in civil matters as he had been dauntless and
successful in the late war. He was no inconsiderable antagonist in debate, and throughout his life he was the idol
of the western people of North Carolina." After his
death, his family scattered, some returning to Virginia,
others going west. One of his sons, Hugh Harvey, removed to Missouri, where he became a prominent citizen,
and died there in 1859. Another son, Joseph Jefferson
McDowell, removed to Ohio, and was the distinguished
and able member of Congress from the Hillsboro district
from 1843 to 1847, having previously served with credit in
both branches of the Ohio State Legislature. While a
member of Congress, he attracted attention by his zealous
advocacy of the annexation of Texas, and his insistance
upon a vigorous prosecution of the war with Mexico. He
was a general of the Ohio militia, and an ardent Democrat.
His wife was Sarah Allen McCue, a daughter of Rev. John
McCue, an eminent Presbyterian minister, who succeeded
Dr. James Waddel in the pastorate of the Tinkling Spring
Church. The wife of Rev. John McCue, and mother of
Mrs. McDowell, was a daughter of James Allen, of Augusta county; one of her sisters was the mother of Gov-
ernor Allen Trimble. Two of the sons of Hon. Joseph
Jefferson McDowell removed to Richmond, Kentucky,

where one of them married a daughter of Judge Breck, and the other a Miss Rodes. Sarah, daughter of Colonel Joe McDowell, of the Quaker Meadows, married John Matthews, a native of Augusta county, who moved to Fayette county, Kentucky, where he died, in 1814; they had four children, one of whom was Rev. Joseph McDowell Matthews, of the Methodist Church, well known as the able and successful president of female colleges at Nicholasville, Kentucky, and Hillsboro, Ohio. Dr. Matthews was three times married, and left three children, one by his first and two by his second wife. Margaret, another daughter of Col. Joe McDowell, of the Quaker Meadows, and Margaret Moffett, married her kinsman by the half-blood, the distinguished Governor Allen Trimble, of Ohio, and was the mother of Rev. Joseph McDowell Trimble, of the Methodist Church; of Madison Trimble, of Hillsboro, Ohio; and of Colonel Wm. H. Trimble, of the same place. The latter represented Highland county in the legislature several terms, with marked ability. Though fifty years old when the civil war broke out, his inherited military spirit asserted itself; he recruited the Sixtieth Ohio Regiment, of a thousand men, and fought at their head in the battle of Cross Keys. The misfortunes of war transferring him to the command of Colonel Miles, the brigade which he commanded made a most gallant and persistent defense at Harper's Ferry against the assaults of more than three times their number, under Hill and Ewell; it was no fault of his that the slaughter-pen was captured by the Confederates. A fall from his horse compelled his resignation just as promotion was tendered him. Celia and Clarissa McDowell, daughters of Colonel Joe and Margaretta Moffett, married their relatives, Chrismans, and some of their relatives live in Jessamine county, Kentucky. Colonel Joseph McDowell was truly a worthy block from the gnarled Scotch-Irish tree which gave to this country a race so prolific of soldiers. His widow, Margaretta, after his death, returned to Virginia, and thence removed to Woodford county, Kentucky, where she died, in 1815. Mary, the second daughter of Colonel George Moffett and

Sarah McDowell, also married her relative, Captain or Major Joseph McDowell, a son of "Hunting John" McDowell, of the "Pleasant Garden." Her husband was the first cousin of the Major or Colonel Joe, who married her sister, Margaret. His father, "Hunting John," was the first of the McDowells to move to the Catawba country. Draper narrates that when Charles McDowell called the leading men of the Catawba valley together, in 1780, and, to meet the present emergency, suggested that they should repair to Gilbert Town, and there take British protection, as the only means of saving their live stock, which were essential to the support of the country—justifying it as a temporary expedient—"Hunting John" absolutely refused to adopt the suggestion. With others who agreed with him, he proposed to drive all the stock they could collect into the deep coves at the base of the Black Mountain, leaving to others the humiliating office of taking protection, in order to save the remainder. The distinguished Indian fighter, Captain John Carson, and the Davidsons, and others, were selected to take protection, which they did, deeming it justifiable and not unpatriotic under the circumstances. His son, Joseph McDowell, who married Mary Moffett, was born at the Pleasant Garden, February 25, 1758. A boy when the Revolution broke out, he immediately went into active service in the patriot army. He soon rose to a captaincy in the Burke regiment, of which his cousins Charles was the colonel and Joseph the major. He was with it in every fight in which it was engaged. At King's Mountain, while Major Joseph, of Quaker Meadows, acted as colonel, Captain Joseph, of Pleasant Garden, acted as major. Hence the dispute as to which of the two it was who commanded in that fight. They were equally brave, equally patriotic, equally able. Captain Joe, of the Pleasant Garden, is the one known in history as major, while he of the Quaker Meadows is known as colonel. Both were at the Cowpens, where Tarleton succumbed to the sturdy blows of the wagoner, Morgan. Serving from the beginning to the close of the war for independence, Major Joe possessed

the fighting characteristics which distinguished the breed
in all its branches. In the Rutherford campaign he killed
an Indian in single combat. Educated as a physician, his
distinction as a statesman was not less than that he won
as a soldier. As Joseph McDowell, Jr., he served in the
North Carolina House of Commons from 1787 to 1792.
McDowell county, North Carolina, was named for him.
He was also a member of the North Carolina Convention
of 1788, and was generally regarded as the brightest intellect of any of the North Carolina connection. He died in
1795, leaving several children. The late Colonel James
McDowell, a distinguished citizen of Yancey county,
North Carolina, was one of his sons; the Woodfins, of
the same county, are his descendants. John McDowell,
of Rutherford, an able member of the House of Commons
from 1820 to 1823, was another of his sons. One of his
daughters married her cousin, Captain Charles McDowell,
of Burke, son of General Charles and Grizel Greenlee.
Still another daughter married her cousin, Caleb, son of
Samuel McDowell, the oldest son of Captain John and
Magdalena Wood. After the death of Major Joseph Mc-
Dowell, his widow, Mary, married Captain John Carson,
the Indian fighter, already mentioned as having taken
British protection in 1780, and afterward a member of
Congress. By him she had a number of children, the
most conspicuous of whom was Hon. Samuel P. Carson, a
native and resident of Burke county, and equally distinguished for his activity of mind, energy of character, warm
and enthusiastic temper, and patriotic sentiments. Elected
to the state senate from Burke in 1822, he was re-elected
in 1824. In 1825, he was elected to Congress over Dr.
Robert B. Vance, and remained in that body as a useful
member until 1833. In his second contest with Dr. Vance,
in 1827, debates between them grew bitter and personal.
Dr. Vance sneeringly charged that Captain John Carson,
the venerable father of his antagonist, had been a Tory,
founding his assertion upon the fact that he had taken
protection under the circumstances already stated. The
aspersion was immediately and heatedly resented. The

duel that followed, in the fall of 1827, at Saluda Gap, in South Carolina, resulted in the fall of Dr. Vance with a severe wound, from which he soon died. Hon. S. P. Carson was succeeded in Congress by Hon. James Graham. Soon after 1833, he removed to Arkansas, in which state he died, in 1840. The esteem in which the breed was held in North Carolina is well attested by the fact that, from 1778 to 1850, Burke county was scarcely at any time without one of the connection in one or the other branch of the general assembly, in Congress, or in some other position of honor and trust—Charles and the two Joes, John M., the younger Charles, John, J. R., and James McDowell; John, William, and S. P. Carson; David and John Mitchell Greenlee; the Tates, Woodfins, and others;—and they still hold their own, there and elsewhere, in the old North State.

CHRISMANS.

When Joist Hite, the adventurous and intelligent German, made the first settlement in the valley of Virginia, in what is now the county of Frederick, his sons-in-law, Bowman and Chrisman, settled near him, on the Opequan, and soon thereafter the Scotch-Irish began to rear around them their habitations. Their "meeting house," a substantial stone building surrounded by oak trees, stood about three miles from Winchester, on the road leading to Staunton. The names of Bowman and Chrisman are of German origin. Both became famous in the Indian wars. The brave Captain John Bowman, who married Grizel Greenlee, and fell at Monsour's Mills, was a descendant of Hite. The Chrismans also spread themselves through the valley and into North Carolina. One of them, also a descendant of Hite, married a daughter of Joseph McDowell, Sr., of Quaker Meadows, a sister of General Charles, who married the widow of Captain John Bowman, and of Colonel Joseph, of the Quaker Meadows; the Hites, Bowmans, Chrismans, and the North Carolina McDowells, had been neighbors in Frederick county. This Chrisman, and the sister of the McDowells of the Quaker Meadows, had a number of children. Two of

them, Hugh, and Joseph Chrisman, Sr., came to Jessamine
county, Kentucky, where yet live many of their descendants, who have extensively intermarried back among their
McDowell kindred, as will be seen in its proper connection. We return to

THE MOFFETTS.

Magdalen, the third daughter of Colonel George and
Sarah (McDowell) Moffett, married James Cochran.
George M. Cochran, of Staunton, and John Cochran, of
Charlottesville, were their sons. George M. Cochran, Jr.,
great-grandson of Colonel George Moffett, married his
relative, Margaret Lynn Peyton, daughter of John Howe
Peyton—eminent as a lawyer, as a statesman, and as an
orator—and his second wife, Ann Montgomery Lewis,
who was a daughter of Major John Lewis and Mary Pres-
ton, a granddaughter of Colonel William Lewis, known
as the "Civilizer of the Border," and a great-grand-
daughter of the Irish John Lewis, the first settler in the
Beverly manor. John Cochran, grandson of Colonel Moffett, married Margaret Lynn Lewis, another daughter of
Major John Lewis. Colonel George Moffett's daughter,
Martha, married Captain Robert Kirk, of the United
States army; and his daughter, Elizabeth, married James
Miller, the owner of large iron works in Virginia. George
Moffett married a Miss Gilkerson, and removed to Ken-
tucky; while James Moffett, another son of Colonel
George, married Hannah Miller, sister of the above-named
James Miller. Colonel Henry McDowell Moffett was the
son of James and Hannah Moffett.

JAMES McDOWELL.

James, the second son of Captain John McDowell and
Magdalena Wood, was born at the Red House, near Fair-
field, Rockbridge county, in 1739. He died early, in 1771,
but not before he had gained the confidence of the community in which he had been born and lived. Intrusted
with the sheriffalty of his county, he was on his way to
Richmond on the business of the important office when
the summons came. He married Elizabeth Cloyd, by

whom he had six children; she lived until 1810. Their daughter, Sarah, married her cousin, Major John McDowell, of whom hereafter. Elizabeth married David McGavock, and, removing to Nashville, Tennessee, became the ancestress of the numerous family of that name in that locality, than which no other in that state is more eminently respectable and worthy; there the name of McGavock is synonymous with honor, integrity, and valor. James, the youngest son of James McDowell and Elizabeth Cloyd, inherited the magnificent estate left by his father, and there, planting vines and fig trees, continued to reside until his death. Better than the large wealth that descended to him, and to which he added, he inherited also with his name the high moral qualities, good sense, and soldierly instincts of the McDowells. In 1812, as a colonel in the American army, he won honor and fame. He married Sarah, one of the daughters of the first Colonel William Preston, and granddaughter of John Preston and Elizabeth Patton, from whom so many distinguished men and noble women of that and other names have sprung. Colonel William Preston was himself an active participant in the Revolutionary struggle. As his assistants and deputies, John Floyd, John Todd, Douglas, Hancock Taylor, Hancock Lee, and others, made their first surveys and explorations in Kentucky, the Indian hunting land and battle ground. Colonel James McDowell and Sarah Preston had three children. Susan, their oldest daughter, married Colonel William Taylor, a prominent lawyer of Alexandria, and from 1843 to his death, in 1846, the able representative in Congress from that district; their son, Dr. James McDowell Taylor, was, in 1886, still an active practicing physician in Rockbridge; another son, Rev. Robert Taylor, married Elizabeth McNaught, and had two daughters, one of whom, Margaret P., married a Smith, and lives in Missouri; their daughter, Susan, married Hon. John B. Weller, a native of Ohio, who removed to California in the early emigration of 1849, came back in 1852 as United States senator, held the place with distinguished credit until 1857, was governor of California from 1858–60, minister to Mexico, 1861, and died in 1875, leaving a son, John B. Weller, Jr., who has gained prominence as a lawyer in the Golden State; another son, William Taylor, is a successful lawyer in California; and still another, Thomas Benton Taylor, who married a daughter of Rev. Dr. Nathan L. Rice, the celebrated Presbyterian divine, is a leading member of the bar of Chicago. The second daughter of Colonel James McDowell and Sarah Preston, Elizabeth by name, was the wife of Hon. Thomas Hart Benton, for thirty years the able and distinguished United States senator from Missouri, and a man as remarkable for his extraordinary force and decision of character as he was for the splendid physical courage which never flickered, and which age was powerless to cool. The efforts of "Old Hickory" to bully him met with failure and disaster; it was one of the few instances in which Jackson mistook his man. At various times in the career of Colonel Benton, allusion was made to an alleged act of dishonesty while he was still a boy at college—charges unnecessary now to be discussed. A sufficient answer to all such imputations upon his integrity is found in the fact that, during his thirty years of arduous, faithful, and able service in the senate, no whisper of venality was ever made against him; that he lived simply, had no extravagant habit or vice, and that he died poor. One of his daughters married General John C. Fremont, and another, that true patriot and gallant soldier, Colonel Richard T. Jacob, of Kentucky. Both were women of inherited talents and remarkable strength of character.

Governor James McDowell.

The third child, and only son, of Colonel James and Sarah (Preston) McDowell was also named James; as a gentleman, graceful and accomplished; as a man, the soul of honor and truth; as a congressman, United States senator and chief executive of his native Virginia, beloved, able, and most honorably and highly distinguished. Generally the McDowells were men of action, born soldiers, practical and sensible, not given to gush nor to display in words, and little gifted with fluent speech. Those of North Carolina were good talkers as well as ready fighters, but as speakers they were strong and earnest rather than brilliant. But this James McDowell, senator and governor, got from the Pattons, through his Preston mother, the rare gift of true eloquence and graceful oratory, combined with reasoning powers of a high order. These were seldom aroused to the magnificent height of their full splendor; but on the few occasions when their owner was spurred on by the excitement of intellectual conflict, and had his metal tested by the heat of actual combat, they burst forth with the brilliancy of real genius, which none can ever show who have not the spark divine, and with a surprising and resistless fervor which swept all before it and captured every auditor. To enter into a detail of the incidents of his virtuous life or public career would be foreign to the purpose of the writer. His noble wife was his first cousin, one of the talented daughters of General Francis Preston, noted for the exhibition of handsome talents as a congressman from Virginia, and for courage and good conduct as an officer in the War of 1812; he was the son of the first Colonel William Preston, and grandson of the first John Preston, of Virginia, both of whom have already been referred to. General Francis Preston's wife was the daughter of Colonel William Campbell, who was given the command at King's Mountain, at the instance of Isaac Shelby, who had planned the campaign; at whose instance, also, Campbell had marched his command from Virginia into North Carolina, and who, with Sevier, Winston, and the two Joe McDowells were the real heroes of the fight; in subsequent engagements, especially at Guilford Court House, Colonel Campbell won honor and renown. Colonel Campbell's wife, the mother of Mrs. Preston, and grandmother of Mrs. McDowell, was one of the sisters of the great orator of the Revolution, Patrick Henry; their mother, Sarah Winston, came of a prolific race, remarkably gifted with a high order of eloquence, graceful manners, and great mental force. The wives of Rev. Dr. Robert J. Breckinridge, of Kentucky, the ablest of Presbyterian divines, and of John B. Floyd, of Virginia, Secretary of War under President Buchanan, were Mrs. McDowell's sisters, while their husbands were her own and Governor McDowell's cousins. William C. Preston, the learned scholar, the gifted orator, and able statesman, of South Carolina, and General John S. Preston, a brilliant orator and gallant soldier of the same state, were her brothers. One of Governor McDowell's sons, Dr. James McDowell, married Elizabeth Brant, a wealthy lady of St. Louis, went to France and was for years a successful physician in Paris; his daughter, Sallie Benton McDowell, married her relative, Wickliffe Preston, of Lexington, Kentucky; and his son, Brant McDowell, of St. Louis, is said to be the only living male descendant of the name, of James McDowell and Elizabeth Cloyd. Governor McDowell's daughter, Sallie Campbell Preston, married, first, Governor Francis Thomas, of Maryland, and, afterward, Rev. John Miller, of Princeton, New Jersey. His daughter, Sophonisba Preston Benton, married the late Colonel James Woods Massie, a professor in the Virginia Military Institute. Susan Preston, another daughter of Governor McDowell, married Colonel Charles Carrington, of Richmond, Virginia; and still another, Margaret Canty, married Prof. Charles P. Venable, of the University of Virginia; while the youngest daughter, Eliza P. B., married the late Major Barnard Wolffe. Thomas Lewis McDowell, youngest son of the governor, died in the Confederate army; his widow, Constance Warwick, and their only child, Susan McDowell, live in Richmond, Virginia.

JUDGE SAMUEL McDOWELL.

The oldest son of Captain John McDowell (son of old Ephraim, of Londonderry) and the three times married Magdalena Wood, was Samuel; born in the Colony of Pennsylvania, in 1735; removed to Virginia in 1737, after his father had made the settlement in Burden's Grant; and who became, in future years, the progenitor of the Kentucky branch of the name and race. His father dying during his childhood, the education he received, though

neither collegiate nor classical, was far better than that
usually obtained in a border and debatable land, even
when it is held by a race so intelligent and enterprising as
the Scotch-Irish, by whom the valley was peopled; his
familiar letters to his children, indicating not only strong
sense, unaffected piety, and an affectionate heart, but also
educated intelligence, were admirably written.   Archibald
Alexander, who had been liberally educated in the old
country, and with whose descendants his own intermarried, was one of his teachers; the McClungs, Paxtons, Stuarts, Lyles, Irvines, Reids, Moores, Campbells were his
school-fellows and playmates, the companions of his youth,
the associates and friends of his manhood.   The most valuable lessons taught him were those of self-reliance, love
of liberty, and fear of God; that these were sown on good
and fruitful soil, the record of his whole life attests.   Like
other youth of the hardy race among whom his early life
and, manhood were passed, the exposed situation of a
frontier settlement inured him from infancy to the endurance of hardship and to indifference to danger.   In the
troubles with raiding Indians, in the more serious vicissitudes of the French and Indian war, the dawn of his manhood saw frequent and meritorious military service, in
which he acquitted himself with credit, and obtained most
valuable experience.   In Henning's Statutes, his name
appears, in an act passed by the Virginia Assembly in
1758, in the list of soldiers from Augusta county engaged
in the arduous campaigns of that war, and in 1775, a large
tract of land was surveyed for him in Fayette county,
Kentucky, and awarded to him for his services.   Withers
errs, in his "Chronicles of Border Warfare," in stating
that John McDowell was in Samuel Lewis's company at
Braddock's defeat.   John McDowell had been killed thirteen years before the disastrous battle.   It was his oldest
son, Samuel McDowell, who was a private soldier in that
company at that battle and in the following campaigns.
His kinsman, Andrew Lewis, was the lieutenant of the
company; Thomas, William, and Charles Lewis, and a
number of McClungs and Paxtons—the kinsmen of his

wife—were his companions in arms. In Dunmore's war, in 1774, he was captain of a company from Augusta county, his name appearing in that capacity on the original official list of the brave men who, under the leadership of his intrepid kinsman, Andrew Lewis, beat back Cornstalk and his painted warriors at Point Pleasant. A copy of this list is in the hands of Mr. Hixon, the historian. It was Samuel McDowell, at the head of his brave men from Augusta, who, after Colonel Charles Lewis had fallen, and the gallant Colonel Fleming had been carried desperately wounded from the bloody field, and the line of battle of the Virginians was wavering and yielding ground, charged along with Colonel Field, of the Culpepper men, drove back to their coverts the advancing, whooping, triumphant Indians, and snatched victory from the jaws of disaster. In the stubborn retreat of the savages, the chivalrous Field, who also had done his part well in 1755, fell. The official records show that Captain Samuel McDowell, in command of a company of scouts, did frequent and valuable service during that memorable campaign in which the power of the Shawanese was broken, both before and after the bloody battle. In the Revolution, he was colonel of a regiment of militia from Augusta, which guarded the mountain passes, kept in subjection the western and southern Indians, and gloriously participted in General Greene's North Carolina campaign, the turning-point of the war. At Guilford Court-house, under the immediate command of Colonel Samuel McDowell, the regiment again and again drove back the British regulars, acting the part of veterans, and maintaining its ground until assailed in flank by the British cavalry, and left unsupported. In this attack and retreat, its major, Alexander Stuart, the ancestor of General J. E. B. Stuart, had his horse killed, was captured, but fortunately escaped unwounded. In its ranks, the distinguished Judge Archibald Stuart fought as a private soldier. When a part of the regiment fell into disorder and scattered, Colonel McDowell, with the remainder, continued with the army; and when, against his protest

3

and remonstrance, the men returned to their homes, he continued with .General Greene, and participated in the pursuit which drove Cornwallis to Wilmington.

For several terms preceding the Revolution, the freeholders of Augusta, which then included what was afterward formed into Rockbridge, chose Samuel McDowell as one of their representatives in the House of Burgesses, an honor most worthily conferred in troublous times, when none but the foremost, and best, and truest were trusted. In all the meetings and movements in Colonial Virginia which led to the struggle for independence, he had an active part; of every deliberative body which assumed progressively advancing ground against monarchical and parliamentary encroachments upon popular and individual rights, he was a prominent member. In 1765, John Harvie, Thomas Lewis, the near-sighted but able and learned son of old John, and Samuel McDowell, were the Burgesses sent to the assembly from Augusta. That year, the celebrated *Resolutions of Remonstrance* of Patrick Henry had, besides their eloquent author, no more able or zealous advocate than the scholarly Lewis, nor a firmer nor more ardent supporter than Samuel McDowell, kinsmen, and Calvinists by descent and training. The freemen of Augusta pronounced decisively for the position taken by the men they loved as well as trusted, and from them came the clear notes that re-echoed throughout the colony, and were every-where caught up and repeated by the lovers of liberty. In the years intervening before the outbreak of actual hostilities, to Lewis and McDowell was confided the duty of voicing the patriotic sentiments of the people of Augusta. They did not desire nor look to a separation from the mother country; it was a representation in the councils of those who levied taxes upon their property and commerce that they demanded, and without which they would never rest content; they did not propose hastily to fly to arms for a redress of grievances, nor indulge in angry menace nor impetuous clamor; their protests were at once moderate, dignified, and respectful; and it was not until their repeated earnest petitions had been rejected with contemptuous scorn, and every other resource had failed, that they resolved to appeal to the God of Hosts as a remedy for oppression that had to them become intolerable. Ten years later than the ratification of the Henry *Resolutions of Remonstrance* by the people of Augusta, and a year in advance of the formal Declaration of Independence by the convention of delegates of the United Colonies, the people of Augusta chose Thomas Lewis and Samuel McDowell to represent them in the convention composed of delegates from the counties and corporations of the Virginia colony, which met at Richmond on the 20th of March, 1775; and these kinsmen, fitting representatives of this fine historic race, clansmen of an antique type, Calvinists of the strictest sect, received from their constituents instructions well calculated to fire every patriotic heart, which sounded the tocsin that rang throughout the hills and valleys of all the colonies, and were in effect their own declaration of independence. If these instructions were indeed drawn by Rev. Mr. Balmaine, an Episcopal minister, as stated by Meade, it is worthy of note that Mr. Balmaine was educated by Calvinists for the church founded in Scotland by John Knox. Their temper and spirit are sufficiently indicated by a single paragraph:

"Many of us and our forefathers left our native land, and explored this once savage wilderness, to enjoy the free exercise of the rights of conscience and of human nature. These rights we are fully resolved, with our lives and our fortunes, inviolably to preserve; nor will we surrender such estimable blessings, the purchase of toil and danger, to any ministry, to any parliament, or any body of men upon earth, by whom we are not represented, and in whose decisions, therefore, we have no voice."

In obedience to these instructions, Lewis and McDowell addressed to George Washington, Patrick Henry, Ben. Harrison, and the four other delegates from the colony to the Continental Congress which had recently been held in Philadelphia, a letter of thanks for their services and cordial approval of their course, couched in the most elegant language and breathing the most exalted patriotism; receiving from their illustrious correspondents a response which manifests the high appreciation in which they themselves were held. Just one month after those letters were written, the convention met in the old church at Richmond, where the eloquent speech of Patrick Henry was made that set in motion the great ball of the Revolution, and lighted the torch of liberty which has since been as a beacon-fire to the world. Samuel McDowell was a member also of the second convention which met in Williamsburg, in 1776, which instructed the Virginia delegates to the Continental Congress to " *declare the United Colonies free and independent states*, absolved from all allegiance to or dependence on the crown or parliament of Great Britain ;" erected the colony into a state, of which Patrick Henry was made the first governor; adopted the bill of rights and plan of government drawn by George Mason; and elected officers to command the first nine regiments organized in Virginia. Later in the struggle, when the Virginia state government was driven by the British from its capital, he was selected as one of the State Council, a most important and responsible position, and, in the darkest hour of the inchoate federal republic, accepted and ably and fearlessly discharged the high duties of the trust. The battle for public liberty and political independence having been fought out to a successful issue, in conjunction with Colonel Thomas Marshall he was appointed surveyor of the public lands in Fayette county, then comprising one-third of the District of Kentucky; in 1783, he opened an office, at once entering upon the faithful and intelligent discharge of its duties; the position was one that demanded not merely technical skill in the surveyor's art, but, in addition, the highest order of incorruptible personal integrity. During the same year, he presided as one of the judges of the first District Court ever held in Kentucky—at Harrodsburg, March 3, 1783—John Floyd and George Muter being his associate judges, but the latter not attending. Removing his family to what is now Mercer county, in 1784, two years later, in 1786, he was one of the presiding judges at the first county court held in the Kentucky District; henceforth he was known as Judge Samuel McDowell, to distinguish him from his son

of the same name. A decade subsequent to the Augusta
Declaration of Independence, in 1775, the hardy, resolute,
warlike, and restlessly independent settlers in Kentucky,
then a remote district of the State of Virginia, from which
it was separated by hundreds of miles of rugged mountains and roadless forests, began to agitate anew and with
settled purpose the question of political separation from
that ancient Commonwealth—a separation which, so early
as 1775, had been vaguely outlined by George Rogers
Clarke, who, consistently with the tenor of his whole public and private life, and with the principles that regulated
all his conduct, looked not to legal but to revolutionary
methods to reach the end desired. Over the convention
which met in Danville in 1785, and over all the subsequent
conventions which assembled for the consideration of this
momentous question, and the discussion of the means of
attaining the end in view, Judge Samuel McDowell was
chosen to preside—" his social position, his solid attainments, his matured convictions, his high character, his judicial temper, his fine presence, his popular manners, and
his peculiar and varied experience of public life, com-
bining to admirably qualify him for the position, and to
center upon him the attention, confidence, and respect of
the able men who were associated with him in these early
throes of the inchoate state." It was by the moderation
and patient discretion of the presiding officer, and the
calm patriotism of others like him, as well as by the keen
vigilance of Colonel Thomas Marshall, and far more than
by the fierce and direct assaults of others which savored
of personal and partizan animosities, that the " sagacious
policy of calculated procrastination " was adopted, the
schemes of conspirators who plotted to tear Kentucky
from her connection with Virginia, and even from her
moorings to the general government, and to achieve in
lieu thereof a political and commercial alliance with
cruel and treacherous Spain, were thwarted, a solution of
the difficulties of a separation from Virginia legally and
peacefully reached, and all the commercial advantages of
the free and unobstructed navigation of the Mississippi

were finally obtained. In the troublous and unsettled times in Kentucky, he was the "central figure of an historic group, conspicuous, like himself, for courage, intelligence, fortitude, dignity of character, and mental poise. All were representative men—types of a cultivated class, and of a vigorous, aggressive, and enduring race."* After having presided over the nine conventions which considered the question of a separation from Virginia, Judge Samuel McDowell was also president of the convention which, in 1792, framed the first state constitution for Kentucky. He was one of the first circuit court judges, and one of the first district judges of the new state— appointed by old "King's Mountain" Shelby, by whose side he had fought at Point Pleasant; as well as the first United States judge—appointed by Washington, under whose eye he had served in the campaign on the Monongahela, in 1755, and who well knew his worth. In these positions, as in all others, he acquitted himself with credit and honor. Respected for his strong sense, for an integrity that never bended, for an uprightness of conduct as unassailable in public as it was in private life, and for a pleasing simplicity of character, he lived to the good old age of eighty-two years, and died honored of all at the residence of his son, Colonel Joseph McDowell, near Danville, September 25, 1817. Under the law of primogeniture then prevailing in Virginia, he had inherited the whole of the estate left by his father. The clear sense of justice and native generosity characteristic of the man, so soon as he became of age were attested by the voluntary division of his inheritance equally with his brother and sister, the latter receiving almost all of the personalty. He was a Federalist of the school of Washington, between whom and these men of the Valley there was always the closest sympathy; and in his letters to his son-in-law, General Andrew Reid, who was a decided Jeffersonian, his Federal sentiments were enunciated in terms at once vigorous and unique. In religion, he was a Presbyterian—

---

* *Vide* "The Genesis of a Pioneer Commonwealth."

John Knox himself was no more stern nor unyielding. In person, he was tall, erect, and stately. His forehead was high, square, and prominent; his head "long" above the ears; his face long, with a chin and mouth indicating decision, firmness, and high spirit, without heat or passion. The general effect was handsome, dignified, invited confidence, and enforced respect.

On the 17th of January, 1754, at the age of eighteen, Judge Samuel McDowell married Mary McClung. She was a native of Ireland—but, like himself, of Scotch descent—and had emigrated with a sister and four brothers a few years prior to her marriage. The sister and two brothers settled with her in what was then Augusta county. The sister married an Alexander. Her brother, John McClung, also married Elizabeth Alexander, daughter of Archibald Alexander and Margaret Parks, and sister to the William Alexander who was the father of the distinguished Dr. Archibald Alexander, of Princeton Theological Seminary. John McClung and Elizabeth Alexander were the parents of Judge William McClung, of Kentucky. By this fitting union was grafted another strain of silent fighting blood upon the tough McDowell stock, developing in their descendants not in personal rencounters, but in the line of duty and on the battle fields of their country.

Major John McDowell.

John, their oldest son, was born in Virginia, in 1757, receiving the best education that could be obtained in those days of peril, from teachers who had frequently to lay aside the ferule in order to grasp the rifle. The writer is under the impression that he was a volunteer in the campaign against the Indians known as Dunmore's War, but he was not with his father's company at Point Pleasant, nor does his name anywhere appear in the list of the brave men who were under Andrew Lewis in that bloody fight. At the beginning of the Revolution, he volunteered in the patriot army, went at once into active service, and continued therein until the close of the struggle, from which he emerged with the rank of captain and a well-earned reputation for gallantry. He belonged to the Virginia line of the Continental establishment; that is, to the regulars. He was with Washington at the crossing of the Delaware, fought at Princeton and Trenton, and endured the rigors of the winter camp at Valley Forge. At Brandywine he was severely wounded, was in the hottest of the fight at Monmouth, and witnessed the surrender of Cornwallis at Yorktown. With such a record, and a staunch Federalist, he naturally became a member of the Society of the Cincinnati. If he purchased a lot in the town of Lexington, Kentucky, in 1781, as stated by Collins, he did not then remove into the district. He certainly made a purchase at a sale of lots in that town in 1783, and in the following year brought his family to Fayette county, where he made his permanent settlement. In all the Indian campaigns after 1785 he had an active part. Immediately after the establishment of the state, in 1792, he was appointed one of the first three majors commissioned by Shelby, who had fought beside his father at Point Pleasant, had conquered with his kinsmen at King's Mountain, and knew full well the quality and value of the man ; the other two majors, commissioned at the same time, were his brother James and John Morrison. In the War of 1812 he earned distinction in the rank of major. His father had been prominent in every movement that led to the erection of the new commonwealth; but his selection, by the people of Fayette, to represent them in the first state legislature, that assembled in 1792, was a fitting tribute to his own intelligence, worth and admitted capacity for affairs. His associates in the then important trust were such men as Colonel Robert Patterson, Colonel William Russell, Hubbard Taylor, and James Trotter. That he acquitted himself well in civil office, as he had done in the field, is evidenced by his re-election six times to the same position. In 1799, he was a member of the convention that framed the second state constitution, that lasted fifty years. He married his first cousin, Sarah, daughter of James McDowell and Elizabeth Cloyd. 1. Their son, James, married Susan, daughter of Governor Shelby—a most appropriate union of two patriot families; the descendants of these two are numerous. 2. Major John McDowell's son, John, removed to Alabama, and, in Greene county of that state, married Miss Sarah McAlpin. From Alabama he went to Mississippi, and settled on a cotton plantation he owned in Rankin county. His son, William, never married; he belonged to the Fifth Texas Confederate Brigade, was desperately wounded and captured at Gettysburg, and died in prison. Elizabeth married William Slaughter, a Confederate soldier, by whom she has several children. James graduated at the Missouri Medical College, of St. Louis, was adjutant of a Mississippi Confederate regiment, and was killed at Jenkins' Ferry; he was never married. John married a Miss Slaughter, was a soldier in the Confederate army, and died in the service. Solomon McAlpin McDowell was a soldier in the Eighteenth Mississippi Infantry, and was badly wounded and permanently disabled at Ball's Bluff; he married a Miss McLauren. Blanton McAlpin McDowell, the fifth and youngest son of John, entered the Confederate army at fifteen years of age, and died from disease contracted in the service. 3. Major John McDowell's son, Samuel, married Betsy Chrisman, daughter of Hugh Chrisman, of Jessamine county, whose mother was, as already stated, a sister of General Charles and Colonel Joe McDowell, of North Carolina; Lucy McDowell, their only child, became the second wife of Dr. Alexander K. Marshall, son of Dr. Louis Marshall and Agatha Smith; Lucy's only son, Louis Chrisman Marshall,ˑ a farmer in Fayette county, is married to his cousin, Agatha, daughter of Chancellor Caleb W. Logan. 4. Major John McDowell's daughter, Betsy, married Rev. William McPheeters, and 5, Mary was the first wife of Major Thomas Hart Shelby, son of the governor, and an officer in the War of of 1812. She died without issue, and Major Shelby subsequently married a daughter of Edmund Bullock, by whom he had a number of children.

Major McDowell, after the death of his first wife, married, secondly, Lucy Le Grand, descended from a French Huguenot, who, after leaving Bohain, of which he was a native, was naturalized in England, whence he emigrated to New York.   There, in 1699, he united with the Reformed   Dutch   Church—a   Calvinistic   organization. From New York some of his descendants found their way to Virginia, where one of them, Rev. Nashe Le Grand, became one of the most eloquent and best beloved of Presbyterian ministers.   Major John McDowell and Lucy Le Grand were the parents of the celebrated

Dr. Joseph Nashe McDowell,

of St. Louis—a man singularly unlike his kindred in his eccentric temper and erratic career, but of unquestioned learning and genius in his profession, and in other lines of science and thought.   Noted as a skillful physician and surgeon, the city of his adoption owes to him the establishment of its best medical school, while the profession recognizes in him one of its most advanced thinkers, one of its boldest and most skillful operators, and one of the most cultivated of its publicists.   From Dr. Gross, with whom he frequently came in angry collision, his superior talents extorted the admission, that " Dr. McDowell was an eloquent and enthusiastic teacher of anatomy ; he had a remarkable gift of speech, and could entertain and amuse his class in a wonderful degree."   But it was not solely as a lecturer in medicine and surgery that the oratorical gifts of Dr. McDowell shone conspicuously.   Of varied and extensive culture, his gifts made him the delight of literary circles, and the West contained no more eloquent speaker upon political topics than was this able and learned teacher of the healing art.   He abandoned the rigid Calvinism of the McDowells without adopting the gentler tenets of Arminianism.   Discarding their Federalism, his devotion to the Lost Cause made him an exile from his home and country. In Europe died a man whose learning, genius and enthusiasm, had his life been guided by the principles and religion of his fathers, would have placed him at the very head of his profession, and have made him eminent in any walk of life in any country.   Dr. Nashe McDowell married a sister of the able Dr. Daniel Drake—an aunt of Judge Charles

W. Drake, formerly of the St. Louis bar, and now of the United States Court of Claims. He left by her, among other children, a son, who attained distinction as a surgeon and physician in St. Louis. Before his early death, his fame in the West, as a surgeon, and especially as a demonstrator of anatomy, was second to no other.

7. Charles McDowell, son of Major John, by his second wife, married Miss Redd. 8. Betsy McDowell, daughter of Major John, married Henderson Bell. 9. Sallie McDowell, daughter of Major John, married James Allen, a prominent citizen of Fayette. 10. Lucy, the youngest child of Major John McDowell and Lucy Le Grand, was the wife of David Meade Woodson. This gentleman was one of the sons of Samuel Hugh Woodson.

WOODSON

is a good old Virginian name, one of the family, Colonel John Woodson, of Goochland, marrying Dorothea, daughter of Isham Randolph, of Dungeness, and sister of President Jefferson's mother; he was the ancestor of John J. Crittenden's third wife. Samuel Hugh Woodson represented Jessamine county in the Kentucky Legislature in 1819–25, and from 1820 to 1823 was a representative in Congress. His wife was a daughter of Colonel David Meade, an elder brother of Colonel Richard Kidder Meade, of the Revolution, and uncle of Bishop Meade, who gives an interesting account of that family in his "History of Old Churches and Families." David Meade Woodson was the Whig representative from Jessamine county, in 1833, while his brother, Tucker, represented the county and the senatorial district a number of years—more frequently, indeed, than any other one man. David Meade Woodson and Lucy McDowell were married in October, 1831; she died in August, 1836, in Fayette county, leaving an only son, John McDowell Woodson, born June 5, 1834. In the latter year, David M. Woodson removed to Carrollton, Greene county, Illinois. There he filled many prominent positions: state's attorney, probate judge, member of the legislature, member of the convention that framed a constitution for the state in 1847, and for almost twenty years judge of the circuit court. In 1840, Judge Woodson was the Whig opponent of Stephen A. Douglas for Congress, and, after one of the most noted and heated contests that had ever taken place in the state, in which he successfully held his own with the "Little Giant," was defeated by only a few votes. He died in 1877, in his seventy-first year, full of honors and universally esteemed. His son, John McDowell Woodson, graduated at Center College, in the class of 1853, and, after success as a civil engineer, graduated at the Law School of Harvard, and, in 1857, was admitted to the bar. In the legal profession his success has met the full measure of his ambition. In 1860 he was elected a member of the convention that framed a new constitution for Illinois. In 1865 he was elected mayor of Carlinville, to which place he had removed. In 1866 he was elected to the State Senate, and served in that body with ability for four years. He then removed to St. Louis, where he now resides, and where he at once entered upon a lucrative practice, chiefly as attorney for railroads and counsel for other corporations. Reaping abundant reward for his industrious labors, his rapid success enabled him to withdraw from the general practice when his failing health required rest and ease. Mr. Woodson has been twice married, and has issue.

The limits prescribed for this sketch compels an omission of many other descendants of Major John McDowell, who are as numerous as they are eminently respectable.

COLONEL JAMES McDOWELL, OF FAYETTE.

James, the second son of Judge Samuel McDowell and Mary McClung, was born in what is now Rockbridge county, Virginia, in 1760. Enlisting as a private soldier in the Continental army at the age of sixteen, he continued in active service until victory had been won at Yorktown. From the strife he emerged an ensign. At the age of nineteen, while at home on a brief furlough, he married Mary Paxton Lyle, her father, Captain John Lyle, being about to remove to North Carolina, and the young soldier desiring his sweetheart to remain as his wife with his own parents in Virginia. The day after the bridal, he hurried back to his post in the army. The Lyles were of a Scotch-Irish family which had settled in the Grant contemporaneously with the McClungs, Paxtons, and Alexanders, to whom they were allied by blood and frequent intermarriages. The names of Lyle, Lisle, Lyell, are identical; those who bear them spring remotely from the same stock. Their common origin is in the name of de l'Isle— "of the Island"—which indicates that in the ages wrapped in clouds the common ancestor was one of the lords of the Western Islands. In Scotland still the names are found among the higher gentry. In the Valley the name has been one of the highest repute for a century and a half, borne, as it has been, by soldiers, ministers, teachers, and worthy men in the other professions. The wife of Captain John Lyle—mother of the wife of James Mc-Dowell—was Isabella Paxton She was the daughter of John Paxton and Martha Blair—both splendid types of the Scotch-Irish. For Martha Blair, a descent is asserted from Rev. Robert Blair, a learned professor in the University of Glasgow, who abandoned his place rather than acquiesce in the introduction of prelacy by Dr. Cameron; and then accepted the invitation of Lord James Hamilton, of Claneboy, to the pulpit of the congregation of Bangor, in county Down, where he settled, in 1623. The brothers and sisters of Isabella Paxton married, respectively, with Alexanders, Stuarts, Barclays, McClungs, Houstons, Caruthers, Cowans—all honored names. James McDowell removed with his wife to Kentucky, in 1783. Locating in Fayette county, they made their home about three miles from Lexington, on the Georgetown road, the large body of rich land midst whose beautiful groves they settled probably being a part of the tract patented to Judge Samuel McDowell for his services in the French and Indian war. The comfortable house of hewed logs, erected for their temporary accommodation, after the lapse of a century is still standing. It soon gave place to a commodious dwelling, with thick walls and large rooms, the bricks for which were burned upon the spot, while the woodwork within was carved from the magnificent black walnut trees that shaded the luxuriant blue grass of the land. Alas! the black walnut doors, the hand-carved mantels and cornices, the elegant wainscoting, have been covered with white paint, or torn away, to suit tastes that are not more æsthetic because so different. The vocation of James McDowell was that of a farmer, finding in flocks and herds, the waving grain and blue grass, pleasures congenial to his unobtrusive nature. Helping to found the state, and taking the keenest interest in public affairs, he seems to have avoided the conspicuousness attaching to place, and to have had an aversion to civil office of every kind. Yet, from 1783 on, he had an active hand in all the military measures for the defense of the settlers and the district, and is said to have borne an honorable part in every campaign against the Indians. As major of a battalion in the expedition of General Wilkinson, in 1791, he received the most complimentary mention for good conduct from that experienced soldier. The appointment by Shelby, in 1792, as one of the first three majors of the state, was not an empty honor, but, in the situation of the infant Commonwealth, meant something in the line·of his tastes and capabilities. The War of 1812 found him beyond the age for military service, but with the blood of old Ephraim coursing hotly through his veins—every soldierly instinct alive, and active every patriotic impulse. He had organized and commanded the first company of light horse raised in Lexington. At the first call to arms, with his sons, Samuel and John Lyle, the veteran promptly volunteered. His company soon grew into a battalion. While on the march to the front, the rank and command of major were conferred upon him, and his men were consolidated with those of Simrall, who was commissioned as colonel of the regiment. On more than one bloody field in the North-west, he vindicated the reputation for courage and cool daring so long associated with the name of McDowell. By order of General Harrison, the regiment was detached from the main army on the ex-

pedition to attack and destroy the Indian towns, crops,
and stock upon the Mississinewa.   Besides the Kentuckians and others, there went along, at the head of his gallant " Pittsburg Blues," the heroic Captain James Butler,
son of General Richard Butler, who fell at the disaster
that clouds the name of St. Clair, and first cousin to the
brave soldiers of the name at Carrollton ; leading his regular dragoons, there rode Major James V. Ball, the chivalrous Virginian, who married a granddaughter of General
Andrew Lewis, and who made the charge which won at
Lundy's Lane.   The whole force was under the command
of Colonel John B. Campbell, of the Nineteenth Regulars—
a chip from the tree that had grown in the Valley and
branched into Tennessee and Kentucky.   Leaving Dayton
on the 14th of December, 1812, with instructions to avoid
the Delaware towns, and to spare the family of Little
Turtle, who had remained faithful to treaties, the objects
of the expedition were accomplished in a manner to extort the commendation of General Harrison.   The mission was one of destruction.   The march was over ground
covered with deep snow.   The rigors of the winter's air
were terrible.   The first two days, the march was forty
miles ; the next day and night, another forty.   On the
morning of the 17th, a town of the Miamis was surprised,
its defenders killed or captured, the town, stores, and crops
burned, and the stock shot.   During the day, Ball's dragoons and Simrall's light horse advanced further down the
Mississinewa, burned three large Miami towns and many
cornfields, and killed many cattle ; then returned to the
first town attacked, and there encamped ; the devastation
had been complete.
    The camp had been laid off during the absence of Ball's
and Simrall's commands to the lower towns.   Ball occupied the right and one-half of the rear line ; Simrall the
left and other half of the rear line.   Between Ball's right
and Simrall's left there was an interval that had not been
filled up.   Like a trained soldier, Major McDowell required
his men to cut down the branches from the trees, near
their bases, and to place them around their part of the

camp as a sort of abatis, or *chevaux-de-frise*. Campbell had now to decide whether he would push on with men fatigued and frostbitten, and horses suffering for want of forage, incumbered with prisoners, or return. At four o'clock on the morning of the 18th, the revèille was beaten, and the officers met in council at the colonel's camp-fire. Half an hour before the dawn the hideous yell of a large body of savages announced their furious and desperate night attack, and broke up the council. In a few seconds the attack became general from the entrance of the right to the left of Ball's squadron. The audacious Indians boldly advanced to within a few feet of the lines, resolved, with headlong courage, to rush in. The strongest and most formidable demonstration was made at the gap between Ball's squadron and Simrall's regiment. For half an hour the battle raged, the heavy fire was incessant, the savage yells swelling in triumphant expectation. The Indians pressed on. The redoubt first attacked was captured and held by the Indians; Captain Pierce, of Ohio, who had commanded it, was shot twice through the body, toma-hawked and scalped. During the din the voice of Major McDowell, which had gained him the name of "Old Thun-der," could every-where be heard cheering his men. When Major Ball, hard pressed, requested relief, and none could be had except from the infantry posted elsewhere, it was he who had seen that the spies and guides under Patterson Bain were unemployed, and who rodé with Campbell and ordered them to the succor of Ball. He was with Captain Smith, of his own battalion, when his redoubt was so handsomely held, though abandoned by half his guards, encouraging the men by his example. Summoned from the opposite side of the camp to the aid of Ball, "Captain Butler, in the most gallant manner, and highly *worthy of the name he bears*, formed his men immediately, and in ex-cellent order, and marched them to the point to which he was ordered. The alacrity with which they formed and moved was never excelled by any troops on earth."—[*Col-onel Campbell's Report.*] "The Blues were scarcely at the post assigned them, before I discovered the effects they produced."—[*Ibid.*] At last the welcome daylight broke, and loud over all the voice of McDowell was heard ordering his men to mount. Soon Campbell gave the word to charge to Captain Trotter's company, and with McDowell at their head, "they tilted off at full gallop. Major McDowell, with a small party, rushed into the midst of the enemy and exposed himself very much. I can not say too much for this *gallant veteran*."—[*Campbell.*] Through the Indian line the brave McDowell led the Kentuckians—over them, breaking them—then formed at their rear, and, saber in hand, charged back again. "The cavalry returned, and informed me the enemy had fled precipitately."—[*Campbell.*] The battle had been fought, the day was won. In his general orders and report the gallant conduct of Major McDowell received the most complimentary mention by Harrison; but the enthusiasm of the men who witnessed his fearless and intrepid bearing was unrestrained in its expression. In the charge his horse was killed under him; and, as an Indian was in the act of shooting the major himself, the savage fell dead from a timely shot fired by the major's oldest son, Samuel McDowell, who was a sergeant in George Trotter's company. The triumphant issue of these minor battles is never without important result in such warfare, and with such a foe. Tecumseh, at the head of 1,200 of his best warriors, was known to have been at the time in the Mississinewa country; the force engaged in the battle, commanded by a nephew of Little Turtle, a distinguished brave called "Little Thunder," was somewhat less. For the numbers engaged, the loss on both sides was heavy.

Abram Irvine McDowell, a nephew of Major James, and father of General Irvine McDowell, was also in this battle. In regular course Major McDowell was advanced to a colonelcy, and held that rank at the conclusion of the war. Removing from Fayette to Mason, the last years of Colonel McDowell were passed in the latter county, on a farm near Millwood, the commodious residence still standing. Refusing all office except when its acceptance in the mili-

4

tary service involved the risk of his own life in defense of
his country, the natural soldier of his family, Colonel Mc-
Dowell lived to a good old age, surrounded by the abundance he had inherited and earned, respected for his intelligence and unspotted probity, and, when the end came,
died calmly as he had lived uprightly, transmitting to his
numerous posterity the heritage of an honorable name.
Over six feet in height, his person was at once strong,
handsome and graceful; a high forehead surmounting
large, sparkling black eyes, his countenance beamed with
high spirit and infinite good humor; wanting in the habit-
ual sternness which was characteristic of his McDowell
kindred, and yet capable, on occasion, of fierce, white-
heated, and deadly wrath; a gallant gentleman of the olden
school, he united the courtesy and *bonhomme* of the Cavalier
to the inflexible adherence to principle that marked the
Roundhead. His descendants were worthy offshoots of
the McDowell stock. The writer has frequently heard
from his mother, who knew them well and intimately, that
the daughters of Colonel James McDowell were all not
only women of intellect and culture, but were, of their
generation, the most graceful and beautiful women of Kentucky. Of these, the elder, 1, Isabella, married

Dr. John Poage Campbell,

a man of science, a scholarly theologian, and, in many
ways, one of the most remarkable men this country has
ever produced. His father, Robert Campbell, was a native
of Scotland, and, it is believed [*Sprague's Annals*], was of
the Campbells of Kirnan, who were cadets of the house of
Argyle, and from whence sprung the illustrious poet. It
is ascertained, from the concurring records of several families, that the mother of Robert Campbell, Elizabeth
Walker, was born in Scotland, in 1703, and was the oldest
of the seven children of John Walker, of Wigtown,
Scotland. The mother of this John Walker was Catherine Rutherford, daughter of John Rutherford, of
an ancient and honorable family in Teviotdale, celebrated in story and ballad as hard fighting, adventur-

ous soldiers. One account represents this John Rutherford to have been the son, another asserts that he was
either the nephew or the full first cousin, of Rev. Samuel Rutherford, the able and learned author of "Rutherford's Letters," one of the seven delegates from Scotland
to the noted Westminster Assembly, and one of the very
foremost, ablest and bravest of the leaders of the Scotch
Presbyterian Church.—[*Sprague's Annals.*] The two were
certainly of the same blood and very nearly related. Whatever the degree of kindred, the connexion could add
nothing of honor to the characters or reputations of the
gifted, brave, pious descendants of John Rutherford in
America. The wife of John Rutherford was a descendant
of Rev. Joseph Alliene, the distinguished author of "Alliene's Alarm." John Walker went from Wigtown to Ireland, and there married; all of his children were born in
Ireland save Elizabeth, the mother of Robert Campbell.
From Ireland he emigrated to Pennsylvania, whither all of
his children also came; and from that colony they all, or
nearly all, drifted to the Valley of Virginia, settling on
Walker's creek, in Rockbridge county. The sons of John
Walker, of Wigtown, were John, James, Samuel, Alexander and Joseph, who gave their name to the creek on
which they settled, where their descendants became so numerous that they were sometimes pleasantly called the
"Creek Nation."

Besides Elizabeth—the mother of Robert Campbell—
John Walker, of Wigtown, had also a daughter, Jane,
who married, in Pennsylvania, an Irishman named James
Moore, who, with his brother, Joseph Moore, had emigrated to that colony about the year 1726, from whence
they removed to the Valley. Rachel, the oldest daughter
of James Moore and Jane Walker, married William Mc-
Pheeters, also born in Pennsylvania, the son of a Scotch-
Irishman, also named William McPheeters, who was said
to have been descended from a Scotch highlander named
Peter Hume. William McPheeters and Rachel Moore had
ten children, one of whom was Rev. William McPheeters, the
able theologian and eloquent preacher, whose first wife was

Elizabeth, daughter of Major John McDowell; by a third wife Rev. Wm. McPheeters was the father of Rev. Dr. Samuel Brown McPheeters, the able, brave and beloved pastor of the Pine Street Presbyterian Church of St. Louis. Rebecca, a daughter of Wm. McPheeters and Rachel Moore, married Captain John Gamble, a brother of Colonel Robert Gamble, and had by him eleven children, of whom one was the able Presbyterian divine, Rev. James Gamble, of South Carolina and Georgia. Another daughter, Rachel McPheeters, married John Logan, of Rockbridge county, and was the ancestress of a number of able preachers. Elizabeth, the youngest child of William McPheeters and Rachel Moore, married William Campbell, a son of Captain Charles Campbell, of Rockbridge. This Captain Charles Campbell was a cousin of Robert Campbell, and his wife was Mary Anne Downey, whose mother was a sister of William McPheeters, the husband of Rachel Moore.

Mary Moore, the second child of James Moore and Jane Walker, first married one of the chivalrous Paxtons, by whom Samuel Paxton was her son. Secondly, she married, as his second wife, Alexander Stuart, the major of Colonel Samuel McDowell's regiment, who was captured at Guilford. By Major Stuart she was the mother of four children, one of whom was Alexander Stuart, a distinguished judge of the Superior Court of Virginia, Judge Alexander Stuart, of Patrick, an able lawyer and an eloquent orator, and a distinguished soldier in the War of 1812; and *he* was the father of General James Ewell Brown Stuart, the Murat of the Southern Confederacy, the idol of Virginia, a major-general at twenty-nine, who died on the field of battle, as gloriously as he had lived honorably.

Elizabeth, the third daughter of James Moore and Jane Walker, married Michael Coalter. One of her granddaughters married William C. Preston, of South Carolina —scholar, orator and statesman; and a sister of Mrs. Preston married the able Judge Harper, of the same state. Her son, John Coalter, was judge of the Superior Court of Virginia, and afterwards of the Court of Appeals; his third wife was a daughter of Judge St. George Tucker, and half sister of John Randolph, of Roanoke. The eighth child of Michael Coalter and Elizabeth Moore, named Mary, was the first wife of Beverley Tucker, youngest son of Judge St. George Tucker, and half brother of John Randolph.

James, one of the sons of James Moore and Jane Walker, married, in Rockbridge, Martha Poage, a member of a numerous and respectable family in the Valley, one of whom was the first wife of Colonel Robert Breckinridge, while others found their way to Kentucky, where they earned distinction as men of valor. On Walker's creek, among his mother's kindred, James Moore lived, and there were born his sons, John, James and Joseph. About the year 1775, he removed to Abb's Valley, in what is now Tazewell county—a delightful tract of extraordinary fertility, ten miles long, and about an eighth of a mile wide, with no stream running through it, and surrounded by the lofty peaks of the Clinch and New River mountains. Here, in 1784, his son, James, was captured by Black Wolf, a noted Shawanese chief, and carried into captivity among the Ohio Indians. Here, in 1786, James Moore himself, his sons, John, William and Alexander, and his daughters, Rebecca and Margaret, and an aged Englishman, named Simpson, were murdered by a band of Cherokees; and his wife, his daughters, Jane and Polly, and a seamstress, Martha Ivins, were captured and carried off. Shortly afterward, Mrs. Moore and Jane were tortured and burned to death at the stake, the former bearing, without a murmur, the agonies inflicted upon her, encouraging her daughters with her conversation, and lifting up her voice in prayer to her Redeemer. Thus was the whole family cut off by one fell blow, excepting the captives, James and Polly, and Joseph, who was at school in Rockbridge. Five years from the time James was captured, and three years from the time that Polly, then only eight years old, witnessed the torture of her mother, after incredible sufferings, they were restored to their kindred in Rockbridge. James Moore married and lived to a great age in Rockbridge. Polly, upon

her return, lived at first with the family of her uncle, Wm.
McPheeters, who then resided about ten miles southward
from Staunton, near the Middle river. Afterwards, she resided with her uncle, Joseph Walker, who had married her
aunt, Jane Moore, his cousin, on Buffalo creek, about six
miles from Lexington, Virginia. She had taken with her,
from Abb's Valley, two New Testaments, which she kept
throughout all her captivity. At the age of twelve years
she was received into the communion of the Presbyterian
Church. When she grew up she married Rev. Samuel
Brown, a distinguished Presbyterian divine, and the loved
pastor of the New Providence Church. Of her eleven
children, five of her sons were able and devout Presbyterian ministers, another a ruling elder, and a sixth a com-
municant; one of her daughters married a Presbyterian
minister, and another a pious physician. One of her sons
was Rev. James M. Brown, so long the occupant of the
pulpit in Charleston, on the Kanawha. It was the latter
excellent man who adopted and befriended the singularly
gifted Irish lad who became the eloquent Dr. Stuart Robinson—a robust leader of men, and aggressive soldier of
the Cross.

Jane, eighth child of James Moore and Jane Walker,
married her relative, Joseph Walker. Her daughter, Margaret, married Rev. Samuel Houston. One of her sons
was Rev. Samuel Rutherford Houston, the zealous and
faithful missionary to Greece. It is singular how the best
fighting qualities go with the most brilliant pulpit abilities, when the stock is Calvinistic.

The Campbell of Kirnan who married Elizabeth, oldest
child of John Walker and Catherine Rutherford, had, by
her, eight children. Of these, three certainly came to Augusta county, Robert, John Walker and Jane. The latter married Alexander McPheeters, a relative of William
McPheeters, who married her kinswoman, Rachel Moore.
Her son, Robert McPheeters, was a ruling elder and worthy
citizen of Augusta. Major John Walker Campbell married, but had no children. Their cousin, Captain Charles
Campbell, who married Mary Anne Downey (her mother

was Martha McPheeters), was the father of Dr. Campbell, of Lexington, Virginia; of John W. Campbell, of Petersburg; and of William Campbell, who married Elizabeth McPheeters, his relative, and sister of Rev. Wm. McPheeters. The precise date of the arrival in Augusta county of Robert Campbell with his brother and sister, can not be stated; but at some time prior to 1744, as the records show [*Peyton*], he purchased 350 acres of land from the patentees of the Beverly Manor, and on this tract he built his home; afterwards he sold, to trustees appointed for the purpose, "the glebe lands," as the lands set aside for the support of the Episcopal Church were called. By Governor Gooch he was appointed one of the early magistrates of Augusta. All that is known of him demonstrates him to have been not only a religious, but also an intelligent and educated man, highly esteemed in the peculiar community among whom he cast his lot, exercising a salutary influence in all matters for the advancement of religion and education, and active in providing for the common defense. When an elderly man, before the beginning of the present century, Robert Campbell removed to Kentucky, locating, at first, in Fayette county, near Lexington; afterwards, becoming associated with General Thomas Bodley, General Robert Poage, and Hughes, in the purchase of ten thousand acres of rich cane land in the Mayslick neighborhood, he removed to Mason county, there made his final settlement, and there he died. Robert Campbell was already of middle age when, in the family of a fellow-countryman and co-religionist, in Augusta county, he met with and married his friend's daughter, Rebecca Wallace—of a Scotch Presbyterian family which had early settled in the Valley, and has since spread itself over the South and West, every-where esteemed for the virtue and intelligence of its members, prominent in all social circles, and frequently found in high official place. In Augusta county, in 1767, the fruit of this union, John Poage Campbell, was born; a man to whom was transmitted, through the generations, the intellect, the eloquence, and the high and combative spirit, with the religious tenets of his renowned ancestor, and whose attainments were even more varied, liberal and elegant. The easy circumstances of his uncle, Major John W. Campbell, who had adopted him, gave him the advantages of the very best schools in Virginia; after thorough training in the academies, he graduated, in 1790, at Hampden Sidney; then studied medicine with his kinsman, Dr. David Campbell, a native of Virginia, but a graduate of the University of Edinburg, whose inaugural thesis, dedicated to Theodoric Bland and Robert Mumford—both earnest patriots of the Revolution—printed at Edinburg, in 1777, and couched in the purest and most elegant latinity, attests the perfection to which classical scholarship was carried at that day. The skepticism of his youth having been corrected and dispelled, he became a student of theology under Drs. Graham and Hoge, Dr. Archibald Alexander being a fellow-student; completing the course, in 1792 he became associated with Dr. Hoge, as co-pastor of the Presbyterian Church at Lexington, Virginia, and, in 1793, was elected one of the trustees of Liberty Hall, now the Washington-Lee University, serving until 1795, and being present at eighteen meetings out of twenty.—[*Hixson.*] In the latter year removing to Kentucky, where all religion seemed imperilled by a so-called " free thinking" infidelity, which developed its pernicious ultimate results in the horrors of the French Revolution, and distinguished that social convulsion from the struggles for religious and political liberty in England and America—" in defense of his imperilled faith, he at once plunged into a controversial career." " The land jobbing, litigation, religious skepticism and ecclesiastical dissension, and the chronic political turbulence and intrigue under the leadership of military adventurers, commercial speculators, and unscrupulous politicians that then afflicted this newly-erected state—engendering a sort of Jacobinism in religion, politics and social life"—needed to be confronted by a spirit as bold, an intellect as acute, a learning as broad and accurate, and an eloquence as fervid as that possessed by the young Calvinist. From his first charge at Smyrna, in Fleming county, his fame rap-

idly spread; soon every Presbyterian pulpit in Central
Kentucky knew him as the most daring, resolute, inflexible, and as one of the most eloquent of the soldiers of the
Cross. A thorough scholar, not only in the classics and
in modern languages but also in the natural and exact
sciences, and with a literary style in composition at once
chaste and elegant, as a pulpit orator Dr. Campbell has
never had a superior, and but few, if any, equals in the
West. With a fervid eloquence that swept all before it,
as a theologian he was at once learned, profound and critical; as a logician and controversialist he was the most
dangerous, as he came to be one of the most dreaded, of
opponents. Said Dr. E. P. Humphrey of him: "As a
preacher he was distinguished for weight of matter, brilliant diction, the flashing of a deep-set, dark-blue eye, elegance of style, and gracefulness of delivery." Old Dr.
Louis Marshall, himself one of the most accurate scholars
and first thinkers of the country, regarded him as the
greatest intellect and most wonderful orator he had ever
met; he united with the church under Dr. Campbell's administration, and named a son after him. Drs. Timothy
Dwight and Archibald Alexander, the elder John Breckinridge, and other public men of like standing, his contemporaries, admirers and friends, placed an equally high
and just estimate upon him. It is worthy of note, as indicating the order of his well-poised mind and his undeviating adherence to his own convictions, that while, in 1806,
over the signature of *Vindex*, he most ably "vindicated the
principles and practices of his fellow-churchmen against
the rash and harsh charges of a clerical antagonist, who
had passed the most bitter and sweeping censure upon
"the private and religious character of all who held
slaves," Dr. Campbell was one of the first clergymen in
Kentucky to urge the policy of legal and constitutional
emancipation, and, consistently with his utterances, to set
an example in the philanthropic work, by the liberation
of his own slaves." His convictions upon this subject
finally led to his removal to Ohio. Prof. Tyndall, in his
remarkable address to the " British Association for the Ad-

vancement of Science," in 1874, says that Sir Benjamin
Brodie,-the distinguished English physician, first drew his
attention to the fact that, "as early as 1794, Charles Darwin's grandfather was the pioneer of Charles Darwin;"
and the New York *Nation*, shortly afterward, spoke of
"the perhaps over ingenious connection of Darwinism
with the philosophy of Democritus." "Now, all concede
that the germs of the Darwinian theory were derived, by
the elder Darwin, from the writings of the early philosophers, including the writings of Democritus, a learned
physician. Notwithstanding the notable variation by descent the doctrine has undergone, its germinal idea is undoubtedly traceable, through the elder Darwin, to a remote classical source. A striking illustration of the thoroughness, the accuracy, and the high quality of Dr. Campbell's scholarship is the fact, that, as early as 1812, in his
criticisms upon the theories of the elder Darwin, as developed in his *Zoonomia* and the *Botanic Garden*, he anticipated
Sir Benjamin Brodie and Prof. Tyndall, of our own day,
in the detection of the germinal ideas from which the Darwinian theory of evolution is derived. Said Dr. Campbell, in his "Letters to a Gentleman at the Bar"—the
celebrated Joseph Hamilton Daviess : "It had been thought
that a vast accession of light had flashed upon the world
when the author (Dr. Erasmus Darwin) published his celebrated work. It was hailed as a new era in philosophy. . . . But, . . . the philosophy was not new;
the design of the poetic exhibition was not new, nor did
the manner of the author possess a shadow of a claim to
novelty. The doctrines had long ago been taught by Pro-
tagoras, Strato, Democritus, and Leucippus. Epicurus had
improved on the Democritic philosophy, and his admirer
and disciple, Lucretius, had touched its various themes in
a fine style of poetic representation. All that Dr. Darwin
did, was to modernize the doctrines of the atomic philosophy, and embellish them with the late discoveries made in
botany, chemistry and physics. . . . Our philoso-
pher . . . tells us that the progenitors of mankind
were hermaphrodites, monsters, or mules, and that the

mules which did not possess the powers of reproduction
perished, while the rest, who were more fortunate in their
make, propagated the species which, by gradual and long-
continued amelioration has been molded into its present
shape and figure." Dr. Campbell here quotes a passage
from the 5th book of Lucretius, in which the same doctrine is taught, and another from Aristotle, to prove that
the same hypothesis is traceable to Empedocles, who flour-
ished at a still earlier date. In brief, he conclusively
demonstrates that the idea of the struggle for existence,
and of the survival of those species best fitted for the conditions of that struggle, "was familiar to ancient thinkers." Since the appearance of that epochal work, "The
Origin of Species," later investigators, unconsciously adopting the conclusions of Dr. Campbell, have re-discovered
the vague, fluctuating and elusive line of descent upon
which the Darwinian theory was slowly evolved.* The
acute theologian and ripe scholar did not exaggerate the
dangers which threatened Christianity. The younger
Darwin, himself, in adopting his undemonstrated theory,
rejected his previous belief in all revealed religion. His
doctrine of evolution strikes at the very foundation of the
faith. Than Dr. Campbell no abler antagonist to this de-
structive idea has since entered the lists. His active in-
vestigation in the field of archæological inquiry, even before the time of Rafinesque, illustrated the versatility of
his genius, and the variety of subjects of which he was the
accomplished master. His labors were concluded at Chillicothe, in 1814, at the age of forty-six years. While actively engaged in the practice of medicine, and in botani-
cal and antiquarian research, and at the same time preaching with his usual impressiveness, vigor and eloquence, he
caught a severe cold, which soon terminated his life. "In
person he was tall, slender and graceful; his countenance
was composed, thoughtful and grave; his complexion
clear and pale; his carriage manly and erect;" his temper

---

* *Vide*, sketch of Dr. Campbell in the History of Mason County.

bold; of unyielding firmness; his predominant characteristic, manliness. His wife was a fit helpmeet for such a man; a woman of cultivated intellect and rare personal graces, great energy, sound judgment and ready tact. She survived him, residing with her family at Lexington until her death in 1838. Her son, Dr. James McDowell Campbell, born in 1804, received his academical education at Transylvania University, his medical education at one of the Cincinnati schools. He practiced medicine at Burlington, Iowa, where he died in 1837. Her son, Dr. John C. Campbell, born in 1812, received his academical education at the Miami University, then under the presidency of Dr. Bishop, and graduated in medicine at the medical school of St. Louis, now the medical department of the State University. He is now a prominent and wealthy citizen of Nebraska City, Nebraska. In the years 1855, '7, '9, '61 and '62, he was a member of the Territorial Legislature of Nebraska, two years of the time in the senate. In 1871 he was a member of the convention called to frame a new constitution for the State of Nebraska. His daughter, Henrietta Campbell, married, at Nebraska City, in 1887, Mr. George Sumner Baskerville—a familiar name in old Virginia. He is a son of Colonel William Baskerville, a distinguished lawyer of Mecklenburg, who represented the south-east district of Virginia in the state senate before the war, during which he was a member of the Confederate Congress. The son entered Hampden Sidney, in which he took a four years' course; he then spent two years at Yale Divinity School, and graduated at the Theological Seminary, at Hartford, Connecticut, in 1882. Margaret Madison Campbell, daughter of Dr. John Poage Campbell and Isabella McDowell, was the sensible, cultivated, most interesting, amiable wife of Thomas J. Pickett, of Mason county; a man of the most honorable character, of the most scrupulous and inexorable integrity, a shrewd judge of men, of acute and broad intellect; a gentleman of rare taste and varied culture. A most worthy and faithful representative of his county in the state legislature, his voluntary withdrawal from all public life deprived the state of one of its best minds. His sterling worth and generous nature were made conspicuous in vicissitudes before which a manliness less robust and true would have succumbed. Mr. Pickett was one of the sons of Colonel John Pickett, an early settler in Mason county, which he acceptably represented in both branches of the state legislature. Colonel James C. Pickett, the elder brother of Thomas J., was distinguished as a legislator, as a diplomatist, and as a man of letters. William, the father of Colonel John Pickett, a native of Fauquier county, was a Revolutionary soldier, a valued captain in the regiment commanded by Colonel Thomas Marshall, and a member of the Burgesses. The mother of Colonel John Pickett was a Metcalfe, of the same blood as that of the " Old Stone Hammer," governor of Kentucky. The first wife of Governor Metcalfe's father was also a Pickett. The family were of Fauquier—" the fighting Picketts," they are called in Virginia and South Carolina—as noted for their graceful wit in the social circle, as they have been distinguished for gallantry in the field. Campbell, Pickett and Metcalfe were good shoots to graft upon the McDowell stock. The only son of Mr. and Mrs. Thos. J. Pickett, is Dr. Thomas E. Pickett, of Maysville, a graduate of Center College and of the University of Pennsylvania.

2. Sallie, the second daughter of Colonel James McDowell, married Oliver Keene, of Fayette county; her son, Oliver Keene, Jr., married a daughter of the late Sidney Clay, of Bourbon county, and granddaughter of General Green Clay, of Madison, and his daughter is the wife of Colonel Shackleford, of Richmond. One of Sallie Keene's daughters married Dr. Churchill J. Blackburn, a prosperous physician and farmer of Scott county; another daughter married a Boswell, and removed with her family to Philadelphia. The wife of Mr. Riggs, the Washington banker, an accomplished and beautiful woman, was her daughter.

3. Samuel, the colonel's oldest son, who was sergeant in Captain Trotter's company, and shot the Indian at Mississinewa, married Polly Chrisman, of Jessamine. She was a daughter of Joseph Chrisman, Sr., of Jessamine county, whose mother was a sister of Colonel Joe and General Charles McDowell, of North Carolina, and who was himself a brother of Hugh Chrisman, whose daughter, Betsey, married Major John McDowell's son, Samuel. William McDowell, son of Samuel and Polly Chrisman, is a farmer in Jessamine. One of the daughters of Samuel McDowell and Polly Chrisman, Sarah, married William Steele, and was the mother of John Steele, a substantial farmer of Jessamine, and of William L. Steele, a successful merchant of Nicholasville, where his good sense and high moral character have won for him respect, esteem, and confidence, and who is recognized as possessing the cool, deliberate courage which has been for centuries the McDowell characteristic.

4. Juliet, the third daughter of Colonel McDowell, married Dr. Dorsey, an early physician in Fleming county. She left two daughters, one of whom was the sensible, judicious, excellent Christian woman who became the wife of Hon. L. W. Andrews, whose father, Robert Andrews, was a native of Pennsylvania, of Irish descent. Mr. Andrews himself was born in Fleming county in 1803; educated in the neighboring schools and at Transylvania University; studied law under Judge Roper, and was licensed in 1826. As soon as eligible, he was appointed county attorney of Fleming; then made a gallant and successful race for the legislature in 1834, and was re-elected in 1838. In 1839, he was elected representative in Congress, after a brilliant and heated race, in which, as the Whig candidate, he defeated John C. Mason. In 1841, he was re-elected, and served until 1843; then, having surrendered all his estate, the accumulations of an honorable industry, to discharge obligations incurred for others, he declined a re-election in order to devote himself to his profession. In this he was shrewd, discriminating, industrious, and successful. In

1857, he was elected to the state senate for four years, and was one of those who saved Kentucky to the Union. In 1861, he was again chosen to represent Fleming in the legislature, in which body his course was that of a conservative, firm, patriotic friend of the Union. He resigned, in 1862, to accept a nomination for judge of the circuit court of his district, to discharge the duties of which position, in the precarious situation of the state and people, a man of sense, discretion, character, and decision was required. For six years he held the office, and left it amid the plaudits of a people who recognized his worth. Of quick perceptions, a ready wit, easily adapting himself to the emergencies of the court-house, an amusing, fluent, and most effective public speaker, of marked individuality, and, over and above all, incorruptibly honest, and patriotic, and generous, whether at the bar, in Congress, or upon the bench, Judge Andrews has been distinguished. Fleming county has had no citizen who has exercised a wider influence over her people. His daughter, Juliet, married William L. Sudduth, an estimable citizen and graceful gentleman of Bath. Their son, W. A. Sudduth, born in 1854, graduated at Center College, in 1874, is at the head of the Fleming bar.

5. Hettie, fourth daughter of Colonel McDowell, married John Andrews, brother of Judge L. W. Andrews. Her daughters married brothers, Shepherds, and live in Texas.

6. The second son of Colonel McDowell was Captain John Lyle McDowell, a courageous soldier of the War of 1812, in which his father and brother fought. Volunteering as a mere youth, in 1813, he followed Shelby to the front, participating in all the sanguinary engagements in the North-west, in which Kentuckians, under their martial governor, won fame and honor. He did well his part, as became his lineage. As modest as he was brave, it was his to lead a life of duty in a private station. He inherited the farm in Fayette first owned by his father; selling which to the husband of his daughter—Clifton Ross—he

removed to a large estate owned by him, in Owen county, on the Kentucky river. After an unstained and upright life of eighty-four years, he died, in December, 1878, at the residence of his son-in-law, Captain Samuel Steele, in Frankfort. His wife, Nancy Vance, was a daughter of Richard Scott, whose mother was a Montgomery, a near relative of General Richard Montgomery, who fell at Quebec. Through the Scotts, she was nearly related to the late Judge Wm. S. Botts, of Fleming, and, through the Montgomerys, to the Deshas. Captain Steele, who married one of their daughters, was the son of William Steele and Rebecca McClung—the latter a daughter of John McClung and a sister of Judge William McClung; John McClung was a brother of Mary, the wife of Judge Samuel McDowell; and thus, Captain Steele and his wife were kinspeople. Captain John McDowell's son, James, a farmer, married Lizzie Green, lived long on the bank of the Kentucky river, in Owen, and now resides in Missouri. Alexander Boyd McDowell, a Confederate soldier in McCullough's Missouri cavalry, was killed in battle at Colliersville, Mississippi; his widow, Mrs. Fannie McDowell, and only daughter, Mildred, live at Sedalia, Missouri.

Major Hervey McDowell.

Another son of Captain John Lyle McDowell is Major Hervey McDowell, of Cynthiana. With a large, well-formed head, a high, square forehead and prominent brow; a very large, clear, pale blue eye that looks squarely at you, and sometimes glitters like steel; a full jaw and chin, indicating the utmost resolution and force; an athletic person—with the features that are peculiar to his race, Major McDowell combines, to a remarkable degree, the family traits. About his manner there is a quiet reserve; his appearance and bearing impress all who meet him as those of a man absolutely impenetrable to fear, and as absolutely incapable of falsehood or any kind of meanness. The soldiers who fought by his side in the Confederate army describe his courage as heroic, his coolness and composure

under the heaviest fire as phenomenal.   These characteristics were most amply tested.   Graduating at the military
school near Frankfort, in 1856, and at the Medical College
of St. Louis, in 1858, he abandoned a large medical practice at Cynthiana, in 1861, to recruit a company for Roger
W. Hanson's Confederate Second Kentucky Infantry, in
which he was made a captain.   With this regiment he remained until the close of the war.   Captured and badly
wounded in the head at Fort Donelson, he was a prisoner
for six months at Camp Chase and Johnson's Island.   Exchanged at Vicksburg, in September, 1862, he returned at
once to his command and to the front.   At Hartsville, in
November, 1862, he was in the thickest of the fray.   At
Murfreesboro, he was in the desperate charge of Breckinridge's Division, in which Hanson fell, was shot through
both arms, and wounded in three other places.   At Jackson, Chickamauga, Mission Ridge, Dalton, Resaca, Dallas,
Kenesaw, Peach Tree Creek, in the intrenchments at Utay
Creek, in all the fights around Atlanta, at Jonesboro (where
he was again captured), in several battles in South Carolina—one of them on the old battle ground of Camden;
wounded for the seventh time at Resaca, and six times
again in other battles; in Kentucky, Tennessee, Mississippi, Alabama, Georgia, and South Carolina; in prison, in
camp, on the march, in the hottest fights of the bloody
war; in victory and in defeat; always uncomplaining,
calm, energetic and daring, he exhibited the best qualities
of a soldier.   Promoted to the majorship for gallantry on
the field at Chickamauga, and to the lieutenant-colonelcy
for meritorious conduct at Jonesboro, covering the Confederate retreat before Sherman's march to the sea—the
regiment having been mounted for the purpose—no man
in that service has a more honorable record.   Returning
to Cynthiana after the cause of the Confederacy had gone
down forever, he resumed his practice of medicine, spent
several additional years in study and in practice in St. Louis,
returned to Cynthiana again in 1869, and has since been
as conspicuous for success and skill as a physician as he

5

had been for good conduct as a soldier—the two callings, arms and medicine, in which so many of his name and kindred have been distinguished. In St. Louis, in 1869, he married Louise Irvine McDowell, daughter of Alexander Marshall McDowell, a planter of Alabama and first cousin to his own father. They have several children. He is a Presbyterian elder, and has been active and useful in the promotion of education.

7. The youngest child of Colonel James McDowell and Mary Paxton Lyle was Dr. Ephraim McDowell, of Mason county, a handsome, graceful gentleman and a successful physician. His first wife was Ann, daughter of General Robert Poage, who commanded a brigade in the war of 1812. General Robert Poage was a descendant of the Robert Poage who "proved his importation" at Orange Court House in 1740, and whose daughter was the first wife of Colonel Robert Breckinridge and mother of General Robert Breckinridge of Kentucky. Dr. McDowell's second wife was Lucretia C. Feemster. One of their sons is Dr. Lucien McDowell, of Flemingsburg, who was first a captain and then a surgeon in the Confederate army. Dr. Ephraim McDowell's daughter Mary married Frank Garrard, a grandson of the second Governor of Kentucky. They live in Pendleton county. Dr. Ephraim McDowell had another son, James, who was a Captain of a Missouri company in the Confederate army. He died from the effects of wounds received while fighting at the front in the battle of Springfield, Mo.

Judge William McDowell.

The third son of Judge Samuel McDowell and Mary McClung, William, was born in Rockbridge, March 9, 1762. He also saw active service during the Revolution, not in the Continental army, but as one of the Virginia militia. The private letters of his father show that he was frequently in arms to protect the settlers in Kentucky. To him tradition assigns the reputation of having been the most thoroughly educated, most learned and accomplished of all the sons of his father. His education was obtained at the best schools in Virginia; of the opportunities they afforded, his honorable ambition spurred him on to take full advantage. The lawyer of his family, in that profession he was at once able, distinguished, and successful. Coming with his father to Kentucky, in 1784, and locating at first near Danville—then the religious, educational, social, and political center of the district—he immediately became not less prominent in public affairs than he was at the bar. His name, with those of his father, Judges Speed, Ormsby, Todd, Innes, Muter, and Wallace; Governors Shelby, Scott, Garrard, and Greenup; Willis Green, Humphrey Marshall, and others, is signed to the paper calling a meeting to establish the " Kentucky Society for the Promotion of Useful Knowledge," dated at Danville, December 1, 1787.—[*Collins.*] At the session of that same year, he acceptably represented Mercer county in the Virginia Legislature. The first senator from Mercer county—after serving from 1792 to 1796 he was re-elected in 1800, and, two years thereafter, was chosen to represent the same county in the house. Appointed by Governor Shelby, in 1792, the first auditor of the state, he was succeeded, in 1796, by George Madison, whose accomplished sister he had married. By the Virginia Legislature of 1787, he was appointed one of the first trustees of the town of Danville.—[*Henning.*] His high character, united to his real ability and solid attainments, commended him for appointment as United States District Judge for Kentucky to President Madison, the cousin of his wife. He held the office for years, with distinction to himself, discharging its duties with such marked ability and impartiality as to win respect from all, and with such grace as made him popular and beloved. During his incumbency of this office, he removed to Bowling Green, where he died, full of honors, and after a life well spent. Judge William McDowell married Margaretta Madison. daughter of John Madison, a brother of the father of President Madison. Her father was the son of Ambrose Madison and Frances Taylor, the latter a member of the

distinguished race from which came John Taylor, of Car-
oilne, which gave to the United States a hero president of
that name, and from whom also the Pendletons, respectable as lawyers, judges, senators, congressmen, gentlemen, and soldiers, are descended.   General Samuel Hopkins, of Kentucky, also came from a union of this Taylor
and Pendleton blood with that of the substantial Welsh
people whose name he bore. The wife of John Madison and
mother of Margaretta was Agatha Strother, daughter of
William Strother, of Stafford county, and Margaretta
Watts. "Old Rough and Ready" came from a union
of this Strother blood with that of Dabney and Taylor.
The sisters of Agatha Strother married the able and
learned Thomas Lewis, the renowned Gabriel Jones, and
the gallant Captain John Frog. Mrs. Frog was the mother
of the hero of the same name.   John Madison, the father of
Margaretta, was the first clerk of Augusta county, a
member of the first vestry formed within its limits, active
in setting on foot the exploring expeditions into Kentucky, and one of the most prominent, useful, and influential men in Augusta during the Revolution.   One of the
brothers of Margaretta was James Madison, the first
American-born bishop of the Episcopal Church of Virginia—able, learned, and accomplished.   Another of her
brothers, General Richard Madison, married a daughter of
the first Colonel William Preston, of Virginia, and was
the progenitor of a large family extensively intermarried
with their Preston kinspeople—the Bowyers, Peytons,
Lewises, and others.   Her brother, General Thomas Madison, married Susanna Henry, a sister of the great orator.
Margaretta's brother, Gabriel Madison, one of the early
pioneers of Kentucky, and who frequently held important
public positions in the district and state, married Miriam
Lewis; the Banks family, of Henderson, are his descendants.   Margaretta's brother, Roland, also one of the pioneers, married Anne, daughter of General Andrew Lewis;
his descendants live in Indiana and Maryland.   Yet
another brother of Margaretta was the distinguished
Major George Madison, the hero governor of Kentucky,

whose wife was a daughter of Major Francis Smith, of the Revolution, and a granddaughter of the first John Preston. Governor Madison's only daughter married William Alexander, and was the mother of the wife of General Frank Blair. Than with this Madison-Taylor-Strother cross, the McDowells have made no better alliance.

1. Judge William McDowell's son, Samuel I. McDowell, represented Warren county in the legislature in 1823, '24, as appears from the journal of that body, of which he was an active and useful member. He married Miss Nancy Rochester, and left issue.

2. Judge William McDowell's daughter, Lucinda, a beautiful and cultivated woman, with a character as elevated as her person was graceful and lovely, married Dennis Brashear, a very handsome and well-educated man, who died early in life, and of whom there is but little record. Their daughter, Mary Eliza Brashear, was the second wife of Joseph Sullivant, of Columbus, Ohio, by whom she was the mother of six children; the oldest daughter, Lucy Madison, is the wife of General James A. Wilcox, of Columbus, a gallant soldier in the Federal army; Pamela Sullivant, the second daughter, described by those who know her best as a woman of rare intellectual gifts, a brilliant conversationalist as well of strong individuality, and who is certainly a most charming writer, is the wife of Robert Samuel Neil, a son of one of the robust and enterprising pioneers of Ohio, and the owner of a large stock farm near Columbus. Lucas Sullivant, the oldest son of Joseph Sullivant and Mary Eliza Brashear, was a professor of anatomy in the Starling Medical College, of Columbus, and died young. Lyne Starling, the second son, entered the Federal army at the outbreak of hostilities, and remained in it until the close of the war. As lieutenant of ordinance, captain and major of the One Hundred and Thirteenth Ohio Regiment, at Dallas, Chickamauga, Kenesaw, Peach Orchard, Atlanta, and in the "March to the Sea," he vindicated his claim to a large share of the McDowell-Madison-Taylor-Strother blood.

Pamela Brashear, the oldest daughter of Dennis Brashear and Lucinda McDowell, married John Trotter, a son of the Captain George Trotter who fought at Mississinewa, under Major James McDowell, and who for gallantry was made a colonel; the mother of John Trotter was a sister of the distinguished statesman and orator, Governor John Pope. Pamela Brashear had no children by this marriage with Trotter, after whose death she married Charles Alexander, an uncle of the late "Lord" Robert A. Alexander, and of the present A. John Alexander, of Woodburn, Woodford county. After Dennis Brashear's death, Lucinda married General Merrill, of Lexington.

3. Mary, second daughter of William McDowell, was the first wife of the late Major George C. Thompson, of Mercer county, Kentucky, a son of George Thompson, one of the early pioneers of Kentucky, and a near kinsman of Hon. John B. Thompson, United States senator. Major Thompson represented Mercer frequently in the legislature, was a man of large wealth and influence. Their children were Colonel Wm. M. Thompson, formerly of Keokuk, Iowa, and now of Florida; and Mrs. Mary Kinkead, widow of the late Frank Kinkead, of Woodford—a woman of intelligence, of great purity and elevation of character, who employs her large wealth in works of benevolence and religion.

4. Judge William McDowell's son, William, married a Miss Carthrac. She was the daughter of John Carthrae, of Rockingham, Virginia, and Sophia Lewis, daughter of Thomas Lewis and Jane Strother, and thus doubly related to her husband.

5. Agatha, the fourth daughter of Judge McDowell, married James G. Birney, the abolition candidate for president in 1844. Mr. Birney's father, James Birney, was a native of Ireland, who had settled at an early day on a farm near Danville, and whose wife was one of the daughters of John Reed, also an Irishman, who had emigrated to Virginia about the middle of the eighteenth century, and was one of the pioneers of Lincoln county, where he built his fort, in 1779. Many men of distinguished talents

trace their ancestry to this John Reed and Lettice Wilcox, his wife. His youngest son, Thomas B. Reed, was the eloquent United States senator from Mississippi. The late Wm. D. Reed, Judge John Green, Rev. Dr. Lewis Warner Green, Willis G. Hughes, and James Gillespie Birney, were among his grandsons. The wives of Major James Barbour, of Dr. William Craig, of Dr. Ben. Edwards, of Judge Cyrus Edwards, of Judge Paul Booker, of Sidney Clay, were among his granddaughters. Revs. Joshua F. and William L. Green, James and Rev. Lewis G. Barbour, Rev. Dr. Willis G. Craig, Dr. Willis G. Edwards, of St. Louis, and General Humphrey Marshall, were among his great-grandsons. The history of James Gillespie Birney is that of Kentucky, the South, and of the country. His son, General William M. Birney, is engaged upon a work which will present the details of his life, and which it is unnecessary to anticipate. His oldest son by Agatha Mc-Dowell, James G. Birney, an intellectual and cultivated man, an able and learned lawyer, won distinction and wealth at the bar in Michigan, was lieutenant-governor of that state, and was the accomplished Minister of the United States at The Hague. In the war he was a colonel, and did good service. The second son, William M. Birney, an elegant scholar, was for some years professor of English literature in the University of Paris, France; returning to this country, engaged in the successful practice of the law in Cincinnati and Philadelphia; was all through the war as a colonel and brigadier in the Federal army; and now, in the afternoon of his life, enjoys a lucrative practice at the bar of Washington City; one of his daughters has been successful in literature. The third son of James G. and Agatha Birney was the handsome and chivalric David Bell Birney, talented as a lawyer, and successful in business in Philadelphia; as colonel of a Pennsylvania regiment, he was one of the most daring fighters under the gallant Phil. Kearney, was promoted to the rank of general for distinguished gallantry in the field, and died from exposure, in 1864.

6. Eliza, the youngest child of Judge William McDow-

ell, married Mr. Nathaniel Rochester, of Bowling Green, and left several children, one of whom, Agatha Rochester, married Mr. Strange, of Bowling Green.

SAMUEL McDOWELL, OF MERCER.

To distinguish the fourth son of Judge Samuel Mc-Dowell and Mary McClung from his father and nephews of the same given name, he is designated as of Mercer county. Born in Rockbridge, March 8, 1764, his tender years prevented him from going into the patriot army at the beginning of the Revolution. Before its close, however, he disappeared from home, at the age of seventeen years, joined Lafayette as a private soldier in the final campaign against Cornwallis, remained with that command until the end of the struggle, which he witnessed at Yorktown, in the siege and fighting at which place he took a lively hand. His service was brief, he made good use of the time at his disposal, and was "in at the death." His father, suspecting the cause of his disappearance from home, wrote to his elder brother, James, to keep a sharp lookout for him among the new recruits. Finding him footsore and sick, James wrote to their father to let him have his fill of the realities of war as the best antidote for his military penchant. The interval between the close of the war and the removal of the family to Kentucky was passed in the completion of his education. With them he removed to Mercer county, in 1784, there located, and there continued to reside during the remainder of his honorable life. In the defense of the district, he saw frequent additional service as a soldier, and accompanied General Charles Scott in his expedition against the Indians of the North-west. In General Hopkins' expedition against the Indians of Illinois, he was a valued officer, though his age then nearly reached half a century. Washington gave another evidence of his confidence in and regard for the family by appointing him the first United States Marshal for Kentucky, when the state was organized, in 1792. In subsequent years, the office has frequently been vastly more lucrative, but it has never been of greater importance than in that epoch of confusion and conspiracies. With unimpeached probity, and the utmost fidelity, he discharged the duties of the position during the remainder of the first and all of the second term of Washington, all that of John Adams, and part of that of Jefferson. He could not swerve from his devotion to the Federalism of Washington to secure the good-will of "the apostle of Democracy," and was by him dismissed, and Colonel Crockett appointed as his successor. His letters disclose his conviction that his removal was attributable to the unfriendly representations of Senator John Brown, who, from being a friend, had become an active and malevolent enemy of all the family. It was natural and inevitable that so ardent a Federalist should also have been equally as zealous as a patriot. His letters show that even at so early a day he was keenly alive to the pernicious tendencies of the principles of disintegration which then threatened the future of the country, and culminated in the attempt to dissolve the Union. They also disclose spirit and culture, and show him to have been a well-informed, educated, thoughtful man of sense. A deeply religious man, without parade or austerity, his character was as attractive as his temper was amiable. Possessed of a natural pride in his name and kindred, an earnest belief in their merits, and a warm desire for their advancement, those will not be surprised who read in one of his letters to his brother-in-law, General Andrew Reid, of Rockbridge, under date of September 22, 1813, an exclamation of delight at hearing that General Reid's son, Samuel McDowell Reid, who had volunteered, and was doing good service in the war, was "likely to be an honor to the name"—an anticipation that was most happily realized. Nor will the reader wonder at what follows: "*The name is rising in Kentucky*, all that the Democrats can say to the contrary, notwithstanding." But the explanation of this gratified pride will in vain be sought for in any dwelling upon their social station, though that was high, as it had always been; or in any boast of their increasing wealth, though they were among the largest land-holders of the state; or in any allusion to the political honors that had been bestowed on them in a state where Federalists were unpopular. The explanatory lines that follow reveal the man, as they are characteristic of the race: " There were seven of the family out last fall (*i. e.*, in the war) and winter, *and they all behaved well.* . . . Brother Joseph is his (Shelby's) adjutant-general, and my son John his assistant. William McD.'s sons, Sam. and Madison, and James McDowell's son John are also with him. . . . My son Abram was out with the army all last winter; he was with Colonel Campbell at Massasineway. He went out last spring as assistant quartermaster-general from this state; he was taken down with the fever in July last, and has not yet entirely recovered. I could hardly prevent him from going out with Shelby. . . . I believe it is the wish of all Kentuckians that the war should be prosecuted with vigor." In a letter of an earlier date, August 10, 1807, he wrote: "Kentucky is all in a buzz again. Federal Republicans and Democratic Jacobins all join to fight the British. . . . Nothing has happened . . . that has excited so general disgust as the outrage of the Leopard on the Chesapeake. . . . But one sentiment appears to prevail in the heart of every Kentuckian—the hope that our administration will take spirited and manly measures, . . . and let the British see that the Americans have respect for their *honor*, as well as their interest, and the courage to defend it. . . . The people of Kentucky are beginning to have their eyes opened, and to discover that the Federal Republicans are the only true friends to their country. Humphrey Marshall is elected representative from Franklin county by a large majority, in defiance of the Democrats and Spanish conspirators, and John Rowan is sent to Congress from one of the most respectable districts in the state."

Among the very earliest settlers in the Valley of Virginia, were Scotch-Irish Presbyterian families, named Irvine, kinsmen of the McDowells, and probably descended from brothers of Ephraim McDowell's wife, who emigrated with him to Pennsylvania, and some of whom fol-

lowed him to Burden's Grant. Their names are found
among the soldiers of the French and Indian War, as well
as in the war of the Revolution, from both Pennsylvania
and Virginia. Members of the family were among the
first settlers of Mercer county, neighbors to their Mc-
Dowell kin. Among the magistrates who held the first
county court in Mercer, in August, 1786, were John Irvine, Samuel McDowell, Sr., and Gabriel Madison. One
of this family, Anna, daughter of Abram Irvine, became
the wife of her kinsman, Samuel McDowell, of Mercer.
Eleven children were born to these well-mated kinspeople.
1. John Adair McDowell, their oldest son, was born in
Mercer county, May 26, 1789; was well educated at the
best schools in the state; studied law in Mason county
under Alexander K. Marshall, who had married one of his
aunts, and who was one of the ablest lawyers in the state,
as well as one of the most intellectual members of that
extensive family. John Adair McDowell was with
General Samuel Hopkins in his expeditions against the
Illinois Indians in the fall of 1812, rendering valuable
services to that officer. When Governor Shelby called
upon the men of Kentucky to meet him at the mouth of
the Licking with their rifles, with the inspiring promise,
" I will lead you," his old friends, the McDowells, were of
the earliest to respond, and John Adair McDowell again
went to the field. Shelby at once placed him on his confidential staff, and as an aide he was with the hardy, brave
old soldier at the Thames, and throughout all the arduous
campaign. When very young, he had married Lucy Todd
Starling, a daughter of William Starling and Susannah
Lyne, who were then residents of Mercer county. After
the close of the war, Major McDowell was induced by
Lucas Sullivant, who had married a sister of his wife, to
remove to Columbus, Ohio, whither he went, in 1815, immediately entering upon a successful career as a lawyer.
In 1819, he was appointed attorney for the state; he was
a member of the Ohio Legislature in 1820, '21; his abilities and attainments received appropriate recognition in
his appointment as Judge of the Circuit Court for the

Columbus District, a position to which he gave dignity, and held at the time of his death, in the prime of a vigorous manhood, in 1823. Handsome in person, of graceful manners, amiable temper, and decided character, he won affection and respect from all; death alone interfered between him and the highest honors of his adopted state. 1. His daughter, Anne, born in 1810, married John Winston Price, of Hillsboro. Her husband was a descendant of the second William Randolph, of Turkey Island, whose wife was a Miss Beverly; also of the gifted Winstons, from whom came Patrick Henry, the Prestons, of South Carolina, and General Joseph E. Johnston, of the Confederate army. Mr. Price had been a law student under his relative, Chief Justice Marshall, and was for many years Judge of the Court of Common Pleas for the Hillsboro District. They had many children. 2. Another daughter of Major John Adair McDowell married Hon. John A. Smith, a lawyer of Hillsboro, who was honored by the people among whom he lived by election several times to the state legislature, to two constitutional conventions, and as congressman for the district for several terms. They also have a large family.

Abram Irvine, the second son of Samuel McDowell, of Mercer, and Anna Irvine, was born April 24, 1793. A soldier in the War of 1812, he fought at Mississinewa. Going to Columbus, Ohio, he was, for many years, clerk of the supreme court, of the court of common pleas, and of the court in bank, and was, at one time, mayor of Columbus—an urbane man, much beloved and respected. His wife was Eliza Selden, daughter of Colonel Lord, whom he married in 1817. General Irvine McDowell, of the United States army, who attained the highest military rank of any of the name, was his oldest son; Colonel John McDowell, a good soldier in the Union army, now living in Keokuk, Iowa, was another son; and Malcolm McDowell, also an officer in the Union army, a third son; while his daughter, Elize, married Major Bridgeman, of the regular army.

Dr. Wm. A. McDowell.

The fourth son of Samuel McDowell, of Mercer, and Anna Irvine, by name William Adair, was born at the family residence in Mercer, March 21, 1795. He was educated in the schools in the neighborhood of Danville, the best in the state, and at Washington College, Lexington, Va. In a letter of his father, already quoted, under date of September 22, 1813, mention is made of seven of the name being in the army, among them his elder brothers, John Adair and Abram Irvine. In another letter, also addressed to General Andrew Reid, at Lexington, Virginia, dated April 14, 1814, his father said: "My son, William, will hand you this. I have sent him to Washington Academy to stay one year. . . . He has been living with Dr. Ephraim McDowell for twelve months past, studying medicine. I wish him to study science, and intended sending him to the University at Lexington, Kentucky; but the fever has been so fatal there, and still is, *and parties are so violent*, that I have sent him to your country." . . . In another letter to General Andrew Reid, dated September 16, 1814, his father wrote: "This evening I received a letter from William, informing me that he was drafted, and was just about starting to Richmond. . . . I hope you will write me soon, and let me know how William went. . . . He is young and inexperienced, and I feel uneasy about him." . . . So he also had a part in the War of 1812, and it is known that he did some actual fighting; and if he ran with the others, at Bladensburg, there is precious little ground to blame him for that. He was in General Winder's command. At the conclusion of the war, he returned to Washington Academy, then renewed his medical studies with Dr. Ephraim McDowell, at Danville, and received his diploma from the Medical College of Philadelphia. Returning to Danville, he entered upon the practice of medicine with Dr. Ephraim McDowell, whom he assisted in some of the difficult operations which rendered the latter famous throughout the world. From 1819 to 1838 he resided, and most successfully practiced, in Fincastle, Virginia; then, removing to Louisville, he continued there, with a brief interval passed in Evansville, Indiana, until his death. In 1843, he published an interesting volume of original and striking observations upon the subject of pulmonary consumption. In Fincastle, August 24, 1819, Dr. McDowell married his kinswoman by the half blood, Maria Hawkins Harvey. She was the daughter of Matthew Harvey, a Revolutionary soldier, whose wife was Magdalen Hawkins, daughter of Benjamin Hawkins, a gay, handsome and graceful cavalier, who had run away with and married Martha Burden, daughter of Benjamin Burden, Jr., and Magdalena Wood, the widow of Captain John McDowell, killed by the Indians in 1742. Thus, the blood of Benjamin Burden, the grantee, and of John McDowell, without whose aid he could not have fulfilled the conditions of the grant, met in the union of Dr. McDowell and his lovely kinswoman—still beautiful when the writer saw her, thirty years ago. Ben. Hawkins and Martha Burden had five other children besides the wife of Matthew Harvey, one of whom was a daughter, Sarah Hawkins, who married Thomas Mitchell, the son of James Mitchell and Captain John McDowell's sister, Margaret. The son of this Thomas Mitchell and Sarah Hawkins was the old cashier at Danville of the same name. And thus, again, the blood of McDowell, Mitchell, Burden and Hawkins mingled.

JUDGE BALLARD.

1. Sarah Shelby McDowell, oldest daughter of Dr. Wm. Adair McDowell and Maria Hawkins Harvey, married Bland Ballard, nephew and namesake of the noted pioneer and Indian fighter. Mr. Ballard attained a high position as a lawyer in Louisville, but his frankly-avowed sentiments in opposition to slavery and its extension, excluded him from political honors. When the office of United States district judge was vacated by Hon. Thomas B. Monroe, in 1861, Mr. Ballard was appointed to the position by Mr. Lincoln, and held it until his death, eighteen years thereafter. The situation of the state and her people during and after the war; the passage of the Freed-

men's Bureau and Civil Rights bills, and other similar measures, by Congress; the new and frequently-changing laws for the collection of internal revenue, and other enactments of a similar nature, bringing before Judge Ballard, for decision, many intricate questions, involving principles never before adjudicated in this country: combined to render the duties of his position at once delicate and perplexing. To the discharge of these duties he brought the powers of a clear, well-balanced mind, professional attainments that were highly respectable, and the vigor of decided and firmly-rooted convictions. Judge Ballard's widow and a number of children survive him; among others, a son who bears his name, and a daughter who is the incarnation of the graces.

2. Henry Clay McDowell, the oldest son of Dr. William Adair McDowell, was well educated, graduated with credit in the Louisville Law School, and won his own way to a successful practice in the profession. For some years he was the partner of Judge Ballard. Inheriting the political opinions of those who preceded him, he was one of the earliest in Kentucky to enlist in the Union army, and as aide to General Alexander McDowell McCook, with the rank of captain, he saw much active service, participating in the hard fighting of the campaigns of the Army of the Cumberland. He left the service to accept, from Mr. Lincoln, the position of United States Marshal for Kentucky. A splendid specimen of physical manhood, tall, well proportioned and vigorous, black haired and dark eyed, graceful in carriage and manners, at once amiable and spirited, just minded and sensible, it is natural that, while adhering to his own convictions, he should enjoy the respect and esteem of those who differ from him the most widely. Captain McDowell married Annette, daughter of the hero son of Kentucky's " Great Commoner "—Lieutenant-Colonel Henry Clay, who watered the field of Buena Vista with the rich current of his life's blood. The wife of Colonel Henry Clay was one of the daughters of Thomas Prather, a man of the highest character, who, as one of the early merchants of Louisville, and perhaps the most successful

and wealthy of his generation, sustained a reputation for the most scrupulous honor, second to that of no man in the country. The wife of Thomas Prather was one of nine beautiful sisters, the Misses Fontaine, daughters of one of the earliest of the pioneers, and descendants of Jacques Fontaine, born at the village of Chatelas, and long the pious Huguenot pastor of Royan, whence he fled on the Revocation of the Edict of Nantes. The descendants of this noble man, under his own name, and that of Maury, and others, have been eminent in Virginia, in the West and South, as Episcopal ministers, as scientists, and in all the learned professions. One of the sisters of Mrs. Clay was the beautiful first wife of Rev. Dr. E. P. Humphrey, and another, the first wife of the distinguished and able Judge S. S. Nicholas, of Louisville. Captain Henry C. McDowell resides at the old "Ashland" home of his wife's grandfather, the patriot orator, Henry Clay.

3. Wm. Preston, second son of Dr. Wm. Adair McDowell, also went into the Union army at the beginning of the civil war, his first service being as adjutant of the Fifteenth Kentucky Infantry, commanded by Colonel Curran H. Pope; afterwards as aide to General L. H. Rousseau, with the rank of major. In the battle of Perryville, he was wounded; at Stone River, his conduct was gallant and meritorious. He married Miss Kate Wright, and lives in Louisville.

4. Edward Irvine, the fourth son of Dr. Wm. A. McDowell, as captain in the Fifteenth Kentucky Infantry, had a record for good conduct and courage in many of the hardest fought battles in the West—an honorable career, which was ended by his heroic death at Resaca; shot through the head while leading his men in a charge upon the Confederate rifle-pits.

Joseph, fifth son of Samuel McDowell, of Mercer, and Anna Irvine, married Anne Bush, settled in Alabama, where he achieved prominence as a lawyer. His daughter, Mary, married Judge Clarke, of Mississippi; Bettie married Dr. Welch, and settled in Galveston, Texas.

Alexander Keith Marshall, the youngest son of Samuel

McDowell, of Mercer, and Anna Irvine, was born in Mercer in 1806. His childhood was passed in Mercer. His mother dying when he was about ten years old, he was sent to Franklinton, Ohio, where he lived, alternatively, with his two elder brothers, and attended school. Later, he received instruction at the academy of the learned and celebrated Dr. Priestley, in Tennessee, where one of his classmates was Andrew J. Donelson; and afterward was sent to the college at Nashville. On attaining maturity, he bought land near Palmyra, Missouri, and while living there, married Priscilla, daughter of General Robert Mc-Afee—the historian of, and a gallant officer in, the War of 1812—who had removed from Kentucky to Missouri. After a brief residence in Missouri, he determined to settle permanently in the South; and while proceeding thither with his wife and their infant, the two latter died tragically in the burning of the "Ben. Sherrad," on the Mississippi, while the bereaved husband made the narrowest of escapes by swimming the great river. Returning to Missouri, after another brief residence there, he sold his lands, and, with his servants, went to Demopolis, Alabama, where he bought a plantation. After a widowerhood of fifteen years, he there married Anna, daughter of Sebastian Haupt, a native of Philadelphia, and son of a rich ship-owner of that city. Mr. Haupt had been for many years a prosperous coffee planter in the Island of Trinidad, and on returning to this country, avoided the rigors of northern winters by settling upon large tracts of rich land which he bought in Greene and Sumpter counties, Alabama. Miss Haupt was an educated and intellectual woman. Her husband, Mr. McDowell, after their marriage, continued to live upon and cultivate a cotton plantation, together with the avocations of a civil engineer, for which he had been educated, until about four years before the war, when he became a resident of Demopolis. He had taken part in the "Black Hawk War," in which he was wounded in the knee, crippling him for life. His condition did not prevent his early enlistment in the

6

southern army, but he was soon detailed from the line to other and more important duties. About the time of the surrender, he was chosen probate judge of Marengo county. In 1868, he sold out what possessions in Alabama the war had left him, and removed to St. Louis, where he remained until 1873, when he became a citizen of Cynthiana, and afterward clerk of the Harrison circuit court. A handsome, stately gentleman, of winning and graceful manners, sunny temper, extensive reading, and attractive gifts, he is also an uncompromising Calvinist. His only surviving daughter, Mrs. Louise Irvine McDowell, is the wife of her kinsman, Dr. Hervey McDowell, of Cynthiana—an accomplished lady, of native talent broadened by elegant culture, whose general and accurate information, not less than her ready and sportive wit, render her the most interesting of correspondents, the most charming of conversationalists. His son, Colonel E. C. McDowell, lives at Columbia, Tenn.

Sallie, the youngest daughter of Samuel McDowell, of Mercer, born in 1801, married Jeremiah Minter, at Columbus, Ohio, March 12, 1819; resided for years in Lexington, Kentucky; then removed to Missouri, where her numerous posterity live.

THE STARLINGS.

Mary, the oldest child of Samuel and Anna (Irvine) McDowell, was born in Mercer, June 12, 1787, and, on the 13th of June, 1805, married William Starling, and at first settled near Danville, Kentucky. An interesting account of Mr. Starling's family may be found in the valuable family memorial published by his nephew, Mr. Joseph Sullivant, of Columbus, Ohio. After leaving the vicinity of Danville, Mr. Starling moved with his family to a fine farm opposite Frankfort, and for some years was engaged in mercantile pursuits in that city. Meeting with business reverses, he removed from Frankfort to Christian county, where he died. His widow, a strong-minded and well-informed woman, of great energy and firm purpose, survived him many years, revered of all for the highest qualities of a noble womanhood. Dying at a good old age, she bequeathed her resolution and courage to a gallant brood. Lyne, the oldest of her hardy offspring, was born in 1806; studied law, and entered upon its practice, in Columbus, Ohio; abandoned the profession to accept an appointment to the clerkship of the court of common pleas and of the supreme court. Resigning this position, after having secured a competence, his business ventures led him, at various times, to New York City, to Illinois, and to the South. The waves of the civil war had scarcely broken upon Kentucky, when this amiable, lovable and courteous gentleman entered the Union service. As chief of staff to General Thomas L. Crittenden, with the rank of colonel, his services were valuable in the organization of the splendid Army of the Cumberland; upon the bloody field of Shiloh, he was distinguished for cool courage and capacity; and for gallant conduct at Stone River and subsequent campaigns in which Crittenden's corps participated, he was promoted to the rank of general. He married Marie Antoinette Hensley. His oldest son, William, was also in the Union army. Lyne, another son, married his kinswoman, Miss Watson, a granddaughter of John J. Crittenden. His daughter, Lizzie, a brilliant woman, is the wife of Robert P. Pepper, of Frankfort.

The second son of William Starling and Mary McDowell, Samuel, was born September 19, 1807. Well read, robust in mind and body, he had passed his half century four years before the civil war. Thoroughly a patriot, with an inherited devotion to the union of the states, his years did not prevent him from offering his services to the imperilled government. As chief of staff to General James S. Jackson, he was by the side of that chivalric officer when he fell at Perryville; then, taking charge of the dead Jackson's Division, he led it into the fight, commanded it to the close of the severe engagement, and displayed high qualities as a soldier; was afterwards an officer of cavalry, and served npon the staff of General Judah. The McDowell race has given to the country no braver man. Colonel Samuel Starling married Elizabeth Lewis. Among the notable alliances of this historic breed, the history of no family is more interesting than that of the wife of Colonel Samuel Starling—one of the most ancient in America; illustrious in its various lines, in arms, in statesmanship, in the professions, and in the deeds of manhood. Of the Welsh colonists, who gave tone to the society of Virginia in the first half of the seventeenth century, not one was more respectable, nor one of higher character and standing, than General Robert Lewis, who, with his kindred, came over about the year 1645, entered lands, and made his home in one of the tide-water counties. His people had been sheriffs, sheriff deputies, county lieutenants, justices, and members of Parliament from Brecknock, Pembroke, Glamorgan, and other counties of Wales, for centuries before he founded in this country a hardy and enduring race; and, to the present day, the name of Lewis belongs to the most prominent of the Welsh landed gentry. He had two sons, John and William. John married Isabella Warner, probably a daughter of the Captain Augustine Warner, also a Welshman, who was a member of the House of Burgesses from York county, in 1652, and again, from Gloucester, in 1658, '59, and a member of the Royal Council in 1659, '60. Another daughter of this Captain Augustine and Mary Warner, Sarah, married Colonel Lawrence Towneley, and was the ancestress of "Light Horse Harry," and of General Robert E. Lee. Captain Warner had also a son, Augustine Warner, born in Virginia in 1642, educated at the Merchants Tailors' School, in London, and at Cambridge, and who was Speaker of the House of Burgesses in 1676, '77—of the house succeeding the downfall of Bacon's Rebellion—and again, in 1680; and was a member of the Royal Council in 1680, '81. The latter was the colonel commandant of Gloucester county, and is known as Speaker Warner, to distinguish him from his father. His wife was Mildred, daughter of George Reade, who was secretary of the colony in 1637, acting governor in 1638, '39, a member of the House of Burgesses, from James City county, in 1649, and frequently thereafter; a member of the Royal Council in 1657, in 1658, in '59, '60, and succeeding years.

From the sons of George Reade, some of the most eminent men of Virginia and the South descended; one
of his descendants was Thomas Rootes, the grandfather of
Howell Cobb, of Georgia. Speaker Augustine Warner
and Mildred Reade had three daughters. The oldest, Mildred Warner, married Lawrence Washington, son of Colonel John Washington and Anne Pope; Mary, the second
daughter, married Colonel John Smith, of Purtons, son of
the Major John Smith who was the Speaker of the House
of Burgesses in 1660, and subsequent years, and became
the ancestress of a family of that and other names, who
were highly respectable as soldiers, scholars, and in public affairs; Elizabeth, the third daughter, married John
Lewis, son of the above-named John Lewis and Isabella
Warner. The second John Lewis was prominent as a
burgess, as a councillor, and as a citizen. His sons were
John, Charles—a distinguished officer in the French and
Indian War — Warner, who married Eleanor Bowles,
widow of Governor Gooch's son, William, and Fielding.
The latter was the patriotic Colonel Fielding Lewis, of
Fredericksburg, who rendered valuable services to the
cause of independence in the Revolution as superintendent
and owner of the manufactory of arms, advancing large
sums out of his own abundant means to supply the soldiers
of the colonies in the darkest hour of their penury and
distress. Lawrence Washington and Mildred Warner had
three children—John, Augustine, and Mildred. The oldest of these, John, married Catherine Whiting, a beautiful
woman and heiress, of Gloucester, and *their* daughter,
Catherine Washington, was the first wife of her kinsman,
Colonel Fielding Lewis, son of John Lewis and Elizabeth
Warner. Colonel Fielding and Catherine (Washington)
Lewis had an only son to live, named John. Augustine,
second son of Lawrence Washington and Mildred Warner,
married, for his second wife, Mary Ball; their oldest son
was George Washington, President of the United States;
their only daughter, Betty Washington, was the *second*
wife of Colonel Fielding Lewis, by whom she had a numerous progeny, notable in themselves and in their de-

scendants. Mildred, the only daughter of Lawrence Washington and Mildred Warner, married, first, Roger Gregory, by whom she had three daughters, Mildred, Frances, and Elizabeth, who married three brothers, Colonel John, Colonel Francis, and Reuben Thornton. She married, secondly, Colonel Henry Willis, the founder of Fredericksburg, by whom she had a son, Colonel Lewis Willis, and a daughter, Anne, who married Duff Green. John Lewis, the son of Colonel Fielding and Catherine (Washington) Lewis, was married five times. First, to Lucy Thornton, youngest daughter of Colonel John Thornton and Mildred Gregory, by whom he had a daughter, Mildred; the sisters of Lucy Thornton married Samuel Washington, brother of the President, General William Woodford, of the Revolution, and John Taliaferro, of Dissington. Secondly, John Lewis married Elizabeth Thornton, daughter of Colonel Francis Thornton and Frances Gregory, by whom he had no child. One of the brothers of this second wife was the gallant Colonel John Thornton, of the Revolution, who married Jane, daughter of Augustine Washington, elder half brother of the president, and was the ancestor of the wife of Senator James B. Beck. And Mildred, one of the sisters of this second wife, was the wife of Charles Washington, younger full brother of the president. John Lewis' third wife was a daughter of Gabriel Jones, widely known in Virginia during his own generation and for years after all who knew him had passed away, as "*The* Valley Lawyer." Governor Gilmer, of Georgia, in his entertaining sketches of that state, asserts that Gabriel Jones was the " kinsman, friend and executor of Lord Fairfax." He was born in Virginia, was educated at Christ Hospital School in London, served an apprenticeship to a lawyer of Temple Bar, and was persuaded to return to Virginia by his relative Hugh Mercer—a fugitive from the battle of Culloden, where he fought for the Young Pretender, who then settled at Fredericksburg, fought in the French and Indian war, was the first colonel of the Third Virginia Infantry, and died the death of a hero at Princeton. Gabriel Jones rose rapidly in his profession; in attainments he was second to no man at the colonial bar; in native ability he was conspicuous among those who stood in the first rank; he was the first King's attorney for Augusta county, appointed in 1746. The wife of Gabriel Jones was a daughter of William Strother, of Stafford county, and Margaret Watts. This William Strother, of Stafford, was one of the sons of Jeremiah Strother, who died in Stafford in 1741, leaving eight surviving children. James, one of the sons of Jeremiah Strother, married Margaret, daughter of Daniel ·French, of King George county, and died in 1761. French, son of this James, married Lucy Coleman, served in the Colonial House of Burgesses and the state legislature for twenty-nine years, was a member of the convention of 1776, as well as of the convention of 1788–9, which adopted the Federal Constitution. This French Strother's son, George French Strother, represented the Culpepper district in Congress, 1817–20, in which latter year he was appointed receiver of public moneys, at St. Louis; married, first, Sally, daughter of General James Williams; married, second, the accomplished and beautiful Theodosia, daughter of the late John W. Hunt, of Lexington, Kentucky. James French Strother, son of the foregoing George French Strother and Sally Williams, was in the Virginia legislature for ten years, and speaker of the house, 1847–8; was in the constitutional convention of 1850, and a member of congress, 1851–3. The sons of the foregoing James French Strother, namely, James French and Philip W. Strother, are both judges of courts in Virginia; Sallie Strother, daughter of George French Strother and his second wife, Theodosia Hunt, was the late accomplished and gifted Baroness de Fahnenburg. Jeremiah Strother had another son, named Francis, who married Susan Dabney, by whom he had a large family. From the daughters of this Francis' son, John, were descended General E. P. Gaines, of the United States army; General Duff Green, of Rappahannock, and Hon. John Strother Pendleton, distinguished as an orator, diplomatist and congressman. Francis Strother's son, Anthony, was the father of Benjamin

Strother, a gallant officer in the Virginia navy from 1776 to 1779, and an officer in the Continental army thence to the close of the Revolution. This Benjamin was the father of John, who was an officer in the United States army, from the beginning to the close of the War of 1812; was, for many years, clerk of Berkley county, and, at the age of sixty-nine years, volunteered in the Union army, in 1861, and, by his prompt and patriotic example, carried with him many of his neighbors. This John Strother married Elizabeth Pendleton Hunter, and, by her, was the father of David H. Strother, distinguished as a general in the Union army, and known to the world of letters as the gifted "Porte Crayon." The above Francis Strother and Susan Dabney had another son, William Strother, of Orange county, who married the widow Pannill; and their daughter, Sarah, was the wife of Colonel Richard Taylor, of the Revolution, and the mother of "Old Rough and Ready," President Zachary Taylor.

Jeremiah Strother's son, William, of Stafford, and Margaret Watts, had thirteen daughters, and no son. One of these daughters, Jane Strother, was the wife of the able, learned, and patriotic Thomas Lewis, oldest son of rugged Irish John, and colleague of Samuel McDowell and John Harvie in the House of Burgesses and in the conventions of delegates. Agatha, the oldest daughter of Thomas Lewis, married, first, her cousin, Captain John Frogg, who was killed at Point Pleasant; and afterward married her cousin, Colonel John Stuart, of Greenbrier, whose mother was Jane Linn, a sister of old John Lewis' wife. Colonel Stuart was in the battle of Point Pleasant, and was also a gallant officer in the Revolution. Thomas Lewis' son, John, was a captain at Point Pleasant, was there dangerously wounded, and was a Revolutionary officer. Thomas Lewis' daughter, Elizabeth, married Thomas Merriwether Gilmer, and was the mother of Governor Gilmer, of Georgia. Thomas Lewis' daughter, Sophia, married John Carthrae, and it was their daughter who became the wife of William S. McDowell, son of Judge William McDowell and Margaretta Madison. Charles, the third son and eleventh child of Thomas Lewis and Jane Strother, married Miss Yancey, and lived in Rockingham, and by her was the father of the distinguished General Samuel H. Lewis, of that county. The latter first married his relative, Anne, granddaughter of Colonel Charles Lewis, who fell at the Point, by whom he had eight children, among them Charles H. Lewis, the United States Minister to Portugal in 1873, and John Francis Lewis, United States senator from Virginia, 1874. The second wife of General S. H. Lewis was a daughter of the able and learned Judge John Tayloe Lomax; and Hon. Lunsford Lomax Lewis, Judge of the Supreme Court of Appeals of Virginia, is his son by her. Another daughter of William Strother, of Stafford, married John Frogg, and was the mother of the Captain John Frogg who was killed at the Point. A fourth daughter of William Strother of Stafford, was the wife of John Madison, the first clerk of Augusta, some account of whose family will be found in connection with his daughter, Margaretta Madison, wife of Judge William McDowell. Gabriel Jones, the great lawyer of the Valley, and Margaret Strother, had but one son, Strother Jones; the latter had but one son, William Strother Jones, who married Anna Maria, daughter of Charles Marshall, one of the sons of Colonel Thomas Marshall. The descendants of William Strother Jones are as respectable as they are numerous, and have extensively intermarried among their Marshall kindred and that connexion. Margaret, one of the daughters of Gabriel Jones, married John Harvie, the same who was a burgess in 1765, was one of the Virginia signers of the Articles of Confederation, and was for many years register of the Virginia Land Office. These two were the parents of General Jacquelin Harvie, who married the only daughter of Chief Justice Marshall, and of John Harvie, who married his cousin, Margaret Hawkins, and lived and died in Frankfort—a man of fastidious sense of honor, scrupulous integrity, and chivalric courage, president of the Bank of Kentucky, member of the board of internal improvements, and a valued member of the legislature.

Another daughter of Gabriel Jones and Margaret Strother, Anna Gabriella, married John Hawkins, who, the writer believes, was a nephew to the Ben. Hawkins who married Martha Harvey. This John Hawkins was a soldier of the Revolution—adjutant of Colonel Marshall's Third Infantry Regiment. As just stated, his daughter, Anna Gabriella, married her cousin, John Harvie, and was the mother of John S. and Lewis E. Harvie, and Mrs. Breathitt, of Frankfort. A third daughter of Gabriel Jones and Margaret Strother was, as already stated, the third wife of John Lewis, son of Colonel Fielding Lewis of Fredericksburg, and Catherine Washington. John Lewis and Margaret Jones had a son, Gabriel Jones Lewis, who was born in 1775, came to Kentucky when a young man, and before the beginning of this century was much about Frankfort and Lexington, where he was the trusted agent and adviser of large numbers of Virginians having claims and interests in Kentucky. He married, in 1807, Mary Bibb, a sister of the able and distinguished Judge George M. Bibb and of the late John B. Bibb, one of the noblest and best of men. They were the offspring of Rev. Richard Bibb, a learned and eloquent minister of the Episcopal Church of Virginia. Gabriel J. Lewis and Mary Bibb were the parents of Elizabeth Lewis, who became the wife of Colonel Samuel Starling, of Hopkinsville. Colonel Samuel Starling's son, Lewis, lost his life as a soldier in the Confederate army. His son, Fielding, died in the Union service, as a lieutenant of the Eighth Kentucky Cavalry, in 1863. His son, Thomas, married Fannie Killebrew, and had by her five children. His daughter, Mary Starling, married William R. Payne, who survived the marriage only a few days. Mrs. Payne, in intellect, in culture, in elevation of mind and character, in courage, in earnest religion, is a worthy descendant of these illustrious lines; higher praise can not be given any woman. The fourth wife of John Lewis was Mary Ann Fontaine, the widow Armistead—her father, of that excellent Huguenot stock; her mother, a Winston, of the same blood as Patrick Henry, the South Carolina Prestons, and Mrs. Madison. John Lewis' fifth wife was Mildred Carter, widow of Robert Mercer, a son of the Princeton hero; she was a daughter of Landon Carter, her mother being a daughter of Colonel Lewis Willis. It is a noteworthy circumstance that the two first wives of John Lewis were granddaughters of his great-aunt, Mildred Washington, by her first husband, Roger Gregory, and his fifth and last wife, her great-granddaughter by her second husband, Colonel Henry Willis. A grandson of this lady, John W. Willis, was among the surveyors in Kentucky in 1774. The party was assailed by the Indians—some killed, the others scattered. Willis and two companions escaped in an Indian pirogue, or dug-out, descended the Kentucky river to the Ohio, then went down that stream to the Mississippi, and thence to New Orleans—probably the first white men who ever made the trip. John Lewis advanced to Wilkinson the money and goods to make his expedition down the Mississippi in 1787—the first trading expedition ever ventured between Kentucky and the Spanish and French of Mississippi and Louisiana. And Merriwether Lewis, a descendant of General Robert Lewis, the Welshman, and a kinsman of John Lewis, was the first man to explore the western territory from St. Louis to the Pacific.

Edmund Alexander, youngest son of William Starling and Mary McDowell, was born in Logan county, Kentucky, in 1827. His vocation was that of a merchant, before the war doing a large business in New York. He entered the Union service, raised the Thirty-fifth Kentucky Cavalry, which he commanded as its colonel. At the attack upon the salt works of Abingdon, Virginia, he commanded a brigade. When peace was declared, he engaged in mercantile pursuits in Hopkinsville, where he married Annie L. McCarroll. He was elected sheriff of Christian county, and, when a candidate for re-election, was basely murdered. He had all the courage and manliness by which the breed were distinguished.

After the lapse of more than three-quarters of a century teeming with mighty events—revolutions, the rise and overthrow of empires, the fall of dynasties, the strides of populations, and wonderful discoveries in material science —it is still pleasant and instructive to peruse this letter from a patriotic gentleman of the olden school:

"MAY 29, 1809.

Dear Friend:—I received yours of the 9th of November, and of the 11th of December, 1808. I have not had an opportunity (except by mail) before this to answer them. I thank you for the good advice you give me, and for the interest you express for my welfare. As to *style* in living, I despise it; but I am now, and always have been, excessively fond of the company of my friends, and have always been able to treat them as well as they could me. . . . You seem to think me a 'political sinner.' . . . If a strong attachment to the Federal Constitution and to the union of the states is sin, I am guilty. If a wish to be governed by law, and not by men, is sin, I am guilty. If a disposition to submit to the laws of the United States, and to have them well executed, is sin, I am guilty. If measures to make it the interest of the people of the United States to remain united, be wrong, I am guilty. If to oppose any thing that I think has a tendency to weaken the Union, is wrong, I am guilty. These are all the principles I have ever contended for. . . . I felt anxious to clear my character of some of the charges I understood were made by the Browns against me. . . . I am your friend, etc., SAMUEL McDOWELL, JR.

To ANDREW REID, ESQ.,
Lexington, Virginia."

How many Union men in Kentucky, all of whose sympathies were with the institutions and people of the South, will find in this, the prophetic declaration of the principles that constrained them sorrowfully to fly to arms in behalf of their country, to prevent its destruction, and to submit to the arbitrament of battle the issue forced upon them! The writer, with his father and three of his brothers, had fought in the Revolution; he, his brothers, sons and nephews were soldiers in 1812; it seems right, natural and inevitable that nine of his grandsons, besides a number of his great-grandsons, should have vindicated the principles they inherited, by following in the civil war the flag he loved.

Colonel Joseph McDowell, of Danville.

The fifth son of Judge Samuel McDowell and Mary McClung, Joseph, was born September 13, 1768. A child when the Revolution commenced, and still a boy when it ended, yet was his character molded by the stirring events transpiring around him, and by the patriotic deeds to the narration of which he was an eager listener. Coming to Kentucky, with his father, in 1784, his youth was passed in intimate association with the men who, in the Danville conventions, prepared the way for separation from Virginia, and who established and gave its peculiar tone to the commonwealth. In the Indian campaigns, in which Kentuckians were engaged in the North-west, between the dates of his attaining the age for military service and the treaty which followed the victory of " Mad Anthony " Wayne, he was a prompt and brave participant. He was a private in Brown's company, in Scott's expedition of 1791. He was in both expeditions under General Hopkins, in 1812. The reputation for good sense, sound judgment, military capacity and courage won therein, induced his appointment, by Shelby, to the position of adjutant-general upon the staff of that hard fighting commander. He served from the beginning to the close of Shelby's campaign in the North-west, and was at the Thames, where Tecumseh fell. For good conduct and valuable service rendered in that campaign and battle, he received complimentary mention, not only by his immediate commander, but also from General Harrison. The occupation of Colonel Joseph McDowell was that of a farmer. Disdaining all shams, and himself one of the most unassuming of men, his was eminently a veracious character; in the perfect uprightness and simplicity of his life, there was a constant beauty. One of the most amiable, quiet and unobtrusive of men, of all his sex there was none more resolute and determined. A ruling elder of the Presbyterian Church for many years, and devoutly religious, in his observance thereof there was no parade. In the decline of his honorable life, after he had withdrawn from all active participation in public affairs, the writer was witness to the respectful deference shown him by the entire community among whom he lived. He died, in Danville, June 27, 1856, at the good old age of eighty-eight years. The excellent wife of Colonel Joseph McDowell was Sarah Irvine, sister to Anne Irvine, who married his brother, Samuel—a relative, whose symmetrical character made her, in every way, worthy of such a man. Samuel, their oldest son, married, first, Amanda Ball, granddaughter of John Reed, already mentioned, and a cousin of James G. Birney. Of this marriage, the sole issue was a daughter, who was the wife of Dr. Meyer, of Boyle county. This Samuel McDowell, married, secondly, Martha Hawkins, by whom he had children, among them Samuel and Nicholas, both farmers in Boyle county. Colonel Joseph McDowell's oldest daughter, Anna, married Abram I. Caldwell, descended from one of the most reputable of the Scotch-Irish families of the Valley, and a farmer of Boyle; they have a number of children living in that county. Sarah, the second daughter of Colonel Joseph McDowell, married Michael Sullivant, of Columbus, Ohio. Of wonderful energy and the most sanguine temper, Mr. Sullivant engaged in gigantic agricultural enterprises, first upon his inherited acres in Ohio, and afterwards in Illinois. He is best known to the world as the once owner of the princely estates of "Broadlands" and "Burr Oaks," in the latter state. Throughout the most tremendous operations, and amid the saddest vicissitudes, he preserved an untarnished honor and the sunniest of tempers. Large hearted as well as of herculean stature; free handed as he was unreserved and cordial in manner; frank, generous, hospitable and cheery, his image will continue with the living as the most pleasant of memories. The only son of Sarah McDowell and Michael Sullivant, Joseph McDowell, is a prosperous farmer near Homer, Illinois. Annie, one of their daughters, is the wife of E. L. Davison, now of Louisville; and Lucy, another daughter, is the wife of Wm. Hopkins, a grandson of General Samuel Hopkins, and resides in Henderson, Kentucky. Margaret Irvine McDowell, the third daughter of Colonel Joseph, of Danville, was the first wife of Joseph Sullivant, of Columbus, a younger brother of Michael. Mr. Joseph Sullivant's second wife was Mary Eliza Brashear, granddaughter of Judge William McDowell. He was a man of cultivated tastes, devoted to scientific pursuits, too public spirited for his own welfare in a pecuniary sense, and did much to develop literary and scientific ambitions and enterprises in his native Columbus. In many ways a public benefactor, in all ways he was a useful citizen, and at all times a gentleman. He lived to a venerable and respected old age. His first wife died in giving birth to their only child, Margaret Irvine Sullivant, the wife of Henry B. Carrington, a brigadier-general of volunteers in the Union army, colonel of the Eighteenth Regular Infantry, now on the retired list—a gallant and capable officer. Mrs. Carrington is dead; two worthy sons survive her. Magdalen, the fourth daughter of Colonel Joseph McDowell, of Danville, married Caleb Wallace, a lawyer, of Danville; her husband was a grandson of Judge Caleb Wallace, of the Kentucky Court of Appeals, whose wife was a sister of Colonel William Christian. Mrs. Magdalen Wallace is still living, in Danville, blessed with two manly sons, McDowell and Woodford.

DR. EPHRAIM McDOWELL.

The sixth son of Judge Samuel McDowell and Mary McClung, Ephraim, was born in Augusta county, now Rockbridge, Virginia, November 11, 1771. In his early boyhood, he had the advantage of the best schools in his native state; at the age of thirteen years, he came with his father across the mountains and through the wilderness to Kentucky. In Danville, then the seat of the best and most intellectual society in the west, and under the instruction of scholarly teachers, the remainder of his boyhood was passed. At Bardstown, and at the academy in

Lexington, Virginia, his thorough classical education was
completed. There followed two years of close application
in the study of medicine, in Staunton, Virginia, under Dr.
Humphreys, a graduate of the University of Edinburg.
Perhaps it was this circumstance that persuaded him to
take advantage of the opportunities afforded by the abundant means and liberal ideas of his father to further prosecute his medical studies at the University of Edinburg.
Thither he repaired in 1793, '94, remaining two years.
There he had for his preceptor and friend the great surgeon, John Bell, "a man of splendid genius, of high intellectual endowments, an eloquent teacher, and a bold,
dashing operator." Not waiting to take his degree, he
immediately, upon his return to America, settled at Danville, and there entered upon that professional career the
results of which placed him among the greatest of human
benefactors. With the prestige of foreign study, its commencement was auspicious; the fame of his successful
operations rapidly spreading, patients flocked to him from
all parts of the South and West; he found himself well
nigh overwhelmed by a large surgical practice demanding
many of the most difficult and severe operations. The entire profession now accord to him the credit and praise of
being the originator of ovariotomy. Only twelve years
after he had entered upon the practice, in 1809, at the
little town of Danville, upon the person of Mrs. Crawford,
an heroic Kentucky woman, he *first* performed that most
difficult of feats in surgery, the actual removal of an ovarian
tumor, the patient surviving the operation thirty-two
years, in vigorous health, and dying at length in her
seventy-ninth year. This he did without a precedent in
the whole history of surgery since the world began; without a guide in any of the books, from the experience of
others or of his own; without the use of anæsthetics;
without assistants with whom to share the glory of successful achievement or the responsibility of failure. For
years he had no imitators. Eight years elapsed before his
modesty permitted him to report its successful accom-
plishment. Then the ablest surgeons in Europe and

America, proclaiming success in such an operation to be
an impossibility, discredited the statement that the entire
profession had been eclipsed by one whom they were disposed to regard as a country practitioner. The most savage and satirical of his assailants, Dr. James Johnson, the
able and learned editor of the "London Medico-Chirur-
gical Review," lived to "ask pardon," in 1827, for his
"uncharitableness, of God, and Dr. Ephraim McDowell, of
Danville." The concurrent testimony of the profession is
that, in his origination of ovariotomy, Dr. McDowell
"added forty thousand years to the sum of human life."
The virtues which were consecrated to the saving of
human life, and the mitigation of human suffering, were
sought to be perpetuated by the appreciative and grateful
profession in Kentucky in the erection of a costly and
graceful monument to his memory, which adorns the town
in which he lived. Dr. Gross, one of the ablest and most
distinguished of American surgeons, justly said of him :
"Had McDowell lived in France, he would have been
elected a member of the Royal Academy of Surgery, received from the king the Cross of the Legion of Honor,
and obtained from the government a magnificent reward—
as an acknowledgment of the services he rendered his
country, his profession, and fellow-creatures." His professional history is that of the greatest advance in surgical
science of modern times. With a broad and elevated
mind, and a heart gentle and tender as that of a woman,
he was not afraid of the sight of blood ; pre-eminently
bold, his exceptional skill was aided by an unfailing nerve.
He was no mere money grubber ; careless as to pecuniary
rewards, for the poor he had a kindness and a charity that
were inexhaustible. Six feet in height, his complexion
was florid, eyes black, presence commanding, and his activity and muscular power remarkable. He died in 1830.
Dr. McDowell was thirty-one years old when he married
Sarah, daughter of Governor Shelby. Their only son was
named after Judge Caleb Wallace. He married a Miss Hall,
of Shelby county, Kentucky, and after a residence of some

7

years on a farm in Boyle county, removed to Missouri, where
he died. Wallace McDowell's son, John Hall McDowell,
was a gallant soldier in Cockrill's Missouri Brigade of
the Confederate army, and in 1865, a few days after the
battle of Selma, Alabama, died in the hospital at that place
of consumption contracted in the army. Wallace Mc-
Dowell's daughter, Florence, a very beautiful and charming woman, married her kinsman, Thomas H. Shelby, a
grandson of the governor. Mary, one of the daughters of
Dr. Ephraim McDowell, married Mr. Young, of Shelbyville. Another married Mr. Deadrick, of Tennessee. A
third married Major David C. Irvine, a prominent citizen
of Madison, which he represented with ability in the state
senate. A fourth daughter married Major Anderson, of
Boyle county, and moved to Missouri; their son, Ephraim
McDowell Anderson, was a soldier in the Confederate
army, and is now living in Paris, Missouri.

The seventh son of Judge Samuel McDowell and Mary
McClung, Caleb Wallace McDowell, was born April 17,
1774, and married his relative, Elizabeth McDowell, daughter of Colonel Joe McDowell, of North Carolina—Joe of
" The Quaker Meadows"—and Margaret Moffett. Their
only daughter married her kinsman, Joseph Chrisman, Jr.,
of Jessamine county, Kentucky. Joseph Chrisman, Jr.,
was a son of Hugh Chrisman, whose mother was, as has
been stated, a sister of Colonel Joe and General Charles
McDowell, of the Quaker Meadows, North Carolina. One
of the daughters of Joe Chrisman, Jr., married a Mr.
Lewis, and her son, Joseph McDowell Lewis, has in him
five crosses of the McDowell blood. The other daughter
of Joe Chrisman, Jr., married Hon. Marcus Cruikshank,
of Talladega, Alabama.

In this connection, the reader will remember that Joseph Chrisman, Sr., of Jessamine, was a brother of Hugh,
and also a son of a sister of the McDowells of the Quaker
Meadows; and that his daughter, Polly, married Samuel,
son of Colonel James McDowell, of Fayette. It was
George Chrisman, a son of Joseph, Sr., who married Celia,
the daughter of Colonel Joseph McDowell, of the Quaker

Meadows. Jane, one of the daughters of George Chrisman and Celia McDowell, married Gov. L. E. Parsons, of Alabama; and another daughter married Jordan Scott, of Jessamine. A son of Joseph Chrisman, Sr.—Lewis by name—married a Miss Lyle, of Fayette, and was the father of Addison L. and George Chrisman, of Jessamine. A cousin of Lewis Chrisman—James—married a daughter of Henderson Bell, whose wife was a daughter of Major John McDowell and Lucy Le Grand. Of a verity, are these McDowells and Chrismans most wonderfully and fearfully mixed.

THE REIDS AND MOORES.

The two oldest children of Judge Samuel McDowell and Mary McClung, born October 9, 1755, were twin sisters, Sarah and Magdalen. The former married Caleb Wallace, a graduate of Princeton—a Presbyterian minister at the time of the marriage. She died soon, and without issue. Mr. Wallace abandoned the ministry, became a successful lawyer, and was one of the first judges of the Kentucky Court of Appeals. Magdalen married Andrew Reid. Their oldest daughter, Sarah, married Andrew Moore, whose father, also named Andrew, was a soldier in the French and Indian War. The son distinguished himself for gallantry at Point Pleasant. General Andrew Moore, as he was designated, was a member of Congress from the Lexington, Virginia, district from 1789 to 1797; he was re-elected in 1804, and that same year was elected to the United States Senate, filling the place until 1809. He died in 1821. His oldest son was a member of Congress from 1833 to 1835; was a member of the convention that passed the ordinance of secession in 1861, against which he voted. Then a very old man, the efforts of Henry A. Wise to dragoon him into the support of secession met with humiliating failure. Afterward, he served in the Confederate army. His wife was Evelyn, daughter of William Alexander, of Rockbridge. Their daughter, Sallie Moore, married her cousin, John Harvey Moore. The second son of General Andrew Moore and Sarah Reid was David E. Moore, a lawyer of high standing in Lexington, Virginia.

He married Elizabeth Harvey, a daughter of Matthew Harvey and sister of Mrs. Wm. A. McDowell, and had by her eight children; of whom, his son and namesake, David E. Moore, is a prominent member of the bar of Rockbridge. Virginia married Tedford Barclay, and Elizabeth is the wife of the scholarly Prof. Alexander Nelson.

A daughter of Andrew Reid and Magdalen McDowell married a Mr. McCampbell, and their daughter married a Venable, of a family distinguished in Virginia for literary attainments. The second and third daughters of Andrew Reid and Magdalen McDowell also married members of the Venable family. The fourth daughter married Judge Abraham Smith, of Rockbridge.

The fifth daughter of Andrew Reid and Magdalen McDowell, married Major John Alexander, of Lexington, Virginia. Their son, John Alexander, is a lawyer of ability, and a citizen of prominence in Lexington, and their daughter, Agnes, was the wife of Rev. Beverley Tucker Lacey, the noted Presbyterian divine.

The only son of Andrew Reid and Magdalen McDowell, was Dr. Samuel McDowell Reid, a skillful and distinguished physician of Lexington. He married a Miss Hare, and his daughters married, respectively, Prof. James White and Colonel John S. H. Ross. His son, bearing his own name, is a wealthy and reputable citizen of Rockbridge.

THE BUFORDS.

Martha, the third daughter of Judge Samuel McDowell and Mary McClung, was born June 20, 1766; grew to be a woman of strong sense and indomitable will; her letters still in existence show her, also, to have been well educated, pious and patriotic, and a capital correspondent; letters written in good English and captivating style, filled with religion, politics, family news and delightful gossip; such letters as few graduates of Vassar are capable of writing. In October, 1788, after the removal of the family to Kentucky, she married Colonel Abraham Buford, who had been a lieutenant at Point Pleasant, in the independent company from Bedford county, commanded by his cousin,

Captain Thomas Buford, whose blood helped to buy the victory. Afterwards, Abraham Buford was a gallant and patriotic officer in the Revolution, and did good service in more than one battle. Placed in command of a regiment of raw Virginians, he marched to the relief of Charleston, but arrived too late to join the garrison before its surrender. Pursued by the intrepid Tarleton, with his veteran legion, and overtaken at Waxhaw, his undisciplined command was almost annihilated, quarter being refused; 113 were killed outright, 150 were too badly hacked to be removed, while only 53 could be brought as prisoners to Camden. Colonel Buford lived to do good and hard fighting after that, to acquire a magnificent body of land in Scott county, Kentucky, as the reward for his services, and to marry Martha McDowell. The colonel and his wife were both staunch Federalists—the latter a sound Presbyterian. Their oldest son was Charles S. Buford, an accomplished scholar and an excellent gentleman; two of whose sons were officers in the Federal army, and whose oldest daughter, Pattie, was the wife of the chivalric General James S. Jackson—as handsome as he was brave, with the beauty of Alcibiades and the frank courage, sincerity, and magnanimity of the lion-hearted Richard. General Jackson's talents were as handsome as his face; his intellect as vigorous as his form was robust. The most splendid type of a Kentuckian, he was the embodiment of generous manliness. In his twenty-fourth year, the Lexington company of volunteers for Colonel Humphrey Marshall's regiment in the war with Mexico deemed him the fittest person to command them, and elected him their captain. Finding that his friend, Cassius M. Clay, was about to be left out of the service by General Owsley's refusal to appoint him to a colonelcy, Jackson resigned his captaincy in order that Clay might be chosen to the place, and went under him as a private soldier. In 1857, albeit known to have been an emancipationist, he was elected to the state legislature from Christian, one of the largest slave-holding counties in the state. His service in that body was brilliant. Defeated, in 1859, for Congress, he was elected, in 1861, as a Union man, served during the called session of 1861, but left his seat to go to the front as colonel of the Third Kentucky Union Cavalry. He was with Buell in all his campaigns in Kentucky, Tennessee, Mississippi, and Alabama; for his arduous and efficient service, he was promoted to a brigadier. And at Perryville he died the death he coveted most, that of a hero, at the head of his command, in the heat and smoke of battle. Charles A. Buford was twice married. First, to a daughter of John Adair, Governor of Kentucky, and Mrs. Jackson and his son Henry, who married his cousin, Betty Marshall, were his children by that marriage. Secondly, to Lucy, daughter of Dr. Basil Duke and Charlotte Marshall, who was the mother of his other children—Basil; Charles; Lewis M.; Charlotte; Susan McClung, who married Major Edson, professor at West Point; and Henrietta, who married Thomas Barbee. Another son of Colonel Abram Buford, William S., married a daughter of Hon. George Robertson, distinguished as a congressman, senator, jurist, and publicist. The only daughter of Colonel Abram Buford, Mary, married James K. Duke, a brother of Charles S. Buford's second wife. Mr. Duke was a graduate of Yale, a scholarly man, of refined tastes, and elegant manners and appearance. He was educated for a lawyer, but abandoned the practice, for which he had no liking, in early manhood. He died in 1863. His widow, who was born in 1805, still survives, in a graceful and beautiful old age—a good wife, a devoted mother, a sincere Christian, an affectionate friend; with strong practical sense, simple in her tastes and manners, faithful to every trust and duty, and ambitious of good deeds. Basil, one of the sons of this good and venerable woman, was for many years a prominent lawyer of St. Louis, where his family reside. Charlotte, her oldest daughter, married Mr. Strahan, a Presbyterian minister. Pattie, another daughter, married General John Buford, of the United States army. General Buford's father, Colonel John Buford, was the son of a cousin of Colonel Abram Buford. His mother was a daughter of Dr. John Watson, of Frankfort. General Buford was a graduate of West Point, a captain in the old regular army, and much beloved by his associates. For gallant and meritorious service, and as a recognition of his proved capacity, he was made brigadier-general and assigned to the command of a division of cavalry. In McClellan's peninsular campaign; in the fights with Stuart in Culpepper, and Orange, and Spottsylvania; at Antietam; in the Valley and elsewhere; always active, vigilant and energetic, he won for himself a most enviable fame; and, dying in 1864, from disease, the result of suffering and exposure in the discharge of duty, his memory, as one of the heroes who died that the nation might live, is enshrined in the affections of his grateful countrymen. Another daughter of Mrs. Duke, Caroline, is the wife of General Green Clay Smith; at sixteen a soldier in the Mexican war: a brigadier-general of Union volunteers; a member of the legislature; twice a member of Congress; a governor of one of the territories, and now an eloquent evangelist of the Baptist Church. Another son of Mrs. Duke, William, was a soldier in the Mexican war and an officer in the Confederate army.

THE MARSHALLS.

Mary, or Polly, the youngest daughter of Judge Samuel McDowell and Mary McClung, was born in Rockbridge county, Virginia, on the 11th of January, 1772, and came, with her parents, through the wilderness to Kentucky, in 1784. Among all who knew her, she enjoyed the reputation of a character as lovely as her face was beautiful, and her person and manners graceful. As affectionate and hospitable as she was amiable and pious, it is natural that she should have been as universally admired and loved by her husband's as she was by her own kindred. In October of 1794, she became the honored wife of Alexander Keith Marshall, sixth son of Colonel Thomas Marshall of the Revolution, and younger brother of the chief-justice. The wife of Colonel Marshall, the mother of his fifteen children, was Mary Randolph Keith. Her father was James Keith, a native of Scotland, said to have been born at Peterhead, in Ab-

erdeenshire, where the name and family had been conspicuous for centuries, and where they still abound. The
statement that he was descended from the particular family of Keiths who were ennobled as Earls Marischal and
of Kintore may be true; but, if true at all, his relationship
to those of his own generation who held those titles was
so exceedingly remote that it is not now, by any human
ingenuity, in any way traceable. Fortunately, to his descendants the truth or falsity of the statement is as little
important as it is to the world at large; for in this country there have been those among them, of other names,
who have been the equals of any Keith who ever marshaled the Scottish hosts, or charged at the head of the
Clan Chattan. He was educated in Marischal College of
the University of Aberdeen; was, under Bishop Robert
Keith, a fellow-pupil of Field Marshal James Keith, who
saved the Prussian army, and laid down his own life, at
Hochkirch. In 1715, he abandoned his studies to take up
arms for the Old Pretender, and fought at the battle of
Sheriff Muir. That cause having collapsed, he remained
for several years among the highland fastnesses; but again
proved his fidelity to the Stuarts, by aiding in the abortive
attempt of Seaforth and Marischal to raise the highlands
in 1719. Having been attainted, he then fled to Virginia,
took orders as an Episcopalian minister, and was for many
years rector of Hamilton parish. He married Mary Isham
Randolph, one of the daughters of the first Thomas Randolph, of Tuckahoe, and Mary Fleming. Thomas Randolph, of Tuckahoe, was the second son of William Randolph, of Turkey Island, and an elder brother of Richard
Randolph,—the grandfather of John, of Roanoke,—and of
Isham Randolph,—the grandfather of Thomas Jefferson.
Alexander K. Marshall was born at "Oakhill," Fauquier
county, Virginia, in 1770; removed, with his parents, to
Kentucky in 1785; was educated at home by Scotch tutors,
whom his father always employed for the purpose, and by
whom he was well trained in English literature and in the
classics. After marriage, Mr. Marshall removed to Mason
county, and, on the farm now owned by Colonel Charles

A. Marshall, erected the brick house that is still standing after the lapse of almost a century. Like the most of his brothers, he was a lawyer by profession, and, having a legal acumen as acute as it was broad and comprehensive, and a training as thorough as it was liberal, like them, also, he occupied the head place in the front rank. Collins, in the brief, meager and bald paragraph which he gave to the first man in his generation, in all Northern Kentucky, felt obliged to state that " he was one of the very ablest lawyers of his day." His success was commensurate with his abilities; practice came to him unsought, and without resort to devious arts to obtain it. Careless as to pecuniary rewards for his services, and liberal to the point of prodigality in the hospitality of his home and in all expenditures, he yet added largely to his magnificent inheritance. Of the extent of the latter, some idea may be formed from the statement that he owned more than 10,000 acres of the finest land in Kentucky, on Mill creek, in Mason county, besides numerous other valuable tracts elsewhere. Mr. Marshall's talents were only less showy than they were solid; a strong and argumentative speaker, his efforts were clothed in the graces of rhetoric, to which an animated manner, a full and sonorous voice, and an emotional temperament, gave all the effects of eloquence. One of the most decided and outspoken of the Federal party, his abilities caused his election, from the Democratic county of Mason, to the legislature in 1797, '8, '9, and in 1800. One of the early clerks of the court of appeals, he was appointed reporter to that body, in 1817, and published three volumes of reports, extending to 1821. Tall, large and well proportioned, his manner was at once stately and pleasing; a large head, a high and broad forehead, and sparkling black eyes, gave force to a countenance that was expressive and handsome. Mrs. Marshall died in 1822. All of Mr. Marshall's children were hers. He married again in 1823, a distant relative of his first wife, Mrs. Eliza A. Ball, a very beautiful woman. She was a granddaughter of the heroic General Andrew Lewis.

The career and characteristics of General Lewis are well

known to every reader of American history. Of his son,.
John Lewis, Governor Gilmer, of Georgia—a near relative—in his "Sketches of Upper Georgia," says that he
"was an officer under his father at Grant's defeat. He
was made a prisoner, and carried to Quebec, and thence to
France. Upon his liberation, he went to London. His
very tall, erect, handsome person, his colonial commission,
and suffering as a prisoner, attracted the attention of royalty sufficiently to procure for him a commission in the
British army. He belonged to a corps stationed near London, either the King's or Queen's Guards. After some
years spent in acquiring the idle, dissipated habits of the
corps to which he belonged, he resigned, and returned to
Virginia. Upon his arrival in Alexandria, he was greeted
with a splendid ball. Very few Virginians had been honored with a commission in the regular army of Great
Britain, and still fewer had been permitted to serve in the
troops which immediately surrounded royalty. His fine,
manly person, aided by courtly manners and gallant
spirit, captivated Miss Patty Love, the most dashing belle
of the town. He married, and carried her to the home of
his family in the Valley of Virginia. His residence abroad
had not deprived him of his inclination for enterprise. He
settled a farm upon the extreme of the Virginia frontier."
Governor Gilmer proceeds to give an interesting account of
how his negroes, with the hope that after their master's
death their mistress would return to Alexandria, where
they would not be in constant peril from the Indians, murdered John Lewis, and secreted his body, which was at
last found by following his faithful dog. His son, Samuel, came to Woodford county, Kentucky, and in this state
married one of the daughters of the brave General Whitley. His daughter, Eliza, first married John Luke, of
Alexandria, by whom she had a number of children. After
his death, she married the gallant Major James V. Ball,
who fought so well at Mississinewa, and afterward at
Lundy's Lane. He was promoted to a colonelcy in the
regular army, and died in command of the post at Baton
Rouge. His impoverished widow came to Kentucky, was

befriended by John J. Crittenden, and, while at Frankfort, met and married, as her third husband, Alexander K. Marshall. By him she had no children.

The oldest son of Alexander K. Marshall and Mary McDowell, Charles Thomas, was born July 14, 1800, and lived and died on his handsome patrimonial estate in Mason county—an unambitious but sensible man, whose amiable temper, manliness, and sterling integrity made him a general favorite. He married his step-sister, Jane Luke, and had by her a family of four sons, Dr. Samuel L., Edward, Alexander K., and James; and a daughter, Eliza, who married her cousin, George W. Anderson, a colonel of Union volunteers and a congressman from Missouri. James K. Marshall, the second son of Alexander K. Marshall and Mary McDowell, married Catherine Calloway Hickman, a daughter of the late John L. Hickman, who represented Bourbon county frequently in both branches of the state legislature, and was a prominent citizen. John L., son of James K. Marshall, was an officer in the Confederate army. Bettie, daughter of James K. Marshall, married her handsome cousin, Henry, son of Charles S. Buford by his Adair wife; H. Marshall Buford, judge of the court of common pleas in the Lexington district, is her son.

Maria, oldest daughter of Alexander K. Marshall, was born in Mason county, Kentucky, July 20, 1795. In her beautiful girlhood, before she had attained the age of sixteen years, on the 2d of May, 1811, she married her kinsman, James Alexander Paxton, a man who was as gifted mentally as he was handsome in person, as brave as he was amiable. The Paxtons were among the earliest of the settlers of Rockbridge, of the same Scotch-Irish race as the McDowells, McClungs, Stuarts, Lyles, and Houstons, with whom their descendants have so frequently intermarried. Speaking of the Paxtons, General Alexander H. H. Stuart pronounced them to be the most gallant and the proudest of all the families in the Valley. Their names will be found figuring abundantly and conspicuously among the soldiers who fought in every war from 1755; they occur as frequently in the lists of Presbyterian members, elders, and ministers, and on the rolls of able lawyers. One of them, John Paxton, was probably born in Ireland, came from Pennsylvania to Rockbridge, and there married Martha Blair. Their son, also named John Paxton, was a captain in the Revolution, and died from the effects of a wound received at Guilford Court-house; he married Phoebe, daughter of Captain John Alexander; *his* son, John, emigrated to Lincoln county, Kentucky, married there Elizabeth Logan, and left a large family; the other posterity of the second John are scattered from the Valley to the Pacific slope.

James Paxton, the fourth son of the first John and Martha Blair, was also a soldier of the Revolution, and was accidentally shot by a companion with whom he was hunting. He married Phoebe McClung, one of the daughters of John McClung and Elizabeth Alexander, who were also the parents of Judge William McClung, of Kentucky. John McClung was the brother of Mary, the wife of Judge Samuel McDowell; his wife, Elizabeth Alexander, was the sister of the father of the distinguished Dr. Archibald Alexander, of Princeton. Judge William McClung, brother of James Paxton's wife, married Susan Marshall, and was the father of the distinguished orator, lawyer, statesman, and divine, John Alexander McClung, and of Colonel Alexander Keith McClung, of Mississippi. James Paxton and Phoebe McClung had but one child, James Alexander Paxton, who married Maria Marshall. Isabella Paxton, daughter of John Paxton and Martha Blair, married Captain Lyle, a Revolutionary officer, and was the mother of Mary Paxton Lyle, who became the wife of Colonel James McDowell; it was from *her* that Isabella McDowell, who married Dr. John P. Campbell, derived her given name. Elizabeth, another daughter of John Paxton and Martha Blair, married Major Samuel Houston, of the Revolution, and was the mother of Sam. Houston, distinguished as the President of Texas, as a senator of the United States, and by the patriotic stand he made for the Union. No more pleasant task could be found than to follow this gallant race through all its ramifications, and note the same characteristics of honor, chivalry, talent, and patriotism displaying itself in every generation, in all sections of the South and West, in all the professions, and under many names—Caruthers, Lyle, Cummings, Barclay, McClung, Stuart, Houston, Greenlee, Alexander, Davidson, Grigsby, Blair, Campbell, Pickett, McDowell, and others. But this sketch must be confined to a single line. After James Paxton had been killed, his widow married Colonel Moore, and removed with him to Kentucky, bringing her son by James Paxton with her. When a youth of sixteen, James Alexander Paxton came to Mason county, and continued his studies while residing in the family of his uncle, Judge William McClung. Acquiring an excellent English and classical education, under the instruction of his uncle and of Mr. Marshall, he became also a well-read and disciplined lawyer. Upon this firm foundation, his strong mind and brilliant talents built a fair and seemly superstructure. For years he stood at the head of the bar in Northern Kentucky; the favorite of every social circle; a charming companion, and a faithful friend. Volunteering as a private soldier in the company of Captain Bayless, in 1812, he served as an aide to Shelby at the battle of the Thames. He died in 1825, in the prime of his manhood. His oldest son, A. Marshall Paxton, was a successful merchant in Cincinnati; married a daughter of Philip Bush, and left a daughter, Lydia, who married Frank Blackburn, and lives in Missouri.

His second son, William M. Paxton, has been successful as a lawyer and business man in Platte City, Missouri,— one of the truest and best of men, to whose valuable account of the "Marshall Family," this sketch is indebted for many of its facts and dates. He married Mary Forman.

Mary, the oldest daughter of James A. Paxton, married Benjamin Harbeson, a Pennsylvanian by birth, of Scotch descent; a man who loved the truth for its own sake, and, never forgetting what was due to his own honor, and ever true to that sense, and to his own convictions, was to others always faithful. Remarkable for his intuitive percep-

tion of character, he never formed an unworthy friendship, nor lost a man to whom he had once held that rela-
tion. Lenient and charitable in his judgment of faults
which grow out of fallen human nature, words could not
express his detestation for meanness or duplicity. His
head was large, his hair black and curling, his eyes large,
black and sparkling, his face intelligent and singularly
handsome, and his form that of an athlete. The world
contains but few such men as Ben. Harbeson. And his
wife was one of the good women of the state, as bright
and intelligent as she was handsome and noble in appearance. In 1849, Mr. Harbeson represented Fleming county
in the legislature. His son, John M. Harbeson, is a prosperous banker at Augusta, Kentucky. He married Miss
Fannie Metcalfe, a relative of the governor of that name,
and has two sons and three daughters. Mr. Harbeson is
a mingled likeness of both his parents, possessing many of
the best traits of both, along with their handsome features. James P. Harbeson, is another son of Benjamin
Harbeson and Mary Paxton. He was a captain in the Sixteenth Kentucky Union Infantry, and was promoted to
the rank of major for good conduct. A graduate of the
Louisville Law School, he was, for some years, the law
partner of the able Judge Thomas A. Marshall, who held
his capacity in the highest esteem. Appointed judge of
the Louisville city court, he discharged the duties of the
position with an ability, impartiality and courtesy that
elicited general plaudits. Removing from Louisville to
Flemingsburg, he has gained a fast hold upon the affections and esteem of the community. His native talents
and ability are equal to his ambition. He first married
Mrs. Shreve, by whom he had one son; and, secondly,
Alice Andrews, by whom he has five children. The last
wife is a great-niece of John and L. W. Andrews, who
married, respectively, a daughter and a granddaughter of
Colonel James McDowell. William P., youngest son of
Benjamin Harbeson, married Miss Harris, is a farmer, and
lives in Fleming county. Mary, the only daughter of
Benjamin Harbeson, married D. M. Wilson, and lives on a
cattle ranch in Texas.

The second daughter of James Alexander Paxton and
Maria Marshall, Phoebe A., married her cousin, Charles
A. Marshall, who is the youngest son of Captain Thomas
Marshall and Frances Kennan. Captain Thomas Marshall was the second son of Colonel Thomas Marshall,
and an elder brother of Alexander K. Marshall. Frances
Kennan was a sister of the celebrated pioneer and Indian fighter, William Kennan. Mr. Marshall was educated at the academy of his uncle, Dr. Louis Marshall, in Woodford county. He is a fine classical scholar;
few men have so extensive an acquaintance with history, or understand so well its teachings. A farmer all
his life, he was thrice elected to the legislature from his
native county of Mason—honors by him unsolicited.
More than fifty years old at the outbreak of the civil war,
he recruited the Sixteenth Kentucky Infantry, accepted
its colonelcy, led the advance in Nelson's campaign in
Eastern Kentucky, in 1861, held the post of honor—the
front—at the battle of Ivy Mountain, where his command
bore the brunt of the fight, suffered all the loss, and did
nearly all the execution. In that engagement, he acquitted himself with a cool courage which reflected honor
upon his name and the cause he served, worthy of the
reputation he had borne since boyhood for the most
knightly chivalry. Compelled, by disease, to leave the
service in 1862, he carried with him the love of every soldier of his command, and continued to the end of the
struggle an unflinching friend of the Union. When possessed of power, he did not abuse his authority, but used
it beneficently in the maintenance of law, and in protecting every citizen in the rights of person and property, and
in the enjoyment of liberty. Kentucky never had a son
who, without going out of his way to court popularity,
yet enjoys the respect, confidence and esteem of the people more thoroughly and completely than does Colonel
Marshall. His oldest son, Thomas Marshall, has had an
exceptionally successful and brilliant career as a lawyer at
Salt Lake City; *his* wife was Miss Sallie Hughes.

His second son, William Louis Marshall, left school to

volunteer as a private soldier in the Tenth Kentucky
Union Cavalry, in 1862, at sixteen years of age; was soon
transferred to the staff of General Green Clay Smith, and
served until September, 1863; was appointed to the Military Academy at West Point, which he entered in July,
1864, and from which, four years later, he graduated with
distinguished honor; was for several years a valued instructor at West Point; placed in charge of the Colorado
section of the United States Exploring Expedition, he discovered the pass that bears his name, and is now used by
the Denver and Rio Grande Railroad, and also the gold
placers on the San Miguel river, in the basin named in his
honor; was the engineer in charge of the improvements
of the Tennessee and Mississippi rivers; and later was
placed in charge of the improvements of the harbors of
the western lakes. His rank is deservedly high in the
branch of the service to which he was assigned—the corps
of engineers. His commission as captain dates from 1882.
Herculean in form and strength, essentially soldierly in
bearing and appearance, one of the most cultivated and
able of his generation of the family whose name he bears,
Captain Marshall unites the frankness, the courage, the
scholarly attainments, and best intellectual qualities of the
families of Marshall, Paxton, McClung, McDowell, and
Alexander. In 1885, he married a daughter of Senator
Colquitt, of Georgia. They have one child. The third
and fourth sons of Colonel Charles A. Marshall and
Phoebe A. Paxton, James Paxton and Ben. Harbeson, are
farmers in Mason county—both worthy men. Colonel
Marshall has three married daughters—Elizabeth, married
to Rev. Maurice Waller, of the Presbyterian Church;
Lucy Coleman, to John G. Bentley, a soldier in the Confederate army from the beginning to the close of the war,
a graduate of Roanoke College, and a man of education;
and Sallie, to Edmund Wilkes, Jr., a grandson of the distinguished commodore of that name.

Lucy, second daughter of Alexander K. Marshall and
Mary McDowell, born in 1796, married, in 1818, her cousin,
John Marshall, a son of Captain Thomas, and an elder

brother of Colonel Charles A. Marshall—a man of strong
intellect and a fine scholar, but without ambition. The
late Dr. Alexander K. Marshall, John Marshall, and James
T. Marshall were his sons; the first wife of F. T. Chambers, the wife of James B. Casey, of Covington, and Miss
Mary M. Marshall, were his daughters. Dr. Marshall died
childless, James has no issue, and John never married.
His posterity will die out in the male line. Mrs. Chambers left one son, who is married, and without issue. Mrs.
Casey had many children.

Jane, the youngest daughter of Alexander K. Marshall
and Mary McDowell, was born in 1808, and married, in Columbus, Ohio, in 1824, William Starling Sullivant, an elder
brother of Michael Sullivant, who married a daughter of
Colonel Joseph McDowell, of Danville, as well as of Joseph
Sullivant, who first married a sister of his brother Michael's
wife, and then Lucinda Brashears, a granddaughter of
Judge William McDowell. These brothers were the sons
of Lucas Sullivant, a man of great energy and strength of
character, who was one of the most enterprising and useful of the pioneers of Ohio. Their mother was Sarah, second daughter of William Starling and Susannah
Lyne, and a sister of the William Starling who married
a daughter of Samuel McDowell, of Mercer. Born in
Franklinton, Ohio, in 1803, when the surrounding country
that was not covered with the unbroken primeval forest
was an almost uninhabited prairie, the infancy and boyhood of William S. Sullivant were passed amidst scenes
well calculated to teach the lessons of hardy endurance.
He grew up strong in body and vigorous in mind, graceful in person, and handsome in countenance. His thorough education was obtained at Athens, Ohio, and at
Yale, from which latter institution he graduated in 1823.
The death of his father in that year devolving upon him
the care of an immense landed estate, he did not study a
profession, for which the eminence of his talents, the extent of his attainments, and his fine presence and manners, were so admirably adapted. Yet, immersed in affairs

8

of business as he was at the outset of life, and continued
to be while it lasted, he found a field for his elegant
tastes and scientific research in the study of botany. His
numerous published works are standards in Europe as
well as in America. A more detailed account of the useful life and public services of Mr. Sullivant will be found
in the memorial published by his brother. His first wife,
Jane Marshall, died in 1825, leaving an infant daughter,
Jane, a beautiful woman, who married Robert E. Neil, of
Columbus, Ohio. The oldest daughter of Robert E. Neil
and Jane Marshall Sullivant married Colonel T. A. Dodge,
of Massachusetts, a graduate of the University of London,
a colonel in the Union service, who left an arm at Gettysburg. Their second daughter, Lucy Neil, married Major
W. W. Williams, a naval officer, who won his military
title while serving with the land forces of the Union during the war. For gallant conduct in command of a gun-
boat before Newbern, North Carolina, he received deserved
promotion. The naval service of the country has no better officer.

In this account of a numerous and historic race, nothing more has been attempted than a general grouping of
some of its most prominent members, with a cursory
glance at the leading incidents of their public lives. It
has been pleasant to trace the same mental attributes,
kindred physical characteristics, and similar patriotic impulses, as they seem to have run through the whole breed.
To a theme so prolific, a history so suggestive, it has been
possible to do but the scantiest justice. The hundreds
of true men and noble women who have been barely
named, or passed by in silence, will generously attribute
the omission to want of information, or to the necessity of
placing some limit upon the number of these pages. The
naming of any family that has supplied a greater number
of, or better, soldiers, or so large a number of, or more skillful, physicians and surgeons, may be safely challenged. In
this country, the family had its origin in those who fought
beyond the seas to overthrow the " divine right of kings,"
and to establish constitutional government. Here, in

every war since John McDowell lost his life, in 1742, their
blood has been freely offered in defense of liberty regulated by law—in the French and Indian, Dunmore's, Revolution, War of 1812, with Mexico; while, in the recent
civil war, without numbering other descendants of old
Ephraim who fought on one side or the other, as God
gave them to see the right, those of Judge Samuel Mc-
Dowell alone were more than a hundred. They have
worthily filled all grades in the military service, from that
of the private soldier in the trenches to that of the major-
general in command of the armies of the republic. They
have taken prominent parts in the erection, and in shaping
the organic laws, of states—of Virginia, Kentucky, and
others. They have honorably filled and ably discharged
the duties of every executive office in those states, from
the mayor of a city, or the sheriff of a county, to the governorship of the commonwealth; every legislative office
in the gift of the people, from that of the trustee of a
town, or the member of a council, to that of a senator of
the United States; every judicial office, from that of a justice of the peace to that of judge of a United States court.
While not one of them is known to the writer of whom
any one need be ashamed, their alliances in every direction have been with the most eminently respectable—in
many instances, with the most illustrious. In its various
ramifications, members of the family have not only the
same blood as that of governors, congressmen, senators,
judges, chief-justices, generals—almost without number—
but of that of four of the presidents of the United States,
Washington, Jefferson, Madison, and Taylor. Eminently
calm, thoughtful, and conservative, their influence has
been uniformly given to the maintenance of law, the promotion of education, and generally to the inculcation of
the sound principles of revealed religion. The beneficent
influence which such a race, when united and zealously
co-operating one with another, can exercise—do exercise
and have exerted—over communities in which their lot
may be cast, can not be overestimated. They have been as
modest as they have been brave; and, while other families

may not have been deficient in either of these qualities, *their* worth has been a compound of both. In the history of the race, there may be observed a singular uniformity in their leading traits. Men of great self-reliance and integrity, they have been unostentatious and without social ambition, as if their sturdy personal independence disdained the support of fictitious social prestige. Men of this type seldom grow rich, and rarely appear in the newspapers; but in their localities are always esteemed as solid men—citizens to be trusted, friends to rely upon, and enemies to be respected.

THE LOGANS.

Than that of Logan there are in Scotland few surnames more ancient. As early as 1278, it appears in the royal charters. In 1329, a knight named Robert Logan was in the train of barons who bore the heart of Bruce to the Holy Land, and in the battle with the Moors in Spain, in which the "Good" Sir James Douglas was slain, a Sir Walter Logan lost his life. In the reign of the Bruce, the principal family of the name obtained by marriage the barony of Restalrig, lying between Edinburg and the sea, on which the greater part of South Leith is now built. To such a height did this family attain, that Sir Robert Logan, of Restalrig, married a daughter of Robert II., by Euphemia Ross, and afterward was constituted Admiral of Scotland. This family was destined to a mighty fall. The last Logan who was baron of Restalrig, and who sold it to Balmerino,—Sir Robert—was engaged in the Gowrie conspiracy against the timid James VI.; and after his death, in 1606, his bones were exhumed, and a sentence of outlawry pronounced against him, whereby his lands of Fast Castle, obtained by marriage, were forfeited and lost to his family. Even the name was proscribed, so that many who bore it assumed other surnames. Then there was an ancient Celtic clan of the name, one of whose chiefs married a Fraser, and in a feud with the family of his wife was slain, with most of his clansmen. Another branch lived in Ayrshire, and was designed as "of Logan."—[*Scottish Nation.*] The family which is the subject of this sketch can not be definitely traced to any of those which have been mentioned, nor, if possessed of record evidence to do so, would they esteem it as adding to their worth to establish the connection. For generations before any of them came to America, they had been plain people in Ireland, accustomed to rely upon themselves for their individual respectability as well as for the means of subsistence, and were sturdily independent. Their tradition is, that their ancestor was a Presbyterian who fled from Ayrshire to escape the persecutions of John Grahame, the Bloody Claverhouse, and, with others of his name and kindred, found shelter and refuge among the Protestant plantations in the North of Ireland. Lurgan was the locality of his home. In the following years, descendants of this one found their way to Pennsylvania, whose colonial treasurer, James Logan, for whom the Mingo chief was named, was, in no distant degree, their kinsman. Two of these, James and David Logan, soon left Pennsylvania, and settled in Augusta county. They were very nearly related; it is believed they were brothers. They were both young when they went to Virginia, and both were soldiers in the French and Indian wars; their names appear upon the official lists. James settled near the new Providence Church, in what is now Rockbridge county. He had a son, also named James, who married Hannah Irvine, the daughter of a Presbyterian preacher, by whom he had eight sons and four daughters. One of these sons, John Logan, married Rachel McPheeters, a daughter of the Wm. McPheeters who married Rachel Moore, and a sister of Rev. Wm. McPheeters, whose first wife was a daughter of Major John McDowell, of Fayette county. This John Logan and Rachel McPheeters were the parents of Rev. Eusebius Logan, who died in 1827; of Rev. Robert Logan, of Fort Worth, Texas; of Joseph Logan and the late Mrs. Theophilus Gamble, of Augusta county. Alexander Logan, another son of James and Hannah, moved to Kentucky; one of Alexander's sons, a Presbyterian minister, married a Miss Venable, of Shelby county, and Rev. James Venable Logan, of Central University, is *their* son. Robert Logan, a third son of James and Hannah, was a Presbyterian minister. Rev. Robert Logan had the refusal of the tutorship in Hampden Sidney College when the celebrated John Holt Rice applied for it. He was was born in Augusta, in 1769; was educated at Liberty Hall; he visited Kentucky, and while here married Marga-

ret Moore, from Walker's Creek, Augusta county, Virginia.
She came from the same Rutherford-Walker stock which
gave to this country, and to the Presbyterian Church, Dr.
John Poage Campbell, the McPheeters, the Browns (descendants of Rev. Samuel), the Stuarts, and so many other
pious and able divines. Rev. Robert Logan returned to
Virginia, and finally settled in Fincastle county, where he
was for many years the frontier minister. The late John
B. I. Logan, of Salem, Roanoke county, was his son. Joseph D. Logan, a fourth son of James and Hannah, was
another Presbyterian minister, and one of distinction; he
married Jane Butler Dandridge, a descendant in the sixth
generation of Pocahontas, and of the family from which
came the wife of President Washington; their son, James
W. Logan, married Miss S. W. Strother. After the death
of his first wife, Rev. Jos. D. Logan married Louisa Lee,
one of whose children is Dr. Joseph P. Logan, of Atlanta,
Georgia. Ben. Logan, a fifth son of James and Hannah,
was the father of the late J. A. Logan, of Staunton. One
of the daughters of James and Hannah was the wife of
McKinney, the pioneer school teacher at Lexington, whose
bloody encounter with the wild-cat is related by McClung.
The preaching characteristics of the Irvines, as well as of
the Rutherfords, Walkers, Moores, McPheeters, seem to
have come out strong in this branch of the Logan family.—
[*Waddel's Annals.*]

David Logan, the other of these two emigrant brothers,
married, when young, in Pennsylvania. He probably
went to Virginia early in 1740. On the 22d of May, of
that year, fourteen heads of families appeared at the
Orange Court-house (Augusta county not having been
then established, and the territory being embraced in that
of Orange) to "prove their importation." The first of
these was Alexander Breckinridge, who made oath that
he had imported "himself, and John, George, Robert,
Smith, and Letitia Breckinridge, from Ireland to Philadelphia, and from thence to this colony, at his own
charges, and this is the first time of his proving his and

their rights in order to obtain land." The third to make similar oath was John Trimble, from whom came a conspicuous posterity. The eighth was David Logan, and from the record it is ascertained that the given name of his wife was Jane. The thirteenth was James Caldwell, possibly the ancestor of John C. Calhoun. John Preston came into court with Breckinridge, Logan, and others, but postponed proving his importation until 1746.—[*Waddel.*] The record of Rev. John Craig, the first Presbyterian minister in the Valley, shows that on May 3, 1743, he baptized Benjamin, child of David Logan, and that on March 24, 1745, he baptized David Logan's son, Hugh. Thus are the ages of these two brothers approximated. In 1763, the mother of Benjamin Logan, and widow of David, lived on Kerr's creek. This Jane Logan became the fruitful mother of six children, of whom the writer has knowledge, possibly of others; the sons were Benjamin, John, Hugh, and Nathaniel; the daughters were Mary and Sarah. The emigrant died early, leaving a modest but independent estate to the widow and his offspring, the eldest of whom was but fourteen; but bequeathing them also the priceless inheritance of vigorous intellects in robust bodies, well trained in the principles of morality and religion, self-reliance, fearlessness, and indomitable energy.

GENERAL BEN. LOGAN.

The father dying intestate, the lands descended to Benjamin, the oldest son, the law of primogeniture then prevailing in the colony; but with a disinterestedness of temper which continued to be the characteristic of an eventful life, on arriving at years of maturity, and with the consent of the mother, to whom he was ever an affectionate and dutiful son, he sold the lands, which were not susceptible of division, and distributed the proceeds among those whom the law had disinherited in his favor. Then, to provide for his remaining parent a home not less comfortable than that with which they had parted, he united his own share to that of one of his brothers, and, with the joint stock, purchased a fine farm on the rich bottoms of one of the forks of the James river, securing it to their mother during her life, or so long as she might choose to reside thereon, with the remainder in fee-simple to the brother. Thus early in evidences of filial piety was developed that nobleness of nature and devotion to duty which marked his entire subsequent life, and made honorable the name he left to those who came after. The surroundings of a newly-settled country were not favorable to the education of the children of those in circumstances as limited as those of his father; nor did the widowed mother have it in her power to bestow upon him more than a very imperfect knowledge of the rudiments. Without the slightest knowledge of science or the classics, his mind was almost unaided by letters; destitute of literary attainments, he was compelled to study men rather than books; but he had been early imbued with the principles and practice of a sound morality and Christian piety, and had cultivated the qualities of fortitude, endurance, self-sacrifice, and became capable of high resolve. In 1764, at the age of twenty-one years, in the capacity of a sergeant of Virginia volunteers, he accompanied the expedition commanded by Colonel Henry Bouquet against the Indians of Ohio, and there, in leading the advance, saw his first military service. This able and enterprising Swiss had, in the service of Sardinia, distinguished himself in the battle of Cony, where, " being ordered to occupy a piece of ground at the brink of a precipice, he led his men thither in such a way that not one of them saw that they were within two steps of destruction should the enemy force the position. Meanwhile, calmly watching the movements of both armies, he made his soldiers observe, in order to distract their attention, that these movements could be seen much better by the light of the moon than in broad daylight."— [*Dumas.*] Afterward, entering into the service of the Prince of Orange, he carefully studied the science of war, especially those branches of mathematics which are the foundation of the military art. From this service, passing

into that of Great Britain, he was placed in command of
one of the battalions of "The Royal American Regiments" which shared the dangers of the War of 1755.
The peace with the French in 1762 was immediately followed by the great Indian war under the leadership of the
renowned Pontiac, in which the Shawanese, Delawares,
Wyandottes, and other tribes of the North-west, leagued
together, captured from the English all the smaller posts
of the interior, beleaguered Detroit and Fort Pitt, and
swept with fire, rapine, and murder the frontiers of Pennsylvania, Maryland, and Virginia. Ordered to the relief
of Fort Pitt, Bouquet successfully accomplished his mission, and in August, 1763, defeated the Indians at Bushy
Run. It was under this veteran commander that Benjamin Logan began his military career, and received his first
lessons in savage warfare. The spring of 1764 witnessed
a renewal of Indian atrocities, and to chastise the tribes
between the Ohio and the lakes was the object of Colonel
Bouquet's expedition into their territory. The Virginians
who responded to the call met the force at Pittsburg, and
were at once placed in the front. In all the trials, dangers, and triumphs of the expedition, which was completely successful, Benjamin Logan shared. He was present at the "talk" given by the chiefs of the Delawares
and Shawanese—Castaloga, Beaver, Turtle Heart, and
Kiyashuta—to Colonel Bouquet, on the banks of the Mus-
kingum, in October, 1764, and in November of that year,
at the forks of the same stream, witnessed the delivery by
the Indians of the captives, women and children, whom
they had taken in their various raids and spared from
massacre and torture.

Returning from this task of public duty, and having
seen his mother and family comfortably settled in their
new home, he struck out for the Holston, there to provide
and build another for himself, buying land near where the
flourishing town of Abingdon now stands, which he improved; and, being alike shrewd, thrifty, economical, and
industrious, rapidly enlarged and added to his fertile farm.
It would be an injustice to the character of the man to

permit it to be supposed that the years passed upon the
Holston were engrossed by these exertions to improve his
own fortune, in repairing the estate nearly the whole of
which he had surrendered with a magnanimity seldom
equalled, or in the advancement of material interests of
any kind. On an exposed frontier as he was, there still
was time to think of the religion he had inherited, for
which his ancestors had suffered. One of the first settlers upon the Holston, an emigration which was commenced in 1765, his name is found fifth upon the list of the
signers to the call upon the Rev. Charles Cummings to become the pastor of the united congregations of Ebbing and
Sinking Springs, in Fincastle county. The call, which was
presented to Mr. Cummings " at the Presbytery of Hanover,
when sitting at the Tinkling Spring," recites the spiritual
destitution of the hardy pioneers, and the yearnings they
experienced for the consolations of the Word and the administration of divine ordinances. These were the first
organizations there organized, Mr. Cummings the first
minister in all that then distant region. Associated with
Logan in this call, are the historic names of Trimble, of
the McClures, Montgomerys, Casey, Huston, Craig, the
Gambles, Breckinridge, the Buchanans, Sam. Briggs, of
Colonel William Christian, and John Campbell—Presbyterians, religious and heroic soldiers whose qualities were
exhibited at Point Pleasant, King's Mountain, Guilford,
and on other fields of the Revolution. Such were the associates of his youth, the friends of his manhood. The
men of these congregations " never went to church without being armed, and taking their families with them.
On Sabbath morning, during this period, it was Mr. Cummings' custom, for he was always a very neat man in his
dress, to dress himself, then put on his shot-pouch,
shoulder his rifle, mount his dun stallion, and ride off
to church. There he met his gallant and intelligent congregation, each man with his rifle in his hand. When
seated in the meeting-house, they presented altogether a
most solemn and singular spectacle. Mr. Cummings' uniform habit, before entering the house, was to take a short

walk alone while the congregation were seating themselves; he would then return, at the door hold a few words of conversation with some one of the elders of the church, then would walk gravely through this crowd, mount the steps of the pulpit, deposit his rifle in a corner near him, lay off his shot-pouch, and commence the solemn worship of the day. He would preach two sermons, having a short interval between them, and go home."—[*Foote.*] Such were the lessons by which Logan and his kindred were imbued—where the religious and the military spirit went hand in hand; such the scenes amidst which their characters were formed, broadened, and heightened. There he met with bonny Anne Montgomery, the daughter of one of his neighbors of the Scotch-Irish Presbyterian race, escorted her home from these martial-religious exercises, whispered into her willing ears the tender words of love even while his hand grasped the rifle, and, as the years rolled by, won and married her. In 1774, not long after his marriage, hostilities were renewed by the Shawanese, Wyandottes, Delawares, Mingoes, Miamis, Tawas, and other tribes, who had been incensed by the murders perpetrated by Cresap, and had determined to make a last desperate effort to stay the advancing strides of the all-conquering and all-grasping white man. Among those from the Holston who sprang to arms, in response to the call of Lord Dunmore, were Captain Benjamin Logan and the company of brave veterans who had chosen him as their leader. The statement that he had fought at Point Pleasant, where fell the noble Lewis, the experienced Field, and the Allens true, is an error. Commanded to join the division at Fort Pitt under the immediate command of Lord Dunmore, he, with George Rogers Clarke, Sam. McCullough, Kenton, the unlucky Wm. Crawford, and others, continued with that body in its march through Ohio, and lost the distinction and glory of fighting by the side of Fleming, the Shelbys, McDowell, Campbell, and the Lewises, in the desperate struggle in which the painted braves of the eloquent Cornstalk were beaten back. Prior to this, he had been conspicuous in repelling the forays and keeping in subjection the warlike Cherokees and other Indians of the South.

Returning to the Holston, his imagination was fired, his hopes of adding to his fortune stimulated, and his ambition set aglow, by the accounts brought back by the explorers and hunters of the magnificent forests, the dense canebrakes, the luxuriant pastures, and the fat and sightly lands of the then newly-discovered country beyond the mountains, and watered by the beautiful Ohio. Early in 1775, he set out to see for himself, and to make a settlement, unaccompanied save by several attached slaves. Soon falling in with Boone, Henderson, and other adventurers, journeying with a similar purpose, he united himself to their party, and with them passed along the line of the Old Wilderness road for some distance into Kentucky; then, diverging from them, struck out alone in a westerly direction, pursuing it for a few days, until, charmed with the beauty of the scene, in which the rosiest visions of his dreams seemed crystallized in the landscape, he pitched his tent near the present town of Stanford. John Mason Brown, in his oration at the centennial celebration of the battle of the Blue Licks, asserts that John Todd, " in the early spring of 1775, joined Ben. Logan in the establishment of St. Asaphs' station." Mr. Hixson has in his possession letters (which will be published with his forthcoming carefully-prepared work on Mason county) which lead him to the conclusion that the enchanting scene had been visited by the " Long Hunters," under James Knox, and that the latter had acquired some claim to the site before the foot of Logan pressed the flowers that grew upon the land; and that John Floyd and John Todd were there before Logan. Whether Logan first made the settlement, as the historians generally assert, or whether he passed on, acquired lands in what is now Jefferson, and quickly exchanged them with Knox for the tract at St. Asaphs which had so pleased his eye and delighted his fancy, does not matter. At St. Asaphs, he made his permanent settlement, the third made in Kentucky—those of Boone, at Boonesboro, and of Harrod, at Harrodsburg,

having had a brief precedence—and there he built the fort
which is known in history as St. Asaphs. There, with
William Gillespie, he planted and raised a small crop of
corn during the same year; and, after marking out loca-
tions in the surrounding country for his kindred and connexions, returned alone, during the summer, to the Holston, to spur them to the enterprise, and support them on
the way. That fall, he brought to Kentucky his remaining slaves, and all his cattle, which leaving in the charge
of Gillespie, he once more went back, unaccompanied, to
the Holston to remove his family, which was done shortly
thereafter—in the beginning of 1776, as the histories state.
In the following years, came his brothers and sisters, the
family of his wife, and numerous friends and connexions,
to occupy and build new homes upon the lands he had designed for them, finding shelter and refuge within the
hospitable and protecting walls of the fort he so stoutly
held, and around which they clustered. The date of his
arrival with his wife, and infant son, David, at St. Asaphs,
is stated by Marshall as the 8th of March, 1776. Rendered desperate by the settlement of the "Long Knives"
upon their hunting lands, during the ensuing summer the
Indians swarmed through the woods, and lurked behind
every tree and bush. After vainly endeavoring to induce
the scattering settlers in the neighborhood of Crab Orchard to make a stand and rallying point at his cabins,
Logan found safety for his loved ones behind the walls of
the fort at Harrodsburg, where went also those who had
refused to join him; then, insensible to fear, he returned
to his location, and, with his slaves, planted and gathered
his grain, and continued his clearings. His wife and son
returned to him early in 1777, by which time he had
constructed a stronghold behind which to place them.
Thenceforward, his history is that of the territory he
helped to subdue and wrest from the savage, of the state
among whose founders he was one of the most conspicuous. A tall, athletic, contemplative, well-balanced, and
dignified figure, distinguished his person and appearance.
He was taciturn—the statesman's eye was crowned in him

with the warrior's brow; while a countenance, which evinced an unyielding fortitude and an impenetrable guard, invited to a confidence which was never betrayed. Such is the description given of him by one of his contemporaries, the first historian of Kentucky, who did not like him any too well.

On the 20th of May, 1777, this fort, which he had named St. Asaphs, and which had become the place of refuge for all the neighboring settlers, was regularly besieged by the Indians, more than a hundred in number, the most determined investment ever executed by Indian hostility, and sustained with unabated ferocity and vigilance for weeks, during which the heroic characteristics of the commander of the little garrison were signally illustrated. On the morning before the siege was formally commenced, the Indians found the women belonging to the fort milking outside the gates, attended by a small guard of men, upon whom they fired from their ambush in a canebrake, killing one, mortally wounding another, and disabling a third, named Harrison, who fell outside in the sight of his frantic wife. In vain Logan appealed to his men to accompany him in a desperate sally to rescue their wounded comrade. John Martin alone consented, who, after rushing from the fort with Logan, shrank from the appalling peril confronting him, and sprang back again. The undaunted Logan dashed on alone, raised in his arms the wounded man, placed him on his shoulders, and, amidst the bullets which whistled and sang around them, reached the fort with his grateful burden, unharmed. The fort was defended not less vigorously than it was obstinately assailed, until the ammunition commenced to fail. On the distant Holston were supplies, but who would bring them? The courage of Logan was equal to all emergencies. Imbuing into his men the lofty spirit of his own soul, he left them, under cover of the night; shunned the ordinary roads; flew, on the wings of hope, and love, and duty, over valley and mountain; obtained the needed stores, which he intrusted to the companions he had rallied for the rescue; and, in ten days from his departure, returned alone to the fort, to inspire, to re-animate the flagging energies of his men with hope, and instill into them his own unbending nerve. The rescuers carrying the ammunition marching rapidly, and safely reaching the fort, the garrison, though cut off from the world, thought themselves, with the experienced Logan in command, capable of maintaining the defense. The country continued to be infested by Indians, who frequently appeared before the fort, enforcing the necessity of ceaseless vigilance. The arrival of Colonel John Bowman with his detachment of militia, in September, brought a sense of temporary security to the garrison of St. Asaphs. Marshall relates that, upon the approach of Bowman, one of his men was killed by the besieging Indians, and that papers taken from his person were brought to Logan by the man who found the body; Littell, that during the siege, and before Bowman had come, one of the garrison " ventured, early one morning, to open the gate of Logan's station, and step out; he was immediately shot dead. An Indian, or probably some British savage habited as an Indian, ran forward, took off his scalp, laid a bundle of papers on his breast, and escaped. The dead man was brought into the station, and Colonel Logan took the papers." Differing in this, both writers agree that Logan did not examine the papers until he was entirely alone, and that he found them to be a bundle of proclamations from Sir Guy Carleton, then commander-in-chief of the British forces in Canada. The proclamations were directed to the people of Kentucky *generally*, and to George Rogers Clarke and Benjamin Logan *by name*. These proclamations offered protection to all who would abandon the cause of the republic, and denounced the most terrible vengeance against all those who refused. They drew attention to the futility of expecting security against the Indians from Virginia or the Continental authorities; that Britain was the only earthly power that could afford that security; and promising, if they would only return to their allegiance, all the Indian nations should be withdrawn. To the militia officers, they promised the same rank in the regular army of Great Britain that they held under Virginia, and that, instead of the poor and uncertain pay from the state, they should receive that accorded to officers of the British line. Logan secreted these papers, never mentioning their contents, nor even their existence, until many years afterward, when all danger of their possible effect upon the weak and fickle had passed away. Bowman's party soon leaving St. Asaphs to join Clarke at the Falls of the Ohio, the garrison was once more distressed by the want of ammunition. Again Logan went, alone and swiftly, to the Holston, returning with the needed supplies. Shortly after his return from this second journey, the garrison was reinforced by the arrival of a party led by Colonel Montgomery, who confirmed the spirit of cheerfulness his presence had inspired.—[*Marshall.*] Montgomery also went to join Clarke. During the several following years, Benjamin Logan was almost constantly engaged in the active defense of his own and other settlements. While on an exploring excursion, in 1778, a few miles from his fort he discovered an Indian camp. Returning to St. Asaphs, he rallied his men, and attacked and routed the savages. Shortly after this occurrence, being at the same place alone, he was fired upon by Indians in ambush, his right arm was broken, and he received a wound in the breast. The Indians, seeking to capture him alive, forbore to kill him; they rushed upon him, and so nearly succeeded in accomplishing their purpose, that one of them had hold of his horse's tail.—[*Marshall.*] Scarcely had his wounds healed, when his activity was resumed, alone, or in company with others, shunning neither hardship nor peril by which his country or his friends could be benefited. Two years afterward, in 1780, a party going from Harrodsburg, in the direction of St. Asaphs, were ambushed by Indians; two were mortally wounded, one of whom reached Logan's, and communicated the disaster. With a party of young men about his fort, Logan at once repaired to the succor of the wounded man, whom they found in the weeds in which he had concealed himself—alive, but incapable of traveling. Taking

9

him upon his own broad shoulders, Logan bore the wounded man to Harrodsburg. On their return home from Harrodsburg, his own party was fired upon by the Indians, and one of his young companions wounded. The Indians were repulsed with loss. Then the humanity, fortitude, and strong arms of Logan were again called into requisition to convey the wounded man weary miles back to his fort.—[*Marshall.*] In him, generosity, benevolence, self-sacrifice—the developments of true natural religion— were as characteristic as the unblenching courage which never feared the face of man.

Benjamin Logan was second in command of Bowman's expedition against the Ohio Indians. Leaving Harrodsburg, in May, 1779, following the old buffalo trail to the mouth of Limestone, then crossing the Ohio, and striking into the interior through the gap in the northern hills four miles below, still called by his name, the preliminary measures concerted by Logan were so well executed that the expeditionary force had reached within a mile of the large Indian town of old Chillicothe without having given the slightest alarm to their wary enemy. A halt was made; the spies, at midnight, reported the Indians wrapped in sleep and fancied security; an immediate attack was determined. Logan was to turn to the left, with one-half of the men, marching half way around the town; Bowman, at the head of the remainder, was to turn to the right, and make a corresponding march. When the detachments met at the opposite end of the village, which would thus be completely surrounded, an immediate and simultaneous attack was to be commenced. How well Logan performed his part, is related by the graphic Mc-Clung. Having reached his designated position, he there awaited in vain for Colonel Bowman and the signal of attack. The slow hours crawled on until daylight appeared. Logan concealed his men in the high grass; one of them alarmed a dog, which began to bay; a solitary Indian was aroused, stood upon tiptoe, and peered cautiously around him, without discovering any of Logan's men, who lay close and silent. Suddenly a gun was fired in the opposite end of the town by one of Bowman's men; the Indian ran back, and gave the alarm; the savages at once collected at the council chamber, in the center of the town, armed, and prepared for a desperate resistance. Confidently expecting support from Bowman, the party of Logan, promptly rushing to the attack, took immediate possession of the houses that had been abandoned by the Indians, and, advancing rapidly from one to another, established themselves within close rifle-shot of the Indian redoûbt. Nothing could be heard from Bowman; the position of Logan became critical; the Indians, outnumbering him, kept up a heavy fire upon the cabins which covered his men; he could neither advance nor retreat; while the emboldened Indians gave evidence of a purpose to turn both his flanks. Cut off from his commander, from whom he could hear nothing, and of whose position he was ignorant, he determined to make a breast-work of the planks of the cabins, under their cover to charge upon the Indians, and, in a hand-to-hand contest, to drive them from their stronghold. Had time permitted this gallant resolve to be put into execution, and had it been supported by Bowman, victory was certain—not an Indian could have escaped. While the cool and intrepid Logan was preparing for the movement, a messenger from Bowman brought him orders to retreat. The messenger could give no explanation; but these were the orders. The surprised and disappointed Logan, yielding to the demands of military subordination, reluctantly obeyed. The singular and tumultuous scene that commenced was the inevitable consequence of a command so bewildering. Bowman, seized with one of those unaccountable panics to which the bravest of men are sometimes liable, had lost his head, and had remained exactly where Logan had left him the night before. The Indians, as much astonished at seeing this sudden rout as Logan had been at the disastrous order, sallied out in quest of their human game. Bowman sat still upon his horse, unnerved, speechless. With the aid of the gallant Major George M. Bedinger, of Blue Licks, Logan restored some degree of order to the retreat, but was soon surrounded on all sides by the enemy, who kept up a fatal fire. The sound of the rifle-shots and the instincts of self-preservation having restored the men to their senses, the calm Logan, whom no danger ever appalled or confused, and whose best faculties were called into action by the exigency, formed them into a hollow square, and from behind the sheltering trees returned the fire with such deadly results as quickly repelled the attack. The retrograde march having recommenced, the Indians, reappearing, opened a fire upon front, flanks, and rear, from behind every tree, and bush, and stone. The hollow square was agained formed; the assault again repelled. The Indians continuing to press on, with increasing ferocity and in increasing numbers, and the panic commencing to spread from the commander to the privates, Logan, with Harrod and Bedinger, selected their boldest and best-mounted men, dashed into the bushes on horseback at their head, scoured the woods, forced the Indians from their covers, cut and shot down all they could overtake, dispersed, and routed them. In this charge, Blackfish, warrior and chief, was killed. The march was then re-commenced and continued in order of the hollow square.— [*McClung.*] Logan knew nothing of the classics, may never have heard of Cæsar or the Roman legion. His native military genius inspired the adoption of the tactics of the greatest of the Roman generals.

So constantly occupied in the defense of the interior settlements of the Kentucky district, Benjamin Logan had no part in the secret and successful expedition of Clarke against the Kaskaskias and Vincennes. In 1780, the British commandant at Detroit devised the incursion into Kentucky, under Girty and Byrd, which laid waste the plantations upon the Licking and Elkhorn, destroyed Ruddell's and Martin's stations, and carried terror to every heart. Retaliation having been resolved upon, Colonel George Rogers Clarke proceeded from the Falls of the Ohio, and Logan, who had served with Clarke in the right wing under Dunmore, and with him participated in the only actual fighting done in that march into Ohio, met his

old comrade, with the forces of the interior, at the mouth
of the Licking; Clarke had the command, Logan was
second in authority. The Indian settlement at Pickaway,
on the Miami, was vigorously attacked as soon as reached,
the defenders beaten and dispersed, the town burned, the
crops destroyed, and the cattle killed. The loss on both
sides was heavy. Logan was then detached with his men
to march against the Indian store and settlement some
twenty miles distant—Larimie's store; the Indians, fleeing before him, declined the combat; the store, which was
the main object of attack, and the town, were burned, and
the same policy of destruction was every-where pursued.
From this store, all the Indian expeditions into Kentucky
had been supplied with arms. Compelled by these severe
but necessary measures to resort to hunting for food, the
Indians, for the remainder of the year, left the Kentucky
settlers in peace. During the interval of security thus afforded, Colonel Logan visited Virginia, and, with that filial
piety which marked his life, brought his mother and sister
to Lincoln, where he gave them land, built them a house,
and provided for their future.

In the fall of 1779, Logan was followed to Kentucky by
his father-in-law, the elder William Montgomery, with his
family, and by Joseph Russell, another son-in-law of Montgomery, and his family, who, after finding refuge at St.
Asaphs for a few months, built and occupied cabins about
twelve miles distant, on one of the sources of Green river.
The Indians had no sooner discovered these outlying settlements than they attacked them. Early one morning,
in 1781, the elder William Montgomery stepped to the
door of his cabin, a negro boy by his side, when both were
fired upon, and instantly killed; the head of the negro fell
upon the doorsill so that it could not be closed. Jane
Montgomery, the daughter of the aged victim, sprang to
the door, with a vigorous shove of her foot pushed out the
dead boy's head, shut the door, called for her brother's
rifle, and, with it in her steady hand, bravely defied the
foe, who feared to approach the cabin. She afterward
married the gallant General Casey, of Adair, and was the

grandmother of "Mark Twain," the noted humorist. Betsey Montgomery, a younger sister, twelve years of age, clambered out of the chimney, and, fleet as any deer of the forest, outstripped pursuit, running to Pettit's station, two miles away, whence the alarm was swiftly forwarded to Logan's. William Montgomery, Jr., who lived in an adjoining cabin, hearing the report of the shot that killed his father, thrust his rifle over a crevice over the door of his cabin, and firing twice at the Indians made two of them bite the dust. John Montgomery, another son of the elder, was shot dead while in bed in a third cabin, and his wife was made prisoner. Joseph Russell, the son-in-law, fled from the fourth cabin, leaving his wife, three children, and a mulatto girl, captives in the hands of the savages, who soon beat a retreat. An Indian who had pursued Betsey Montgomery returned in ignorance of what had occurred, mounted a log in front of the cabin of the younger William Montgomery, who fired a third time through the crevice over his door, recording a third victim to his trusty rifle. When the messenger from Pettit's reached Logan's, the horn was sounded, and a determined band soon started in pursuit, aided in following the trail by the twigs Mrs. Russell managed to break from the trees and the bits of a handkerchief she let fall whenever an occasion offered. They found the yellow girl, who had been scalped and left for dead, but who sprang to her feet, on hearing Logan's voice, and recovered. When the Indians were overtaken, they fled at Logan's charge, but, being followed as swiftly by the avengers, did not escape without heavy loss. On hearing Logan's voice, one of the Russell girls exclaimed, "There's Uncle Ben.," when an Indian immediately dispatched her with his tomahawk.

In 1782, information brought by spies that Colonel Clarke was engaged in the preliminary arrangements for an expedition from the Falls to attack Detroit, determined the British commandant of that post to anticipate the movement by precipitating his barbarian allies upon the Kentucky settlements. With hearts inflamed by the sanguinary appeals of the infamous Girty, and the noted

Brandt, the Indians responded to the call to rapine and murder; under the leadership of Colonel Caldwell, the army that had been collected for the purpose suddenly emerged in the interior; and, after bloody atrocities elsewhere, on the night of the 14th of August laid siege to Bryant's station, the gallantry of whose garrison is the theme of McClung's unsurpassed description. Intelligence of the incursion sent to Colonel John Todd, at Lexington, was by him forwarded to Colonel Trigg, at Harrodsburg, and to Daniel Boone, at his fort on the Kentucky river. Committing to Harrod the duty of apprising Logan, Trigg, with such men as were immediately available, hurried to Lexington, where he was joined by the ever-watchful Boone. A large force was quickly collected by Logan, and, led by one in whose courage and wisdom all confided, rapidly marched for the point of danger. Logan himself records his misgivings, when, on reaching Lexington, he ascertained that Todd and Trigg, both gallant, but comparatively inexperienced in savage warfare, and eager for distinction, had rashly marched without him. Then forcing his own march forward, he had advanced a few miles beyond Bryant's, when the bloody and dust-covered stragglers, returning from Blue Licks, told him of that dreadful disaster. Gathering the fugitives, and restoring order, Logan returned to Bryant's, there awaited the arrival of a portion of his men who were hurrying on, and then resumed his march for the Blue Licks. The Indians having retreated, to him was left only the pious duty of burying the mangled remains of the heroes he was powerless to avenge. It was no fault of a soldier so vigilant, active, and enterprising, that the ambitious zeal of the leaders who had fallen brought woe to the widow and orphan, and mourning to all the land for its best and bravest, in place of that assured and complete victory that awaited the united force under the command of a fighter at once so resolute and experienced. The council at the Falls, to concert measures for immediate revenge, was attended by Colonel Logan. In compliance with the agreement, the men who rendezvoused at Bryant's were led by him to the mouth of the Licking, where they were joined by Colonel Clarke with those from the Falls. Clarke again directed the expedition, while Logan was second in command. The Indians, fleeing in dismay before the advance of so large a force, could not be brought to an engagement, and the only compensation and satisfaction gained for Blue Licks was in the work of devastation and destruction which spread ruin and desolation throughout the Indian country. This was effected in a manner so thorough and remorseless as secured Kentucky from any future invasion of such magnitude. Settlers remote from others continued to be harassed and beset by marauding raids, and the constant anxiety which pervaded every mind kept Colonel Logan, and men like him, forever on the alert. His letters to the governors of Virginia show that from the first he had urged an aggressive war against the Indians in their own country as the best means of protecting the Kentucky settlements.

His services and signal capacity for command having received tardy recognition by the distant state authorities of Virginia, by an appointment as brigadier-general, Logan, in 1786, crossed the Ohio river with Clarke, on his abortive Wabash expedition. While in camp at Clarkesville, Ind., it was determined that General Logan should leave his men with Clarke, return to Kentucky, and organize another expedition against the Miami and Mad River Indian towns. The mind turns with sorrow from Clarke's mortifying failure, nor receives consolation by dwelling on its causes. The arrangements contemplated by General Logan were soon perfected, the men assembled, the march pushed onward with a celerity equalled by its secrecy. Mackachack, his first destination, reached, that large Indian town would have been completely surprised, but for the information given by a deserting Frenchman, which enabled the warriors to escape. As it was, twenty warriors were killed and eighty captured. The pen of General Wm. H. Lytle describes the scene in which he was an actor; he professes himself to have been " animated with the energy with which the commander conducted the head of the line. He waved his sword, and, in a voice of thunder, exclaimed, 'charge from right to left' upon the retreating Indians."—[*Howe.*] Among the captives was the aged Moluntha, the great sachem of the Shawanese, with his three wives, one of whom was the celebrated " Grenadier Squaw," the sister of Cornstalk and Tecumseh; and the young Indian prince, Lawba, son of Moluntha and the " Grenadier Squaw," so-called from her immense height, strength, and courage. The boy, who was of the same age as Lytle, clung to him for protection. Unfortunately, among the officers under Logan was Colonel Hugh McGary, still smarting under the censure which attributed to him the precipitation of the tragedy at Blue Licks, and burning with desire for revenge for his comrades. Disregarding the peremptory orders of General Logan to do no harm to the prisoners, McGary, forcing his way through the crowd which surrounded the old chief, his wives and son, demanded of Moluntha if he had been at the " defeat of the Blue Licks," to which an affirmative answer was given. Instantly seizing an ax from the " Grenadier Squaw," in spite of the effort of Lytle to prevent it, and before any one else could intervene, McGary laid Moluntha dead at his feet. The swift seizure of Lytle's arm by others, alone averted the thrust with which he sought to dispatch the murderer, who escaped from the crowd. The town, with the adjacent cornfields, was destroyed. Seven others shared the same fate; but, the alarm being given to the inhabitants, they saved themselves by timely flight. Pity for their condition induced General Logan to take the wives and son of Moluntha to his own home in Lincoln county. Won by the handsome appearance and noble bearing of Lawba, the generous victor adopted the lad, gave him his own name, and educated him with his own children. The speech made by General Logan to the important council of Shawanese braves, subsequently held in the beautiful valley opposite Maysville, of which the captivity of Lawba was in part the subject, has been by Mr. Hixson, the careful historian, most thoughtfully preserved. His affection

won by the kindness of his protector, Lawba continued
the friend of the whites, and, in after years, sealed his devotion by the sacrifice of his life. Marshall, in his account
of General Logan, deemed it not beneath the pen of a
just historian to place on record " his open house and hospitable attention to all emigrants and travelers; and the
solicitude with which he often met them and conducted
them into the country;" surrounded daily by peril the
most imminent, he was yet careful of the amenities of
life; the noble nature of the man never slept.

Nor did the incessant military duties of General Logan
render him neglectful of civil affairs. From Marshall it
is learned that in 1780 he was chosen to the General Assembly of Virginia, and, on the establishment of Lincoln
county, was commissioned as the colonel of its military
forces. In 1781, he was again elected to the general assembly, and attended its session at Richmond. In the
latter year, he was also one of the magistrates who held
at Harrodsburg the first court which sat in Kentucky. In
1783, he was the second sheriff of Lincoln. In 1784,
General Logan—to whom had been committed the defense
of the interior, while Clarke commanded at the Falls—received information of an intended Indian foray into Kentucky upon a large scale; and publicly summoned the most
prominent and influential citizens of the district, from far
and near, to meet in Danville on a designated day, to con-
sult upon and concert measures for the common defense.
The meeting was very largely attended. The result of
the conference was to accept the conclusions of the ablest
lawyers present—that, under the existing laws, there was
no legal means of organizing a force to invade the Indian
territory; men could no longer be impressed; there was
no legal method of providing for the payment of those
who volunteered; and, no matter how imminent the danger, there was no way in which the resources of the district could be called out to meet the emergency. All legis-
lation had to come from Richmond. The necessity for a
government independent of Virginia was thus made apparent. It was agreed that each militia company should

send a delegate to another convention, to be held in Danville on the 27th of December, 1784; this convention met, and was the precursor of all the others. Sent several times after 1781 to the Virginia Assembly, General Logan was also a member of the first convention to consider the question of separation from the mother state, which met in Danville in 1785; a member of the conventions held for the same purpose in 1787 and 1788. He was a member of the convention which framed the first state constitution, in 1792, as well as a member, from Shelby county, of that which framed the second constitution, in 1799. From the establishment of the state, in 1792, until his death, he was frequently a member of the state legislature. In these deliberative bodies, whether in Richmond, Danville, or Frankfort, his accurate information relating to all practical affairs of the district or state, his sound and strong judgment formed in the study of men more than of books, his broad views and intelligent statesmanship, and the terse and judicious utterances with which he made known his well-matured opinions, commanded respect, and gave him a wide and beneficent influence in all public affairs. In 1790, he was appointed by Washington a member of the local "Board of War," for the defense of the district, the other members of which were Isaac Shelby, Charles Scott, Harry Innes, and John Brown. It is doing no injustice to others to say that his influence, activity, zeal, energy, and military experience, contributed equally with those of the heroes of King's Mountain and of the Fallen Timbers, to the efficiency and *morale* of the expeditions against the Indians which were prepared under their direction. Under the constitution of 1792, the governor was chosen by an electoral college, similar to that of the federal government. The second governor, successor to Shelby, was elected by this body in May, 1796. The college was legally constituted of fifty-seven members, of whom fifty-three only voted on the day designated by law. Of those, 21 cast their votes for Benjamin Logan; 17 for James Garrard; 14 for Thomas Todd; and 1 for John Brown. The college, holding that a majority of the whole was requisite to an election, proceeded to a second ballot; Todd and Brown were dropped; and Garrard receiving a majority of the votes was declared elected. Logan, after obtaining from John Breckinridge his opinion that the plurality vote he had received had legally elected him, and that the subsequent action of the college was illegal and void, appealed the question to the senate, which body the statute had made the arbiter of gubernatorial contests. That body dodged the issue by deciding that the law conferring upon it the jurisdiction was unconstitutional.— [*Warfield.*] In December, 1802, while riding alone, General Logan fell from his horse in an apoplectic fit, was found speechless where he had fallen, was conveyed to his home, five miles from Shelbyville, and, in a few hours, died. The inscription upon his tombstone states that he was then sixty years old.

As hardy and as capable of endurance as Boone, Kenton, Harrod, or Harlan—the equal of the most famous of the early adventurers and hunters in woodcraft—in intelligence, in mental endowments, in elevation of character, Benjamin Logan was as superior to this class of the bold and generous pioneers as he was in mere social position and early surroundings. In the judgment of contemporary historians, among the grim warriors who conquered the land from the Indians, and extended the boundary of our country to and beyond the Mississippi, his sole equal in military talents, in far-reaching enterprise, and in capacity for command, was found in the brilliant genius of George Rogers Clarke. Above all others, these two will forever stand conspicuous. Equally self-sacrificing, fully as enterprising, and even more athletic than Clarke, the energy and ardor of Logan were never the results of a desire for individual advancement or of personal glory. While no man felt more keenly or saw more plainly than Logan the disadvantage under which Kentucky labored as a distant province of Virginia, the idea of a revolutionary and illegal separation, meditated by Clarke as early as 1776, never found even a transient lodgment in the thoughts of his reflecting contemporary. The close of

Logan's eventful and honorable life remained unclouded by the vices that force the generous to lament the eclipse that darkened the fame and last days of the daring captor of Vincennes. Content with the honors that came to him naturally and unsought, and devoid of self-seeking, no reproach of ingratitude against his country corroded in the heart nor passed the lips of Logan; nor can it be shown that ambitious visions induced him to accept a military commission from a foreign power to enter upon an act of war in violation of that country's laws. Comprehending in all its magnitude the importance of the free navigation of the Mississippi, and resolute as the foremost in all legitimate, peaceful, and legal measures to secure it, no act, or utterance, or written word of his ever for an instant gave occasion or pretext for the charge that he favored a separation from the Union, or an alliance with a foreign power, in order to obtain that commercial advantage; nor left it to be disputed whether he opposed or favored the proposition. His broad and comprehensive mind realizing the magnificent future that awaited the grand imperial republic of the people, his figure stands aloof from all real or alleged conspiracies, far above and unassailed by the factious warrings and recriminations of jealous and contending politicians.

The Montgomerys.

Traditions ascribing to the wife of General Logan a relationship to the hero of Quebec are of no value and are entitled to no respect. It was not near, nor can the most remote connexion be traced. The identity of the names suggests to the imagination the probability that both may have sprung from families—possibly his kinsmen and clansmen—planted by Hugh Montgomery in Ireland, upon the lands wrung from The O'Neill as the price of his liberty; or from the subsequent emigrations of Protestant Scotch. All that is certainly known of Anne Montgomery's ancestors is, that they were of the Scotch-Irish Presbyterians who peopled the Valley; that they were, in every way, respectable; that their names are found among

the valiant soldiers, among the civil officers deemed worthy
of trust, and among the preachers of God's Word. With
the Logans, Gambles, McClures and Campbells, they struck
out to the Holston, then the frontier. There they did not
acquire wealth, but became independent, and, the stuff of
which they were made being good, maintained in excellent credit the worthy names they had inherited. The
fate that befel her father, and others of her kindred, has
already been stated, and may be found, in greater detail,
in the pages of Collins. Thomas Montgomery, one of the
sons of her brother, William, won distinction as the able
judge of his circuit district. He was the father of the
late Dr. Montgomery, of Lincoln, and of the first wife of
Dr. Lewis W. Green, the learned president of Hampden
Sidney and of Centre College, and one of the most eloquent and scholarly of pulpit orators. Anne Montgomery's sister, Jane, was the wife of Colonel William Casey,
of Adair, after whom a Kentucky county was named, and
was, as has been stated, the grandmother of " Mark
Twain." A niece of Anne Montgomery married a brother
of Colonel Joseph Hamilton Daviess, and, after his death,
became the wife of the late Thomas Helm, of Lincoln;
the wife of the eloquent Joshua F. Bell was her daughter.
A niece of Anne Montgomery was the wife of the late
Judge Ben. Monroe, of Frankfort, an upright judge, a
valued reporter of the court of appeals, and an humble
Christian; this niece was the mother of Colonel George
W. Monroe, a soldier of the Federal army, and of the first
wife of Judge Wheat, of the Kentucky Court of Appeals.
Mrs. Wheat was the mother of Mrs. Cornelia Bush, the
first woman elected public librarian of the state. Did prescribed limits permit, few pleasures would be more grati-
fying than that of following these Montgomerys through
all their ramifications—Caseys, Russells, Clemens, Adairs,
Helms, Bells, Monroes, Wheats, and others—the numerous descendants, scattered far and wide over South and
West, both men and women, generally staunch Presbyterians, every-where, by their intrepidity, self-reliance and
strong, good sense, vindicate the laws of heredity. After

the death of General Logan, his widow married General James Knox, by whom she had no issue. General Knox was a native of Ireland, of Scotch descent, a man of great force of character, and, as the leader of the " Long Hunters," was one of the earliest, as well as one of the most intelligent, of the explorers of the Kentucky wilderness— his expedition setting out in 1769. He raised corn in what is now Jefferson county, in 1775, was a soldier in the Revolution, and represented Lincoln county in the legislature, from 1795 to 1800. He died in Shelby county, December 14, 1822. The widow of both these gallant men died in Shelby, October 18, 1825, aged seventy-three years.

JUDGE WILLIAM LOGAN.

David, the oldest child of General Logan and Anne Montgomery, who was brought in his mother's arms to Kentucky, in the beginning of 1776, grew to manhood, and married; but he and his wife both died shortly thereafter, without issue. William, the second child and son of General Logan and Anne Montgomery, was born in the fort at Harrodsburg, to which his mother had gone for protection that could not then be afforded at St. Asaphs in its isolated situation, on the 8th of December, 1776. Whether he or Harrod Wilson was the first *male* white child born in Kentucky, will remain in dispute. If not the first, he was, at all events, 'the second *male* native; and it is improbable that more than one white *female*, Chenoe Hart, was born in Kentucky previously.—[*Collins.*] His infancy was passed in the fort at St. Asaphs, amidst seiges and all the scenes of strife incident to savage warfare. From his earliest boyhood, he was accustomed to listen to the recital of battles and deeds of generous heroism and noble daring from the witnesses thereof and participants therein, and thus was his character formed and molded. From his father, who was most liberal in his views, he received every advantage that could be afforded by the best teachers in the country; his education was thorough and classical; he was stimulated to exertion by constant collision with other youths possessed of the most brilliant intellects.

The laborious compiler, Collins, states that of the early-
born sons of Kentucky, " he was the most gifted and eminent." Whether this estimate was just or partial, it is
certain that in Kentucky, which is still proud of the fame
of the galaxy of orators and statesmen of that generation
who shed luster over her history, he was early and continuously selected as the most worthy of the highest public honors—not easily won in those days by the common-
place. Selected as a member, from Lincoln county, of the
convention which convened at Frankfort on the 17th of
August, 1799, at the age of twenty-two, to frame the second constitution of Kentucky, he was next to the youngest, yet one of its most useful members. In the important
task of shaping the organic law of the commonwealth, his
father sat as a member from Shelby; his uncle, Colonel
John Logan, was the associate of the able and eloquent
Harry Innes as members from Franklin; General William
Casey, who had married his aunt, was the member from
Green; while Judge Caleb Wallace, whose daughter he
afterward married, was one of the members chosen from
Woodford. Captain Thomas Marshall, a veteran of the
Revolution, one of whose granddaughters became the wife
of the best and ablest of Logan's grandsons, sat as the
member from Mason; Walter Carr, whose son married his
cousin, was a member from Fayette; and Alexander Scott
Bullitt, whose wife was a first cousin of William Logan's
wife, and whose grandson married William Logan's granddaughter, was associated, from Jefferson, with Colonel
Richard Taylor, the father of the rough-fighting President.
The distinguished and brilliant John Breckinridge, afterward Attorney-General of the United States, two of whose
grandsons married two of William Logan's granddaughters, was another member from Fayette; which county
also sent Major John McDowell, whose sister had been the
first wife of Judge Caleb Wallace, whose daughter by a
second marriage was William Logan's wife. Besides these
relatives and connexions of William Logan, Fayette sent
to the convention the able Judge Buckner Thruston, son
of the distinguished Colonel Charles Mynn Thruston, of

the Revolution; Bourbon, the gallant John Allen, who, after attaining the rank of major by hard fighting in the Revolution, gained an enviable fame as a lawyer and jurist in Kentucky; Madison, the robust, energetic, strong-minded, and fearless General Green Clay; Mercer, the sensible and brave soldier, John Adair, afterward governor of the state; Scott, Colonel Robert Johnson, the progenitor of a gallant race, one of whom figured in contemporary history as a hero at the Thames, as an honest national legislator, and as Vice-President of the United States; Nelson, the elder John Rowan, than whom our country has produced no more chivalrous gentleman, and few more eloquent orators or more learned jurists; and Washington, the brilliant Felix Grundy. Surrounded by associates so illustrious, among whom mediocrity would have been dwarfed, the handsome talents of the young Logan attracted attention, and made him conspicuous. He was frequently a member of the state legislature from both Lincoln and Shelby counties; in 1803, when not yet twenty-eight years of age, he was elected speaker of the house of representatives; was selected for that position for the three succeeding terms of the general assembly, the choice being made unanimous in 1806; and was again chosen at the terms of 1808 and 1809. No other man has been chosen to that position so often in Kentucky, nor presided in it with more winning grace. In 1809, he was a presidential elector, and was chosen to that responsible position again in 1813, and for a third time in 1817. Appointed judge of the court of appeals in 1808, he resigned the place in a short time. Re-appointed in 1810, he was noted for the propriety and ability with which he discharged the responsible duties of the trust.—[*Collins.*] In 1819, he was elected a senator of the United States; after a brief service, resigned in 1820, for the purpose of becoming a candidate for governor, to which place he was not elected. In 1821, he was once more sent to the legislature from Shelby. He was now generally looked to for governor in 1824, and the successorship to Adair was con-

10

ceded to him; but, in 1822, he died, in the prime of his manhood and intellect, in his forty-sixth year. The character of his mind was eminently conservative. In 1816, Major George Madison had been elected governor of Kentucky, and Gabriel Slaughter lieutenant-governor. The lamented and popular Madison dying in a few weeks after his inauguration, Slaughter became governor, and appointed John Pope secretary of state. The integrity of Mr. Pope could not be challenged; the elevation of his private character was never disputed; his superior talents were by all conceded. He had long been one of the foremost lawyers of the state; had been a valuable member of the legislature, and had served a term in the United States Senate with eminent ability. But he had been an old Federalist, a political and personal friend of Humphrey Marshall. (The mother of the latter was Mary, daughter of Humphrey Guisenberry, of Virginia. One of her sisters was the wife of John Pope, a relative of the father of Senator John Pope, of Kentucky. The Pope family had long been seated in Westmoreland county, where one of them married Colonel John Washington, ancestor of the President.) These facts made him personally obnoxious to Henry Clay, as well as politically offensive to the Republican-Democratic party then dominant in the state. Failing to coerce Governor Slaughter into removing Mr. Pope, Mr. Clay and his friends sought to depose Slaughter from the governorship, under the pretext that, upon the death of the governor elected by the people, the lieutenant-governor did not succeed him in the office, but became the acting governor only until an election could be had as provided by the legislature. The deposition was sought to be accomplished through the legislature, and an effort was made to pass an act through that body providing for a "new election" of governor. Party feeling ran mountain high. Domestic war seemed threatened as a result of the controversy. Though politically opposed to Pope, Judge Logan refused to act as a partisan in such a matter, and, with equal ability, eloquence, and courage, withstood the demands of the majority of the leaders of his own party, by maintaining that construction of the constitution which was adopted as the true one when passion had subsided—that the lieutenant-governor succeeded upon the death of the governor elect, and should serve out his term. His conservatism was also made conspicuous in the "new and old court" controversy, the first step in which was taken in 1822, before his death, in the attempt made in the general assembly of which he was a member to remove by address the upright and honest Judge Clarke, because he had decided unconstitutional an act of the general assembly that impaired the obligation of a contract. This Judge Logan resisted with that firm courage which was his prevailing characteristic, and with all the ardor of his nature. Amicable in temper, courteous and graceful in manners, with a prepossessing presence, his native talents were improved by culture; in public debate, his argumentation was clothed with the graces of rhetoric; his moral worth was equal to his popularity.

Judge Caleb Wallace.

The wife of Judge William Logan was a daughter of Hon. Caleb Wallace, a native of Charlotte county, Virginia; a graduate of Princeton in 1770; received as a licentiate of the New Castle Presbytery by that of Hanover, at the Tinkling Spring, in 1774; on the 3d of October of the same year, ordained pastor of the churches of Cub creek and Falling river, at which ordination "Father" David Rice, afterward the pioneer Presbyterian minister of Kentucky, presided; filled those pulpits most acceptably, until 1779, when he removed to Botetourt, where he continued to preach until 1783; then came to Kentucky. Here he abandoned the ministry without forsaking his religion or church; adopting the law as a profession, he rapidly went to the front; was a member of both of the conventions of 1785; of those of 1787 and 1788; of that which framed the first state constitution, in 1792, as well as of that which framed the second, in 1799; on the 28th of June, 1792, was appointed by Shelby one of the first three judges of the court of appeals, the other two being Innes and Sebastian;—altogether a shining light and man of mark in those early and stirring days. His second wife, the mother of Mrs. Logan, was Priscilla Christian, a sister of Colonel William Christian. One of their sons, Samuel McDowell Wallace, of Woodford, married a daughter of Major John Lee, of the Revolution, and a sister of John J. Crittenden's first wife. The interesting sketch of Judge Wallace soon to be published will not be anticipated.

Judge Caleb Wallace Logan.

The oldest son of Judge William Logan and Priscilla Wallace was the late Caleb Wallace Logan, of Louisville. Born in Shelby county, July 15, 1819, and receiving in boyhood the advantage of the best schools, he graduated with honor and credit at Centre College, in 1838; graduated at the law school of Transylvania University; entered first upon the practice in Woodford, where he soon obtained prominence; removed to Louisville, and represented that city in the legislature in 1850. A frequent contributor to the press, in the rise and progress of the American party he wrote for the old "Louisville Journal" a series of able articles which attracted wide-spread attention, and were largely instrumental in achieving the success of that party in Kentucky, in 1855. The next year, he was elected judge of the Louisville Chancery Court, and for the six succeeding years discharged the difficult duties of that position with an inflexible integrity that was blind to every thing but the principles of justice as embodied in the law, and with a learning and ability that was unsurpassed. The state was under military control in 1862; Chancellor Logan had been a Union man in principle, but had condemned the course of the administration, and had given emphatic and impulsive expression to his views; the civil strife sorrowed and sickened him. He was not re-elected. For years he had been a leading professor in the Louisville Law School. In 1864, when not yet forty-six years old, he died. A learned lawyer, he also thoroughly comprehended the philosophy and teachings of history, and had been an enthusiastic and critical student of poetry. A strong and forcible speaker, his powers of reasoning and scholarly training were exhibited to better advantage with the pen than in public debate. Argumentative and analytical in mental characteristics, he regarded and treated the law as a noble and elevating science rather than as a mere means of milking money from clients. His talents were rather those of a jurist than of the advocate. He appeared to better advantage in the class-room than in the scufflings of the court-house— in trying to impart to the student his own broad and acute conception of the teachings of the law, to infuse into him his own enthusiasm for it as a humanizing profession, than in exhibiting to a jury the cunning arts of the demagogue and pettifogger. Louisville never had a chancellor of greater integrity, of more extensive or elegant culture, nor of a finer mental fibre. His temper was most genial, his habits social, his manner confiding and kindly; while his intellectual qualities and literary attainments made him one of the most interesting of conversationalists. His eyes were blue, his hair reddish, his complexion florid, his person full. In religion he was a Calvinist.

The first wife of Chancellor Logan was Agatha, only daughter of Dr. Louis Marshall, famed as a scholar and teacher, the youngest son of Colonel Thomas Marshall. Her mother was Agatha, daughter of Major Francis Smith, of the Revolution, whose wife was one of the four daughters of John Preston. The only brother of Mrs. Marshall, John Smith, married Chenoe Hart, probably the first white child born in Kentucky. One of her sisters was the wife of Governor George Madison; another was the wife of Colonel John Trigg; a third, the wife of James Blair, Attorney-General of Kentucky, the mother of the elder Francis P. Blair, renowned as an editor, and grandmother of the younger Francis P. Blair, an aggressive and successful politician in Missouri, a bold and talented member of Congress, and the heroic general in Grant's army. The oldest brother of Mrs. Logan was William L. Marshall, judge of the Baltimore Circuit Court; the second,

Thomas F. Marshall, perhaps the most gifted of Kentucky orators; the third, Dr. Alexander K. Marshall—a man of the finest type of manly beauty, and of superior talents—represented Jessamine county in the constitutional convention of 1850, and the Ashland district in Congress, in 1855–57; and the fourth, Hon. Edward C. Marshall, the brilliant congressman from California, afterward the able attorney-general of that state—not so scholarly as his older brother, Thos. F. Marshall, nor possessed of such powers as a logician, but the master of as keen a wit and more playful and unstudied humor, and capable of rising to the highest flights of eloquence. The talents and literary tastes of Mrs. Logan rendered her a fitting companion for her husband. Agatha, their oldest daughter, married her cousin, Louis Chrisman, son of Dr. Alexander K. Marshall. Mira Madison, their third daughter, is unmarried. Mary Keith, their fourth daughter, married Dr. David Cummings, of Louisville, who died shortly after their marriage, and their only child also died in infancy.

THE BULLITTS.

Anne Priscilla, the second daughter of Chancellor Caleb Wallace Logan and Agatha Marshall, was born in Woodford county, April 26, 1847; and married her third cousin, Captain Thomas Walker Bullitt, in 1870. The Bullitt family has long been seated in Virginia and Maryland, tradition assigning to it a French origin. The first of whom the writer has definite knowledge were three brothers who lived in Fauquier. One of these brothers was the father of Thomas, Cuthbert, and Neville Bullitt, who came to Kentucky at a very early day. Neville was a farmer, and lived in Jefferson county. Thomas and Cuthbert were among the very first to engage in mercantile pursuits in Louisville, amassed large fortunes, and became the ancestors of Alexander C. Bullitt, the well-known editor of the "New Orleans Picayune;" of the wife of the heroic General Phil. Kearney; of the family of the late Dr. Wilson, of Louisville; of Colonel William A. Bullitt; of the Weissengers, and others. Another of these

Fauquier brothers, Thomas Bullitt, was the captain who acted with such conspicuous courage at Grant's defeat, in Braddock's campaign, and on various occasions during the Revolution; who made the first surveys at the Falls of the Ohio, in 1773; who figures in the Indian treaties of that period; and who was the adjutant-general of Virginia in the Revolution. This Colonel Thomas Bullitt never married. He was one of the boldest and best educated of the explorers. Unfortunately, the rivalry between this enterprising man and General Andrew Lewis grew into personal enmity, gave much trouble to Washington, who had been the friend of both, and prevented Colonel Bullitt from reaching the rank to which his talents and meritorious services entitled him to aspire. The third brother, Cuthbert, was an able lawyer and a distinguished judge in Virginia. His wife was a daughter of Rev. James Scott—an educated Scotchman and an Episcopalian minister,—whose wife was a daughter of Rev. James Brown, also an Episcopalian minister, whose wife was a daughter of Colonel Gerard Fawke, of Maryland, and related to the Masons. From other daughters of Rev. James Brown are descended the Moncures, Daniels, Conways, and many of the most prominent families in Virginia. One of the sons of Judge Cuthbert Bullitt bore his own name, and was an eminent lawyer and judge in Maryland. Another son, Alexander Scott Bullitt, came to Kentucky as one of the pioneers in early manhood, and by his own force of character, even more than by his family influence, rapidly rose into prominence. He was a member of the convention of 1788; a member of the convention of 1792, which framed the first state constitution; was president of the convention of 1799, which framed the second constitution; continuously speaker of the senate from the establishment of the state until 1800; the office of lieutenant-governor having been created by the second constitution, in 1800 he was chosen to that position, and continued to preside over the senate until 1804;—a robust, solid, sensible, strong-willed man. Alexander Scott Bullitt married a daughter of Colonel William

Christian, was present when that gallant man was killed by the Indians, and shot down the savage at whose hand he fell. The wife of Colonel Christian was Anne Henry, a sister of the orator, and her mother was Sarah Winston, of a family as singularly gifted as it was remarkably prolific. Alexander Scott Bullitt and his Christian wife, besides several daughters, had two sons, Cuthbert and William Christian. The former was the father of the late Dr. Henry M. Bullitt, of Louisville, and of the wife of the late Archibald Alexander Gordon;—Mr. Gordon was a descendant of Colonel James Gordon, one of whose daughters married Rev. James Waddel, "the blind preacher," whose daughter married Dr. Archibald Alexander, of Princeton. The other son of Alexander Scott Bullitt was the late William Christian Bullitt, of Jefferson county—a man of intellect, courage, and the highest order of personal integrity—an influential member of the convention of 1850, that framed our present state constitution. The wife of William Christian Bullitt was Mildred Anne Fry, a daughter of

Joshua Fry,

who won a just celebrity as teacher of the classics in Mercer county. The children of Wm. C. Bullitt and Mildred Anne Fry were: Joshua Fry Bullitt, an erudite lawyer, who was judge of the Court of Appeals of Kentucky; John C. Bullitt, a successful lawyer and financier of Philadelphia; Thomas W. Bullitt, who married Anne Priscilla Logan; James, a gallant soldier in the Confederate army, and a most lovely character, who was killed while carrying a flag of truce; Henry Massie, a substantial farmer of Jefferson county; Susan, the second wife of Senator Archie Dixon; and Helen, the wife of Dr. Henry Chenowith. It is not often a family in this country keeps up for so many generations. There is something tough about the fiber of this Bullitt stock which makes it wear so well.

THE FRYS.

The first of this family who settled in Virginia was Joshua Fry, a gentleman in social position in England; a graduate of Oxford; and, after his emigration to America, a professor of mathematics at the good old college of William and Mary. It was he who was colonel of the regiment of Virginians which was sent on the first expedition, in 1754, against Fort Duquesne, and which, after his death, was commanded by the lieutenant-colonel, George Washington;—a man of high standing, influence, and cultivation, in those colonial days, was this Colonel Joshua Fry. His wife was in no way connected with Dr. George Gilmer, nor with Dr. Thomas Walker, as erroneously stated by Governor Gilmer, in his " Sketches of Upper Georgia." She was, when he married her, the widow Mary Hill, the daughter of Dr. Paul Micou, a French Huguenot, who took refuge in Virginia from the persecutions following the revocation of the Edict of Nantes. Educated for the bar in France, Dr. Micou abandoned that profession, and entered upon the practice of medicine in Virginia, where he gained independence, and commanded respect not less for his personal worth than by his professional attainments. The reputable families of Virginia which bear the name of Micou are all his descendants. So also, through one of his daughters, are many of the Fauntleroys and Lomaxes, and some branches of the Dangerfield and Brockenboro families. The oldest son of Colonel Joshua Fry and Mary Micou was Colonel John Fry, in whose name Washington made, in Boyd and Lawrence counties, the first surveys ever made in Kentucky. The wife of Colonel John Fry was Sallie Adams, a member of a numerous and influential family of Virginia, among whom may be mentioned Colonel Richard Adams; Dr. Adams, of Richmond; Tabitha Adams, who married Colonel William Russell; and Alice, who was the first wife of William Marshall, a rarely profound lawyer, and brother of Dr. Louis Marshall. The only child of Colonel John Fry and Sallie Adams who had issue was

Joshua Fry, who, after having been a soldier in the Revolution, emigrated to Mercer county, Kentucky, where he had inherited a large landed estate, and, finding the educational facilities limited in that then far western land, opened a school for the instruction of his own children and those of his neighbors. To the thorough training received at his hands, to the honorable ambition which he excited in all brought within the circle of his beneficent influence, many of the most prominent of the generation that followed the pioneers in Kentucky owed the eminence to which they attained. Amiable and benevolent as he was scholarly and accomplished, he was beloved by all who ever saw or knew him;—a fine type of those educated Virginians, thinkers as well as scholars, who impressed the characteristics of their own minds and customs upon the early history of our people, his name will be revered until the fame of the men who won and made the state shall become a forgotten memory. The wife of Joshua Fry the teacher, was Peachy, the youngest daughter of

DR. THOMAS WALKER,

the commissary-general of Braddock's army; better known as a skillful surveyor and scientific engineer than as a physician; still better known for the advantageous treaties he made with the Indians; who, in company with Captain Charles Campbell, Colonel James Patton, and others, had penetrated into Kentucky as far as the Dick's river, in Mercer county, long before the feet of Findlay or Boone had pressed her soil. The children of Joshua Fry and Peachy Walker were: Sallie, who became the first wife of Hon. John Green; Lucy, who married John Speed, judge of the Circuit Court of the Louisville district, and was the mother of Hon. James Speed, Attorney-General of the United States; Martha, who married David Bell, a merchant and native of Ireland, and was the mother of Joshua F. Bell, the brilliant advocate and eloquent orator, a distinguished member of Congress, and one of the men who, in the state legislature, held Kentucky fast and firm to her moorings in the Union. Mrs. Bell was also the mother of the wife of Ormond Beatty, LL.D., the learned president of Centre College. Mrs. Bullitt was the youngest daughter of Joshua Fry. One of his sons, Thomas, was the father of General Speed Smith Fry, who distinguished himself at Buena Vista as captain in McKee's regiment, and on more than one bloody field in the civil war; and of the second wife of Dr. Lewis W. Green. Joshua Fry's son, John, was the father of Major Carey Fry, of the regular army, and of Colonel John Fry, of the Kentucky volunteers.

DR. WALKER'S WIFE.

Were nothing said of the wife of a man so celebrated and useful as Dr. Walker, of the ancestress of so many lines of excellent men and women, a record like this would be incomplete. Yet it is far easier to ascertain who she was *not*, than to definitely establish who she *was*. That her *given* name was Mildred; that when Dr. Walker married her, she was the widow of Nicholas Merriwether; that by her first husband she had a daughter, Mildred Merriwether, who married John Syme, the elder half-brother of Patrick Henry, and had issue; that she brought her second husband a very large landed estate in Albemarle, a part of which was the manor of " Castle Hill," where he lived, and which has recently received new celebrity as the residence of her descendant, Amelie Rives, the authoress;—that much appears in the official record to be found in Henning's Statutes, in an act of the assembly to " dock" an entail. The statement of Governor Gilmer, in his " Sketches of Upper Georgia," that she was the great-granddaughter of Nicholas Merriwether (the grandfather of her first husband), and that she first married Colonel John Syme, " a traveled gentleman of rank and fortune, whose name is still freshly remembered from the delicious, tender, white-rinded, red-meat watermelon, which he brought to this country from the islands of the Mediterranean," is as erroneous as it is amusing. The entertaining writer simply confounded *her* with her own daughter, and confounded her daughter's husband with *his* own

father. The Colonel Syme referred to by Governor Gilmer married Sarah Winston, and it was his son by her
who married Mildred Merriwether, the daughter of Dr.
Walker's wife; after the death of Colonel Syme, Sarah
Winston married Colonel John Henry, a relative of Robertson, the historian, and of Lord Brougham, and by him
was the mother of the orator, and of the wives of Colonel
Christian and of General William Campbell. Equally erroneous, and even more unaccountable, is the statement
published by her descendant, Dr. Richard Channing Moore
Page, in his valuable genealogy of the " Page Family,"
that she was the daughter of either Colonel John Thornton and Mildred Gregory, or of Colonel Francis Thornton and Frances Gregory, and the granddaughter of Roger
Gregory and Mildred Washington (the only sister of General Washington's father, and the godmother of the general himself). The wife of Roger Gregory referred to was
the youngest child of Lawrence Washington and Mildred
Warner, and was born in 1696. The record in the old
family bible of Dr. Thomas Walker shows that his wife
was born in 1721; that her daughter, Mildred Merriwether, was born in 1739; and that she was married, the
second time, to Dr. Walker, in 1741. So that, if Dr.
Page's statement were correct, Mrs. Mildred Gregory
would have been a grandmother at *twenty-five*, and a great-
grandmother at *forty-three*. But additional evidence of
the incorrectness of Dr. Page's statement is found in the
official record contained in " Henning's Statutes," in an
act for settling the estate of Colonel John Thornton, who
died intestate; from which it appears that *his* daughter
Mildred, by Mildred Gregory, was the second wife of
Samuel Washington, the next youngest brother of the
general, which also appears from the letter of General
Washington himself to Sir Francis Heard. And that the
wife of Dr. Thomas Walker was not Mildred, the daughter of Colonel Francis Thornton and Frances Gregory, is
rendered certain by the same letter of General Washington, which shows that *that* Mildred Thornton was the wife
of his youngest brother, Charles Washington. The fact

is, that the wife of Dr. Walker was of an older generation than the daughters of Colonels John and Francis Thornton. Dr. Walker himself was probably older than either of the Thorntons, and his wife was very little, if any, younger than their wives. She *may* have been their *sister;* she certainly was not the *daughter* of either. After the death of Roger Gregory, his widow, born Mildred Washington, became the third wife of Colonel Henry Willis, the founder of Fredericksburg. By his second wife (also born Mildred Washington, and a daughter of the first John Washington's son John), Colonel Henry Willis had a daughter, Mary, who married Hancock Lee, and was the mother of Major John Lee and grandmother of Senator Crittenden's first wife. By his third wife (the widow Gregory), besides his son, Colonel Lewis Willis, he had a daughter, Anne, who married Duff Green, and was the mother of Willis Green, the second clerk of Lincoln county, and a member of the conventions of 1785–88. Mrs. Anne (Willis) Green died, near Danville, about 1820; her tombstone still stands at the Old Reed Fort. Her grandson, Judge John Green, married Sallie Fry, the granddaughter of Dr. Thomas Walker, and she lived in the same house with them, and with other daughters of Joshua Fry, for years before her death, and never had a suspicion that they were the great-granddaughters of her half-sister, as this statement of Dr. Page, if correct, would make them. The youngest son of Willis Green, Rev. L. W. Green—grandson of Anne Willis—married Mary Fry, granddaughter of Joshua Fry and Peachy Walker; but neither of them ever knew of a relationship. The wives of Major James Barbour, of Dr. Ben. Edwards, of St. Louis, and of Dr. William Craig, of Danville, lived on the most affectionate and intimate terms with the daughters of Joshua Fry and Peachy Walker, but there was never any recognition of a blood kinship between them. There *was none.* Dr. Page's statement that Dr. Walker's first wife was the daughter of either Mildred or Frances Gregory, or of either Colonel John or Colonel Francis Thornton, is a mistake. Equally incorrect is Dr. Page's statement that Dr. Walker's second wife was Elizabeth, the daughter of either Colonel John or of Colonel Francis Thornton. For Colonel John Thornton's daughter Elizabeth married John Taliaferro, of Dissington; and Colonel Francis Thornton's daughter Elizabeth married, as his second wife, her kinsman, John Lewis, son of Colonel Fielding Lewis and Catherine Washington. But, whatever may have been her maiden surname, and from whatever family she may have come, Mrs. Walker undoubtedly was the ancestress of a gallant and a noble race, who did their part well in the Revolution, and in every struggle since;—lawyers, physicians, professors, financiers, soldiers, congressmen, governors, senators, members of the national cabinet, and as ministers of the gospel, they have left their impress upon their times and country.

Captain Thomas W. Bullitt graduated at Center College; studied law in Philadelphia; entered the Confederate army as a private soldier, and fought his way up to a captaincy in General John H. Morgan's command; was badly wounded in the service, from which he came out, at the final surrender, with the reputation of a good and brave soldier. At the close of the war, he entered upon the practice of his profession in Louisville, has been eminently successful therein, and enjoys the confidence of a large clientage. To say that he is a worthy combination of the best moral and mental qualities of the different hardy, vigorous, and enduring stocks from which he comes, is to do him the barest justice. He has many children.

After the death of Agatha Marshall, Chancellor Logan married, secondly, Irene Smith, by whom he had one daughter. A kinswoman of the second wife, Fanny Smith, married Colonel Alexander C. Bullitt. One of her sisters is the wife of Judge Joshua F. Bullitt, and another sister was the wife of Senator R. W. Johnson, of Arkansas.

THE McKNIGHTS AND CUMMINGS.

Anne, the oldest daughter of Judge William Logan and Priscilla Wallace, was born in Kentucky, and, in the

dawn of her womanhood, became the wife of Virgil Mc-
Knight. The family of that name came from Ireland to
Pennsylvania, and thence to the Valley of Virginia; but
it was of Scottish origin, and of the Presbyterian faith.
Among the soldiers of the French and Indian wars whose
names are preserved in the colonial records, was Daniel
McNight, as the name was erroneously spelled by the recording clerk. He was of the same family as, and not
improbably the immediate ancestor of, Virgil McKnight,
the able and widely known president of the Bank of Kentucky. George McKnight was an ensign in Colonel
Byrd's regiment of Royal Virginians in 1755. Andrew
McKnight, the father of Virgil, was born in Rockbridge
county, Virginia, in 1773. One of Andrew McKnight's
brothers moved to Ohio, and left issue of his own and
other names in that state. One of Andrew's sisters married an uncle of Dr. John Clarke Young, the eloquent
pulpit orator and learned president of Centre College—
these Youngs also lived in Ohio. Another of Andrew
McKnight's sisters married a Shields, but of them the
writer has no knowledge beyond the fact stated. Andrew
McKnight, himself, married Elizabeth Cummings, who
was born in Rockbridge county, Virginia, in 1771; she
belonged to one of the most noted, and intellectual, and
worthy of the Scotch-Irish families of the Valley. She
was the daughter of John Cummings and Esther Reid.
One of the brothers of Elizabeth, Samuel Cummings, married Sarah Paxton; and one of her sisters, Esther, married
Lyle Paxton, brother of Sarah. It would be interesting
to follow the Cummings family in its numerous other intermarriages with the Paxtons, with the McClungs, Lyles
and Alexanders, all of the faith of John Knox; their posterity contributed many superior men to the ranks of the
liberal professions, especially to the ministry. It would be
foreign to the object of this book to dwell upon their high
social position, which does not always indicate a vigorous
breed. The cultivation that distinguished them, their own
recognized intellectuality, would render useless a vain attempt to trace a connexion between them and the ancient

Comyns who were Lords of Badenoch in Scotland, and from whom the more modern name of Cummings is derived.

THE REIDS.

Among the pioneers of Augusta county, were three brothers, of Scottish extraction, who came from the County Down, in Ireland, where they were born—Thomas, John and Andrew Reid. The oldest of these brothers, Thomas Reid, married a highland woman, named McKean, and had by her three children, two of whom married their cousins, daughters of their uncle, John Reid, Sr., who bore the title of colonel. These two were Colonel John Reid, Jr., who married his uncle John's daughter, Martha; and Nathan, who married his uncle John's daughter, Sarah. The third son of Thomas Reid, Alexander, came to Kentucky. It was this Alexander Reid, or his son, who represented Shelby county in the legislature in 1801, '02, and again in 1806; and it was a descendant of his, an Alexander Reid, of a later generation, who represented the same county in the legislature in 1825, '26, '27. Colonel John Reid, Sr., the second of the emigrant brothers, married Martha Nisbet, and had by her a numerous progeny, besides the two daughters above mentioned as having married their cousins. The third brother, Andrew Reid, Sr., had, among others, a son, Andrew Reid, Jr., who married Sarah, daughter of his uncle, Colonel John Reid, Sr., and Martha Nisbet, and the widow of his uncle Thomas Reid's son, Nathan. This Andrew Reid, Jr., and Sarah Reid, had six children. One of their sons was General Andrew Reid, of Rockbridge, who married Magdalen McDowell, twin-sister of the first wife of Judge Caleb Wallace, and daughter of Judge Samuel McDowell and Mary McClung. One of the daughters of Andrew Reid, Jr., and Sarah, was Agnes Ann Reid, who married William Alexander, and was the mother of Dr. Archibald Alexander, of Princeton. Their residence stood on the ground now occupied by the residence of the late General Robert E. Lee, in Lexington, Virginia, and in which General Custis Lee now resides. A third daughter, Flora, married John Lyle; and Rev. John Lyle, who taught a female seminary at Paris, and established the " Citizen," was one of their sons. This latter married the widow Lapsley, whose maiden name was Irvine, and who was a sister of the wives of Samuel McDowell, of Mercer, and Colonel Joseph McDowell, of Danville. One of their sons was John Lyle, of Boyle county, who also married an Irvine. The fifth child of Andrew Reid, Jr., and Sarah, was Esther Reid, who married John Cummings, and was the mother of Elizabeth Cummings, the wife of Andrew McKnight. Another daughter of Andrew Reid, Jr., and Sarah—also named Sarah Reid—married Joseph Alexander, the fourth son of Archibald Alexander and Margaret Parks, brother of William Alexander (who married her sister, Agnes Ann Reid), and uncle of the great preacher and theologian. Sarah Reid, the wife of Andrew, Jr., in 1766, was murdered, and her body thrown into a creek, by a negro whom she had reproved. Andrew, son of William Alexander and Agnes Ann Reid—brother of Dr. Archibald—married Anne Aylett, and *their* fifth child, Evaline, was the wife of the distinguished General Samuel McDowell Moore, referred to on a previous page.

Andrew McKnight and Elizabeth Cummings had a son born to them in Virginia, James, who married a Miss Paxton in that state. When this child was an infant, they removed to Woodford county, Kentucky, where they bought and lived upon a farm, and where their other children were born. That they were highly respected by all was but natural. For their high character, strong good sense, and quick-witted intelligence, they were *honored* by such men as Dr. Louis Marshall, and others, who could appreciate their worth.

Virgil McKnight,

second son of Andrew McKnight, was born on his father's farm in 1798, received the best education to be had in the schools of the neighborhood, and in his youth became engaged in commercial pursuits. In these he was success-

11

ful, and had already made a handsome competency in
1838, when he was called to the presidency of the Bank or
Kentucky. His marriage to Anne Logan occurred in
Shelbyville, at the residence of her parents, in 1822. He
had not wound up his mercantile business when he accepted the presidency of the bank, which required all his
time; fidelity to the obligations of the trust involved
neglect of his private affairs, and mismanagement by
others swept away the greater part of the accumulations
of years of successful thrift. Before he assumed the duties of that position, in May, 1837, the Kentucky banks
had, in the midst of a monetary convulsion, suspended
specie payments; in consequence, their stock fell in the
markets, and their credit, as well as that of the state, had
become seriously impaired. One of the first steps taken
by him on his accession to the office, which constituted
him a member of the board of commissioners of the sinking fund, was to unite the banks in an effort to repair the
injured credit of the state; and in May, 1838, a large
amount of state bonds were sold on advantageous terms
for the state, mainly to capitalists who had known him as
a merchant, and had faith in his representations. In August of the same year, chiefly in deference to his urgent
advice, the banks resumed specie payments. The stock of
his bank rapidly enhanced in value. The ensuing year,
the suspension of specie payments by the banks of Ohio,
Virginia, Baltimore, Philadelphia, and New Orleans, oc-
casioned such a drain on those of Kentucky to help meet
the demand. from Europe, that another suspension was
deemed advisable, which sent the stock of the Bank of
Kentucky down to seventy-one cents. The Bank of Kentucky had at Philadelphia, in the person of the cashier of
the Schuylkill Bank—a Mr. Levis—an agent for the sale
and transfer of its stock. To support the sinking credit
of the Schuylkill Bank, its cashier made a fraudulent issue
of stock in the Bank of Kentucky, aggregating the immense sum of $1,299,700. The fraud was revealed to the
Bank of Kentucky by a private communication from the
confidential clerk of Levis, and another agent was ap-

pointed for the Bank of Kentucky; this revelation was made in December, 1839. On being charged with his fraud, Levis confessed, and fled the country. The stock of the bank went down at once to fifty-five cents. The bank promptly assumed responsibility for this fraudulent issue by its dishonest agent. Then, in order to obtain legal recourse upon the Schuylkill Bank for the fraud of its cashier, it became necessary to establish that fraud by identifying the genuine and authorized stock and separating it from that which was unauthorized, spurious, and fraudulent. Several clerks and book-keepers employed by the parent bank in Louisville went to Philadelphia, attempted this delicate and difficult task, failed, and, returning to Louisville, declared it could not be accomplished. Mr. Wm. S. Waller, who was at the time the cashier of the Lexington branch of the Bank of Kentucky—a man not only of probity, but of sense, and a most expert and skillful accountant,—went with Mr. McKnight to Philadelphia, and, after a careful scrutiny and study of the whole subject, organized the plan and system which was adopted and carried out, and by means of which the fraudulent issue was successfully traced, the proof of the fraud brought home to the Schuylkill Bank, and recourse obtained upon the assets of that bank to reimburse the Bank of Kentucky for its loss. The credit for originating this most ingenious method belongs exclusively to Mr. Waller. In the conduct of that part of all this intricate business which fell to him as the president and head of the Bank of Kentucky, Mr. McKnight was thrown into contact and intimate association with such men as John Sergeant and Horace Binney, the eminent lawyers of Philadelphia, and with Nicholas Biddle and other financiers. These men were impressed by, and bore record to, his incorruptible integrity, his unusual shrewdness and business sagacity, his strong practical sense, sound judgment, and clear intellect. In the conversion of the assets of the Schuylkill Bank, consisting in large part of mining properties, and requiring many years to do so without sacrifice, skill and ability of a high order were exhibited by Mr. McKnight. His management of that entire vexatious entanglement added to his reputation as a financier, and was so successful and satisfactory to the stockholders of the bank, that they voluntarily presented him with a considerable block of its stock as a substantial evidence of their appreciation. In 1842, the banks of Kentucky once more resumed specie payments, and, under the sensible and conservative management of Mr. McKnight, the stock of the institution of which he was the head appreciated rapidly in value, and in a few years sold at a premium. No financial institution in this country had a higher credit or reputation. When, by its large investments in works of internal improvement the credit of the state was jeopardized, the services of Mr. McKnight as one of the sinking fund commissioners were most valuable; his counsel, which was generally followed, sound and sagacious. In 1861, when applied to by Magoffin for money with which to pay for arms contracted for or ordered, while other banks placed the money at his disposal, or refused the application, the president of the Bank of Kentucky annexed as a condition of the loan, if made, that the arms so purchased should be used solely in self-defense, and to protect the "*State of Kentucky and the Union.*" Magoffin did not want the arms for that purpose; the loan was not made. During all the troublous times incident to the inauguration of civil war, Mr. McKnight, a staunch friend of the Union, contributed a weighty influence in convincing the business men of Louisville and Kentucky that their best interests and only safety were in the maintenance of American nationality. No record of that epoch will be complete which does not make known his prominence. At a later date than that referred to, he returned to Magoffin's application for money an emphatic " No," that resounded throughout the commonwealth. In the fall of that year, when Kentucky took her place for the maintenance of the laws, and money was needed to equip her sons, the bank came promptly forward with its full quota. The history of this institution is the public record of its president. Conservative and patriotic, benevolent and kindly, civil strife had for him nothing but horror. Broad minded and liberal, Mr. McKnight had an intelligent conception of the duties, responsibilities, and highest interests of a great state bank. That those interests could not be promoted by the dishonor of the commonwealth; that its highest degree of prosperity could be best attained by advancing and upholding that of the state, of the community, and of legitimate commerce, were facts to which he was keenly alive. In the midst of panics, he remained calm and clear headed; in times of monetary stringency, the policy of the bank was liberal to the extent permitted by prudence. While many a worthy merchant owed his salvation from bankruptcy to the timely aid extended by the bank under his management, not one can trace his ruin to harsh pressure from that source. Equable and placid in temper, and warm in his attachments, he never permitted his friendships to sacrifice the interests of which he was the guardian, and, if the occasion required it, could repel importunity with sternness. He was just and fair-minded, discerning and dispassionate. When James Barbour was first auditor of the state under the incumbency of Governor Helm, he found a considerable sum accumulated and lying idle in the treasury. He ascertained also that the Bank of Kentucky owned $250,000 of five per cent bonds of the state, and that the commonwealth was entitled by law to buy at par $250,000 of the stock of that bank, which was then selling at a premium. It occurred to Mr. Barbour, then a young man, that it would be a good thing for the state to purchase its bonds, and thus stop the interest, with this surplus money, instead of letting it continue to be idle; or, if that could not be done on advantageous terms, to invest this surplus in stock that would yield dividends more than equal to the interest on the bonds; and, further, that the right to buy this stock at par would enable him to obtain the bonds at a discount. Having previously made an arrangement with another bank for a temporary loan of $50,000, which, with the surplus, would give the sum necessary to buy the stock, at the first meeting of the commissioners of the sinking fund after his plans had been matured, he addressed to Mr. McKnight a proposition to buy from the bank the $250,000 of state bonds it held, at eighty-seven and one-half cents on the dollar. Mr. McKnight peremptorily refused to sell; it suited the bank to hold the bonds, and it had no use for the money. Then, said Mr. Barbour, the state is legally entitled to buy $250,000 of your stock at par, and the state insists upon its right. Mr. McKnight told him to wait awhile—that would be seen about. The board taking a recess, when it reconvened Mr. McKnight accepted the first proposition rather than increase the capital stock of the bank, and sold the bonds at the price designated. The state had thus made for it $32,000—the only money that any of its officers ever did make for the commonwealth. Instead of resenting the turn taken on him, Mr. McKnight recognized the fidelity and capacity for affairs exhibited, and at once gave directions that the first vacancy which occurred in the branches of the Bank of Kentucky should be given to Mr. Barbour; at his instance, that gentleman was soon after elected to the cashiership of the branch bank at Maysville. Those who knew Mr. McKnight only in his business relations could form no idea of the extensive, varied, and accurate information he possessed on all public affairs, his general and thorough acquaintance with history and the higher branches of literature; nor could they suspect the loving and affectionate nature hidden by the mask presented to the public, nor see the gentle tenderness of the natural man disclosed in the circle of his own home. Plain and unassuming in habits, and economical in his own personal expenditures, his nature had contracted nothing of that sordidness nor chilling hardness which are too frequently the result of long continuance in the vocation of a money-lender. His home was the abode of quiet elegance, of a hospitality as free and lavish as it was unostentatious. The house, seldom unfilled with guests, was always bright and cheery—the genial host having no greater delight than in listening to the bright wit, the merry jests, and rippling laughter of the young. He was of medium height,

of bulky frame; his head was large, his forehead broad
and high, with a prominent brow; his hair was sandy, complexion ruddy; his hands soft, white, and shapely; his
eyes deep set, small, very dark, bright, and watchful, and
at times twinkled with fun.

The children of Virgil McKnight and Anne Logan were:
Elizabeth, the wife of S. M. Wing, formerly of Owensboro; Priscilla, who died unmarried; Wm. Logan, who
married Lucy Pickett Marshall; Milton, who married
Mary Breckinridge, daughter of Rev. Wm. L. Breckinridge; and Rose, who married Dr. Stanhope Breckinridge,
a brother of the above Mary Breckinridge. Dr. William
L. Breckinridge, the father of Mary and Dr. Stanhope,
was one of the distinguished sons of Hon. John Breckinridge, the attorney-general. His wife was a Miss Prevost,
whose father, Judge Prevost, was the son of Mrs. Aaron
Burr, by her first husband—a British officer. Mrs. Breckinridge's mother was a daughter of Dr. Samuel Stanhope
Smith, the able and learned president of Princeton College.

WM. LOGAN McKNIGHT

graduated with credit at Center College in the class of
1843, and was made master of arts in 1846. He soon
abandoned the law to engage in mercantile business in
New Orleans, where he was also the faithful agent of the
Bank of Kentucky. In these pursuits, before his early
death ere he had reached his prime he had accumulated
a handsome fortune, which was, in large part, swept away
by the calamities of war. Commercial pursuits did not
dull his elegant and cultivated tastes, nor diminish an enthusiastic interest in all public questions. A fine linguist,
a critical reader of poetry, an admirer and patron of art,
in political discussion he wielded the pen with the hand of
a master. In any community, he would have been a man
of note. In New Orleans, his engaging manners, amiable
temper, and generosity made him universally beloved, as
his high character, blameless life, and acquirements made
him as universally respected. The woman whom he married
could not be called " accomplished;" the free play some-

times given to a cutting wit may occasionally have carried her out of the lists of the "amiable;" but she was one of generous impulses, had an uncommonly extensive acquaintance with books, in conversation was sparkling and brilliant;—a woman of undoubted talent, a loving wife and daughter, the most self-sacrificing of mothers, and a sincere Christian. Her parents were first cousins. Her mother was Eliza Colston—second daughter of Captain Thomas Marshall and Frances Kennan;—a woman of majestic appearance, noble intellect, lofty character, and a dignity in bearing that never unbent; a woman who loved the truth for its own sake, could not patiently listen to exaggeration even in jest, and abhorred all manner of falsehood. Mrs. Lucy Pickett McKnight's father,

Martin Pickett Marshall,

was the son of Charles Marshall—one of the sons of Colonel Thomas Marshall—perhaps the most brilliant of that brainy brood; an able lawyer, who, dying in his thirty-ninth year, had already reached the head of his profession in Virginia. The mother of Martin P. Marshall was Lucy, daughter of Martin Pickett and Lucy Blackwell. Martin Pickett was a successful and wealthy merchant of Fauquier county, a member of the Virginia convention of 1776, frequently a member of the House of Burgesses, and in the Revolution an outspoken and active patriot. One of the daughters of Martin Pickett married Judge Scott—grandson of Rev. James Scott already mentioned—and was the mother of the distinguished Robert E. Scott, of Fauquier. Colonel Charles Marshall, of General Lee's staff, and now a prominent lawyer of Baltimore, is a nephew of Martin P. Marshall. The latter passed his boyhood in the family of his uncle, Chief Justice Marshall, and under his instruction. At the age of eighteen years, he came to Mason county, Kentucky, and completed his legal studies under his uncle, Alexander K. Marshall. He practiced for a few years with success in Paris, Kentucky, and in Cincinnati, attracting attention by his popular talents as well as by his acute legal acumen. Ill ·health

forcing him to abandon a profession for whose highest
walks he was admirably adapted, he retired to a large
body of land he had inherited in Fleming county, cleared
and improved it, built upon it a spacious mansion—long
the seat of hospitality—and in the life of a farmer was as
successful as he had been at the bar. Agriculture did not
monopolize his time. His father and twin-brother, William, had owned many thousands of acres of land in Pendleton and the mountain counties, upon which persons
having no legal right had settled; in recovering possession
of these lands, and in discharging the duties of county
attorney, he was frequently before the courts, winning a
reputation for legal knowledge, shrewdness, and tact second to that of no other in Northern Kentucky. In 1825,
he was the able representative of Fleming county in the
state legislature. In 1835, he was the Whig candidate for
Congress against Judge Richard French—the most astute
and dextrous Democratic politician then in the state. In
that mountain district, there were thousands of disputed
land titles, and many hundreds of voters occupying lands
to which they had neither legal nor moral claim. The superiority of Marshall to his opponent upon the stump was
apparent wherever they met;—no one was superior to
Judge French as an electioneerer. Richer in resources,
more powerful in debate, as an orator more eloquent, Mr.
Marshall towered above his wily antagonist in every discussion. The Democrats grew alarmed. Shortly before
the election, scandalous circulars were distributed misrep-
resenting Mr. Marshall's conduct in the land litigation into
which he had been forced, imputing to him as an offense
the ability with which he had maintained his own and
others' rights. He was defeated. Logic, rhetoric, decla-
mation, wit;—all went down before the power of organization and secret slander. Mr. Marshall was three times a
presidential elector—in 1832, '36, and '40. He was a
Whig, and canvassed his district in these several campaigns. At this period of his life, he was an electrical
public speaker. With the small, well-shaped feet, and
long, slender hands of the Picketts, he had their thrift,

practical sense, and their wit, bright, flashing, and keen as the forked lightning. He excelled in powers of withering sarcasm. A little above the medium height, his person was slender and well formed; his manners, when he chose, conciliatory. His eye was a dark hazel, with an iris that dilated or contracted, and, when animated, was bright and piercing. His forehead was not high, nor very broad, but widest at the eyes, square and compact, and brow very prominent. His mobile face gave expression to the alternation in his moods, to the shifting current of his ideas; changing from gay to grave, from the humorous to bitter scorn, and again to impressive earnestness, as he kindled with his own zeal in the discussion of his topic. His delivery was animated, his gesticulation vehement, his voice full and resonant. In 1850, Mr. Marshall was a member of the constitutional convention. In that body he favored an open clause permitting future emancipation of the slaves, and opposed the system of an elective judiciary. In 1861, the Union men of Mason and Lewis counties elected him to the state senate. The story of the Union cause in the commonwealth is that of his career. All his life he was a man of sense, sagacity, and weight, impressed himself upon the community in which he lived, and in public affairs made himself felt.

Another daughter of Judge William Logan and Priscilla Wallace, Rosa, married Mr. Nourse, of Bardstown. Rev. Wm. Logan Nourse, of the Presbyterian Church, is one of her sons, and the widow of Joseph Wilson, a late member of the Louisville bar, is one of her daughters. The youngest daughter of Judge William Logan—Jane—was the wife of the late Jordan Clark, long the clerk of the Louisville Chancery Court. Her oldest daughter, Anna, married Wm. L., son of the Rev. Wm. L. Breckinridge; and her oldest son, Wm. L. Clark, was an officer in the Confederate army.

John Logan,

the second son of General Benjamin Logan and Anne Montgomery, was born and reared in Lincoln county, was well educated at the best schools in Kentucky, and became one of her foremost lawyers. Shelby county, which had previously been represented by his father and other relatives for years, sent John Logan to the state house of representatives from 1815 to 1825, continuously, with the exception of the assembly of 1822, when he gave way to his elder brother, William. Other honors were awaiting him, when his prosperous career at the bar and as a legislator was cut short by death, in the first days of January, 1826, before he had yet attained the full height of his powers. His person was imposing and handsome, the quality of his mind strong and clear rather than showy. His wife, Anna C., was a daughter of Colonel Richard Clough Anderson, who had won the rank of major by gallantry in the army of the Revolution, who was made surveyor-general of the North-western Territory, and who, settling at "Soldiers' Retreat," in Jefferson county, there reared a notable progeny of sons and daughters.

THE ANDERSONS.

The first of this family known to have settled in Virginia were two brothers, Robert and David Anderson, natives of Scotland, who found homes in Hanover county near the close of the seventeenth century. Robert married Mary Overton. Their son, Robert, married Elizabeth, daughter of Richard Clough, a native of Wales, whose wife was Cecilia Massie. The seventh child of the second Robert Anderson and Elizabeth Clough was the gallant patriot soldier of the Revolution, Colonel Richard Clough Anderson, of "Soldiers' Retreat." He was born in Hanover county, Virginia, January 12, 1750. Traditions cherished by his children relate that he and John Marshall were rival suitors for the hand of Mary Willis, the daughter of Jacquelin Ambler. His rival being preferred, he married, January 15, 1785, Elizabeth, sister of General George Rogers Clarke. By this wife, he was the father of the wife of John Logan, and of the gifted Richard C. Anderson, Jr., a popular and highly-esteemed member of the legislature, for a number of years, from

Jefferson county; a distinguished member of Congress for four years, then speaker of the Kentucky House of Representatives; and who, when he died, in 1826, was the first minister from the United States to the Republic of Colombia. In this latter place, he was succeeded by General Wm. H. Harrison, his own and his father's friend. The second wife of Colonel Richard Clough Anderson, to whom he was married September 17, 1797, was Sarah Marshall, the daughter of Colonel William Marshall, an early settler in Henry county. This Colonel William Marshall was a son of William Marshall,—an elder brother of John, the father of Colonel Thomas Marshall. The wife of Colonel William Marshall was Ann McLeod, daughter of Torquil McLeod, whose wife was Ann Clarke, a sister of the father of General George Rogers Clarke. Colonel William Marshall was the great-grandfather of Wm. S. Pryor, Chief Justice of the Kentucky Court of Appeals. He was the grandfather also of the first wife of the late Judge James Pryor, of Covington. Colonel William Marshall had a sister who married a Durrett, and was the ancestress of the family of that name in Mason; of Judge Stockton, Chief Justice of Iowa; of the wives of George S. and Charles M. Fleming and of the late Steele Andrews, of Fleming county. By his second marriage with Sarah Marshall, Colonel R. C. Anderson was the father of the hero of Fort Sumter, General Robert Anderson; of the late Larz Anderson, of Cincinnati; of the brilliant orator, Colonel Charles Anderson, of Kuttawa; and of the late William Marshall Anderson, of Chillicothe, Ohio. Jno. Logan and Ann C. Anderson were the parents of six children. Their oldest son,

JOHN ALLEN LOGAN,

born March 12, 1812, was a man of ability, and a successful lawyer in Shelby county. In 1850, he was in the ill-fated expedition of Lopez to overthrow the domination of the cruel, treacherous Spaniard in Cuba. Desperately wounded in the battle of Cardenas, on the 19th of May, 1850, and borne to the ship " Creole " in the arms of the accomplished and chivalrous John T. Pickett and of the knightly Thomas T. Hawkins, he died the next day, and his body was committed to the deep. "Buried at sea, May 20, 1850," is the brief inscription on the monument of a man who was fitted to have been useful to his state, an honor to his name, and who merited a better fate.

THE CARDENAS EXPEDITION

was the first that ever sailed from the United States in the interest of the Republicans of Cuba. The expeditionary force consisted of three battalions, which left the port of New Orleans in May, 1850. Don Narcisso Lopez (lately second in military command on the island) was commander-in-chief; A. J. Gonzalez was chief of staff; and the three battalions were under the immediate command of Colonels Thomas T. Hawkins, Theodore O'Hara, and John T. Pickett. The first was a member of a family which has been conspicuous in Virginia since its colonization, and in Kentucky since its redemption from the wilderness. The second, son of the scholarly teacher, Kean O'Hara, was no less celebrated for his fine genius as a poet than for his daring as a soldier. The third was the son of the accomplished Colonel James C. Pickett, distinguished for his successful diplomatic career in Colombia and Bolivia, and whose wife was the daughter of the brave Governor Desha. The son, John T. Pickett, had left West Point to accept a diplomatic appointment under President Polk. William H. Russell, the war correspondent of the "London Times," who met John T. Pickett in later life, described him as " a tall, good-looking man, of pleasant manners, and well educated. . . . He threw himself into the cause of the South with vehemence; it was not difficult to imagine he saw in that cause the realization of the dreams of empire in the South of the Gulf, and in the conquest of the islands of the sea, which have such a fascinating influence over the imagination of a large portion of the American people." The Washington correspondent of the "New York Sun," under date of November 18, 1873, said of him: "He is a striking looking man, fully six feet two inches in height, with a knightly appearance

and demeanor, which bring to mind the men of the sixteenth century." The material of the three battalions
was composed of the flower of Kentucky and the South,
whose ardent natures had been outraged by the wrongs of
Spanish rule in Cuba. They rendezvoused at Yucatan,
and, crowding the whole command aboard the steamer
" Creole," safely ran the gauntlet past Havana, and effected a landing on the coast near Cardenas. Their plan
was to dash into Matanzas, forty miles by rail, before sun-
rise. Matanzas was a populous Creole city, prepared to
pronounce in favor of the Republic, and on board the
steamer " Creole " were a number of leading young men
who were natives of that place. Every thing being in
readiness, Colonel Pickett was the first to land with a detachment of sixty men. It was about three o'clock in the
morning when Pickett and his small command passed
through Cardenas, carrying with them a civic watchman
to prevent an alarm, to the railway depot, on the opposite
side of the town, where they seized the road and its stock,
and before daylight had three locomotives fired up, and
transportation provided for the entire command. A
rocket had been agreed upon as the signal, but, instead
of the main body responding to the signal when given, it
became engaged with the little garrison of the town, and
thus frustrated the original plan of the campaign. Colonel Pickett waited until near sunset for the main body,
and then issued an order to return, and, if possible, to re-
join the command under Lopez, which was falling back
with a view of re-embarking for a new landing. They
had scarcely re-entered the town, however, when the re-
united commands were vigorously attacked by the Spanish troops which had been encamped in the healthy high
lands about nine miles distant, and which were under the
command of a major-general of the Spanish army. Two
of the superior officers of the invading force having been
disabled in the morning, the command during the engagement devolved upon Colonel Pickett, who, after a heavy
fight, succeeded in repulsing the Spaniards, and in effect-
ing an orderly retreat to the coast. They re-embarked on

the " Creole," but had scarcely left the harbor of Cardenas before the Spanish war steamer " Pizarro " came after them in hot pursuit, giving the " Creole " a long chase, and a stern chase, first to Key West, and thence to the harbor of New Orleans. A council of war was held, in the midst of which a pistol fell, and, going off, the ball passed through the leg of Colonel Hawkins. Without the movement or twitching of a muscle to betray the pain he felt, he sat still until the determination was reached, in case they were overtaken to grapple with and board the enemy, and if overpowered to blow up the " Creole," and destroy themselves and the Spaniard together; his associates had no suspicion that he had been wounded until the council had adjourned. The " Pizarro " was in full sight when the " Creole " touched the pier. " What shall we do, Colonel, if she overtakes us?" was the anxious inquiry made by the men of Pickett during the pursuit. " Grapple and board her with cutlasses," was the imperturbable response. Thus ended the disastrous expedition in which the gallant Logan fell;—such were the companions by whom he was loved and honored.

John A. Logan represented Shelby county in the legislature in 1839. He married, in 1837, Rebecca M. Bristow. Of their five children, but one survives, Dr. Richard F. Logan, of Shelbyville, a surgeon in the Union army during the war. The latter married Lucy Lemon, daughter of Samuel Lemon, of Louisville. Dr. Richard F. Logan and his son, Ben., a boy of fifteen years, are the only living *male* descendants of General Ben. Logan in the male line, and bearing the name.

John Logan and Ann C. Anderson had a daughter, Elizabeth, who married a Simpson and is dead. Their daughter, Sarah Jane Logan, married James F. Gamble, and now resides in Louisville, with her daughter, Mrs. Jane Rogers. Another daughter of James F. Gamble and Sarah Jane Logan married Mr. J. H. Lindenburger, the banker, of Louisville. Several sons of Mrs. Gamble live in Chicago.

The fourth son of General Ben. Logan and Anne Montgomery bore his name, was born in Lincoln county, January 3, 1789, was well educated for a physician, and successfully practiced that profession in Shelby; was a surgeon in the War of 1812, participated in the battle of the River Raisin, and was there captured; represented Shelby county in the legislature in 1818, at the same time with his brother John; and died in that county, March 19, 1873, after having enjoyed the respect of the community during an honorable life of eighty-four years.

After the death of the father of Colonel William Crawford (the commander of the ill-fated expedition against Sandusky, and who was tortured to death by his Indian captors), his mother married Richard Stephenson, and had by the latter a troop of stalwart boys and several fine daughters. One of the Stephenson girls married a Pennsylvanian named Pressly Lane, who settled in Shelby county. Another, Polly Stephenson, married Dr. John Knight, who was the surgeon of Crawford's expedition, was captured with that unfortunate officer, and, like him, was reserved for the torture, but made his escape by attacking with a club the Indian who had him in charge. This Dr. Knight also settled in Shelby, which county he frequently represented in the legislature. One of his daughters married a Hall, and was the mother of the wife of Wallace McDowell, and the grandmother of John Hall McDowell, who died in Selma, Alabama, in 1865. Still another of the Stephenson girls, Effie, half-sister of Colonel Crawford, married General Joseph Winlock, who settled in Shelby, represented the county in the legislature, was a useful and influential citizen, and a valiant soldier. Dr. Winlock, the professor at Harvard, was a descendant of General Winlock. One of the daughters of General Joseph Winlock—Effie Stephenson Winlock—married Dr. Ben. Logan. Their only son—James Knox Logan—died unmarried. One of their daughters, Ann Logan, was the second wife of Judge Z. Wheat, of the court of appeals, whose first wife was her kinswoman, and daughter of Judge Ben Monroe. Another daughter of Dr. Ben. Logan—Eliza—married Dr. Robert Glass;

and one of *their* daughters married Rev. Robert Clelland, a Presbyterian minister, while another daughter, Lizzie Glass, married Captain Bacon, of the United States army. Polly Logan, daughter of Dr. Ben., married her kinsman, William P. Monroe. Another daughter of Dr. Ben. Logan, Effie, married W. W. Gardiner, a state senator during the war, and a man of talent. The descendants of Dr. Logan are many, and every-where are reputable and worthy.

Robert Logan, fifth and youngest son of General Ben. Logan, was a soldier in the War of 1812, in the regiment commanded by Colonel John Allen, and was killed at the Raisin, where also fell the heroic Allen, whose wife, Jane Logan, was the oldest daughter of General Logan and Anne Montgomery.

THE HARDINS.

The second daughter of General Logan and Anne Montgomery—Elizabeth Logan—married the celebrated Martin D. Hardin; the union of the blood of the Logans with that of the Hardins was singularly appropriate. All through the records of the French and Indian wars, and of the campaigns with the Indians that followed, the name of Hardin is found among the soldiers—John, Mark, and Martin, their Christian names. Martin lived in Fauquier, in humble circumstances, and there his son John was born, in 1753. Thence Martin removed to the Monongahela, about the year 1765. John, though but twelve years of age, was already skilled in the use of arms. From hunting the deer and bear, he was called, before he had yet passed his boyhood, to take part in repelling Indian forays and in avenging their victims. In Dunmore's campaign, he was ensign of a militia company. Under Captain Zack Morgan the ensuing August he won an enviable distinction, and was desperately wounded in battle. The Revolution commenced just as he had prepared to come to Kentucky. Recruiting a body of sharpshooters, he joined the Continental army as a second lieutenant, was soon promoted and attached to the rifle-corps of General

12

Daniel Morgan. With this force he served until December, 1779, winning the respect of Morgan and the intrepid Colonel Richard Butler, by whom he was frequently intrusted with the most perilous commissions. Having resigned his office, in 1780 he came to Kentucky and located lands, and in 1786 removed his family to what is now the county of Washington. Henceforward, his history is that of the district. In every expedition against the Indians, except that of St. Clair (which a wound prevented him from joining), he had an active part, and held high command. He and James McDowell, as majors, commanded the battalions under Wilkinson. In 1792, he was sent by Wilkinson with overtures of peace to the Indians. If that arch-plotter expected him to return alive, he was the only person who did. That Hardin himself anticipated his fate is certain; but his gallant spirit could not refuse to obey an order which no one else was hardy enough to execute. He was murdered by the Indians with whom he had encamped, not far from Fort Defiance. His wife was Jane Daviess. They had six children, of whom the late Mark Hardin, of Shelby, was one. The wife of Rev. Barnabas McHenry was one of their daughters,—the mother of Judge John H. McHenry, of Daviess, and grandmother of Hon. Henry D. McHenry, of Ohio county, and Colonel John H. McHenry, of Owensboro. Lydia, sister of Colonel John Hardin, was the mother of Robert, Charles A., and Nathaniel Wickliffe. The mother of Ben Hardin was another sister, and his father a cousin. No family in Kentucky has been more noted for the intellectuality of its members, nor has the state ever had a more courageous breed. The oldest son of Colonel John Hardin and Jane Daviess was Martin, who added the D., to distinguish him from others of the same given name. Kentucky had no abler lawyer; his race no brainier nor truer son. He was, indeed, a remarkably able man. He represented Franklin county in the legislature in 1812, '18, '19; was secretary of state under Shelby, 1812–16; a United States senator, 1816, '17; a reporter for the court of appeals, 1808. Martin D. Hardin was one of the ma-

jors of Colonel Allen's regiment at the Raisin; George
Madison, the other. Hardin was in the fight outside of
the stockades; among the fallen there was not a better
soldier. He died in 1823, in his forty-third year. One of
the daughters of Martin D. Hardin and Elizabeth Logan
married A. R. McKee, a brother of the colonel of the regiment "orphaned" at Buena Vista. Another daughter
married Dr. Mark Chinn, who, after graduating at Transylvania, removed to Illinois. One of Dr. Chinn's daughters married her kinsman, W. H. Stuart, of Shelbyville.
A son of M. D. Hardin—Charles Hardin—settled at Jack-
sonville, Illinois. The oldest son of Martin D. Hardin
and Elizabeth Logan—John J. Hardin—was one of the
pupils at the famed academy of Dr. Louis Marshall, in
Woodford county, and left it with the respect of that most
exacting of teachers. After a creditable course in the
academies, he graduated in the collegiate department and
law school of Transylvania University, and then removed
to Illinois, where he engaged in the practice of the law,
for which his talents were peculiarly adapted. Without
being brilliant, he had strong sense, clear and discriminating judgment; the personification of integrity of the
highest order; the embodiment of knightly honor and
chivalry; possessed of an energy that never flagged; with
manners at once kind, grave, and dignified;—his force of
mind and character soon placed him abreast of the first in
his profession, while his manly virtues won the respect
and love of those with whom his lot was cast. Independence in fortune came to him as the reward of his labor.
To the Congress of 1843–45, the Whigs sent him as the
successor of his kinsman, John T. Stuart; he was himself
succeeded by E. D. Baker, afterward a distinguished senator from the Pacific slope, a gallant soldier who fell at
Ball's Bluff; and Baker was succeeded by Abraham Lincoln, whose wife was a kinswoman of both Stuart and
Hardin. The latter had taken an active part in the Black
Hawk War; had for years been general in chief of the
militia of Illinois, and having a natural taste and aptitude
for the science of arms, had been a close student of mili-

tary tactics. As a Whig Congressman, he had opposed the annexation of Texas. When his name was urged for a commission as brigadier-general in the Mexican War, his political antecedents insured the refusal of the appointment by Polk. Yet the first regiment raised in Illinois for that war was recruited by John J. Hardin, who was chosen as fittest to command; the colonel of the second was Bissell, also an ex-congressman. Placed under the especial charge of Colonel Churchill, of the regular army, whose rigid discipline was enforced by Hardin and Bissell, these two regiments rapidly acquired the steadiness under fire and the precision in movement of regulars and veterans. They rendezvoused at Alton, where they were found by Wool, prepared and in splendid condition for his expedition against Chihuahua. In July, of 1846, they were embarked for New Orleans; thence by steamer to Lavaca; and from the latter place, on the 11th of August, began their famous march under General Wool, who commanded the Army of the Center. How this force was united to that of General Taylor, and how the latter, who had become too conspicuous by his triumphs at Palo Alto, Resaca de la Palma, and Monterey, was stripped of the greater part of his army, and nearly all of his regulars, in order that they might swell the forces of General Scott, moving on the City of Mexico from another direction, is a part of the history of Polk's administration. The exultation with which the invincible warrior turned to the Illinoisans, under Hardin and Bissell; to the Kentuckians, under McKee, Clay, and Marshall; to the Mississippians, under Davis and McClung; and, with clenched hand and set teeth, exclaimed, "*These* are my *regulars!*" will not be forgotten while the memory of their heroism at Buena Vista lives. There the gallant Hardin proved the characteristics of his race and sealed his patriotic devotion with his life's blood. The story of the battle is too familiar to require repetition. Yet those who honor the brave men who fell on Angostura's plain, will not weary of the recital which tells how, when the Indianians had given back, and in their disorderly rout had swept away with them a part of Mar-

shall's men, that Bissell's Illinoisans advanced to fill the
gap, withheld their fire, while receiving volleys from the
advancing foe, until the word was given, and then poured
out a sheet of flame which drove back the Mexicans; then,
when again the enemy came surging on, fell back to a
better position, with the precision of a dress parade, and
when their ground was reached, again turned and fired;
how McKee's Kentuckians came rushing to the front, at
double-quick up the eminence, to take their place at Bissell's side; how Hardin, who had been hotly engaged in
covering Washington's battery, where the Mexicans had
been repulsed, passing McKee, went into action on Bissell's right, his men exposed to a heavy flank fire from a
whole brigade of Mexicans who crossed the head of the
second gorge; then, wheeling his men, led them to meet
the flank attack, lifted his sword, and shouted, "*Charge
bayonets; remember Illinois,*" the men following, and hurl-
ing back the Mexicans into the gorge, covering the ground
with their dead, and taking many prisoners. From that
time until his fall, Colonel Hardin was continuously in
action. After Taylor had been tricked by Santa Anna's
treacherous flag of truce, and deluded by the hope that
the retrograde movement to escape a critical situation was
an utter flight, he determined to take the battery that
covered the seeming retreat. Hardin was called to lead
the charge upon the belching cannon, and again shouting,
"*We will take that battery; charge bayonets!*" led the rush
of his regiment, followed by McKee and Clay, and a little
later by Bissell. Santa Anna, surveying the field from
an eminence, saw these gallant and devoted men as they
neared his battery, and massed his brigade to meet the
movement, in a supreme effort for the mastery. Hardin,
violently attacked by overwhelming numbers on the right
flank and in front, changed his bayonet charge to a de-
structive fire; and McKee and Bissell coming up, the
three regiments charged together into the Mexican ranks.
The Mexicans were driven before them, their retreat ap-
parently a flight. Suddenly they rallied, and with fresh
brigades, and led by Santa Anna in person, came back,

in myriads, and assailed with an avalanche of flame
and lead the handful of brave Americans struggling desperately in the gorge.   An aide came to Hardin with an
order from Taylor to retreat.   In the backward movement, the edge of the second gorge had been reached—a
pit fifty feet in depth, with precipitous banks, narrow, affording no chance to load and fire.   The crest of this gorge
was enveloped by the Mexicans, who came pouring down its
sides in all directions, numbering more than five to one of
the brave souls who fought as best they could with club-
bed muskets.   Above the roar of battle, was heard the
shout of Hardin—*"Fight on; remember Illinois."*   Wounded
in the thigh, and prostrated, he still shouted encourage-
ment to his men.   The gallant McKee was the first to die
in this fateful struggle.   The talented son and namesake
of Henry Clay had his leg shattered by musket balls, had
fallen, and had bidden his soldiers to leave him and save
themselves, when a squadron of lancers rushed upon him
and pierced him with many mortal wounds.   In the act of
falling, Hardin had drawn his pistol, and with this he
made one Mexican bite the dust; another bullet struck
the hero in the neck, and five lances were run through his
body.   Around them fell Willis, Zabriskie, eight lieutenants, and many men.   The rear-guard, which covered the
retreat of those who dragged themselves out of the pit,
was commanded by Speed Smith Fry, of Danville.   Looking back, and seeing a Mexican about to pierce the body
of one of the fallen victims with his lance, he seized a
musket from a soldier, and, with unerring aim, tumbled
the savage from his saddle.   General Fry always loses his
head in a speech; he never does in a fight.   The victorious
conclusion of the bloody strife was fought by the artillery; by Davis' Mississippians, with a part of the Indianians; by the Kentucky and Arkansas cavalry, under
Humphrey Marshall; and by May's dragoons.

Colonel John J. Hardin married a Miss Smith, of
Harrodsburg, who, after his death, became the wife of
Chancellor Walworth, of New York.   Colonel Hardin's
daughter—Ellen Hardin Walworth—a woman of fine

talent and literary attainment, resides in Saratoga. To her graphic account of the battle of Buena Vista, in the "Magazine of American History," for 1879, the writer is indebted for many of the details above recited. Her account is the most interesting that has ever been published. Colonel John J. Hardin's oldest son—Martin D. Hardin—graduated with credit at West Point, entered the regular army, and, in the civil war, by distinguished gallantry in battle won the rank and command of a brigadier-general—one of the youngest in the service, in which he lost an arm, and received many wounds. He belonged to the fifth generation of a race of soldiers. General Hardin is now a lawyer in Quincy, Illinois. After the death of Martin D. Hardin, Elizabeth Logan married Porter Clay, a brother of the orator, and for many years register of the Kentucky land office. She died in Illinois, at an advanced age.

THE WICKLIFFES.

Ann, the youngest daughter of General Ben Logan and Anne Montgomery, married the late Nathaniel Wickliffe, of Bardstown. His mother was Lydia Hardin, a sister to Colonel John Hardin. Robert Wickliffe, Sr., of Lexington, and Hon. Charles A. Wickliffe, Governor of Kentucky, postmaster-general, and congressman—both men of force and brain—were his brothers. Less distinguished than either of these, Nathaniel Wickliffe was a man of sense and weight, a good lawyer, who exerted influence in the community. He was for a long time clerk of the Circuit Court of Nelson. That county was twice represented in the legislature by his son, Robert Logan Wickliffe. Another son, Charles, graduated with honor at West Point; had the misfortune to kill his antagonist in a duel; and at Shiloh was killed at the head of the Confederate regiment of which he was colonel. A third son, Nathaniel, a man of refined and delicate beauty, and gentle manners, also fell in the Confederate ranks, on a hardfought field. The youngest son, John D. Wickliffe, was an officer of cavalry in the Union army. The daughters of Nathaniel Wickliffe and Ann Logan intermarried with the families of Nourse, Wilson, Halstead, and Muir, of whom there are many and highly reputable descendants.

COLONEL JOHN LOGAN.

Scarcely less active and prominent than his elder brother in all the stirring events of the early settlement of Kentucky, was the second (or he may have been the third) of the four Logan brothers who came to the district—John Logan. He was a private soldier in the Bouquet expedition, in the company of which the elder brother was sergeant. When Benjamin left their mother on a farm in the forks of the James river, in the care of another brother, John went with him to the Holston, and was one of the earliest of the pioneers of that region, as he afterward became of Kentucky. He was a non-commissioned officer in his brother's company on Dunmore's campaign. To Kentucky he came in 1776, settling in Lincoln county. In August, 1778, he was with Boone, Kenton, Holder, and sixteen others, in the Paint Creek expedition to surprise an Indian town; helped to rout a band of Indians of double their own number; and finding the town evacuated, and ascertaining that a large force had gone to attack the Kentucky settlements, made a rapid march homeward, passing the Indian army undiscovered, and got back in time to aid in the defense of Boonesboro against the siege of Duquesne. When his brother's company was first formally organized at St. Asaphs, he was its lieutenant, and had a conspicuous part in all its enterprises. In Bowman's expedition, in 1779, he commanded that company (which rendezvoused at Lexington, with Levi Todd's and John Holder's), and had a part in fighting at its head, at the Indian town, and on the retreat. Later, he was in Clarke's expedition, as well as in that of General Logan in 1786. In 1787, he commanded the expedition against the Cherokees, of Tennessee, to avenge the murder of Luttrell, in Lincoln county, where he was second under his brother in military rank. Calling his militia together, he went with them to the house where the outrage had been perpetrated, discovered the route the Indians had taken, followed their trail for several days until he had entered the Indian territory beyond the Cumberland, finally overtook and attacked them with vigor, routing them, and retaking all their plunder. These Indians had entered into a treaty with Congress two years before and this they had violated by the incursion. Yet those who had escaped from Logan complained that *he* had violated it by entering into the territory and attacking peaceable Indians. The Indian agent represented the affair accordingly to the governor of Virginia, who directed Harry Innes, then the attorney-general for Kentucky, to prosecute Logan and his party, which he, availing himself of the indirectness of the order, refused to do.—[*Littell.*] It was in 1781 that he was appointed lieutenant-colonel of the first regiment of militia ever organized in Lincoln county. Stephen Trigg succeeded Ben. Logan as the colonel. Afterward, John Logan was colonel of the same regiment, and reported its number to the governor of Virginia as over eight hundred soldiers. He hurried to join Todd and Trigg at the Blue Licks, but the disaster had occurred before his men could reach the field. Nor was he less prominent in civil than in military affairs. The record shows that he was a member of the first court ever organized in Kentucky, at Harrodsburg, in 1781. The name of every member of that court has passed into history as that of a true man and soldier. Of the thirteen of its legal members, two had already fallen in battle; and of the eleven who sat, three fell within the following seventeen months.—[*Collins.*] He was three times sent to the Virginia General Assembly from Lincoln county before Kentucky became a state. In the discussions that molded public sentiment in the rising commonwealth, and in the deliberative bodies that led to its establishment, he had an influential voice. With his elder brother and Shelby, he represented Lincoln county in the Danville convention of 1787; and was the associate of Harry Innes, from Franklin county, in the convention of 1799, that framed the second state constitution. One of the fourteen members from Kentucky in the Virginia convention that had under consideration the adoption of the federal constitution, he felt it his duty to vote with ten others against its adoption. It was fortunate, indeed, that the much villified Humphrey Marshall was there, too, as one of the members from Fayette. From 1792 to 1795, John Logan was the senator from Lincoln. This fact did not prevent his appointment by Governor Shelby as the first treasurer of Kentucky, which office he continued to hold through successive administrations for more than sixteen years. In 1792, he was one of the electors of the senate from Lincoln, his associates being his elder brother, Isaac Shelby and Thomas Todd. It need not be added that he was a man of strong intellect, an active and fearless soldier, of the most incorruptible integrity, sincerely religious, of unblemished life, simple tastes, and unassuming manners. Residing at Frankfort from the time the seat of government was removed from Lexington to that place, his official position brought him in constant contact, while his strong personal qualities promoted intimate association, with the best and foremost men in the state. Without classical training, even wanting in a thorough English education, his native mental force was such as to fill the high standard of Dr. Louis Marshall, who, after his death, in a tribute to his memory bore testimony to the excellence of his character, and to his superior intellectual abilities. Scrupulously faithful to the obligations of the public trust confided to his hands, they occupied his time to the exclusion of his private interests; so that thousands of acres of rich lands were lost to his family by sheer inattention.

THE McCLURES.

The wife of Colonel John Logan was Jane McClure, of the same Scotch-Irish race from which he himself had sprung; descended from a family, which, like his own, had been among the earliest settlers in the Virginia Valley and had been soldiers in all the Indian wars;—members of which had gone early to the Holston, and many of whom came with or followed their Logan connexions to Kentucky. Their names are found among the officers and soldiers who fought under Logan, Whitley, and Boyle; several fell victims to the hatred of the savage. One branch of the family, which settled in Russell county, had several members prominent in public life. The wife of Colonel John Logan was a sister of William and Captain Robert McClure, two of the most daring, the coolest and most successful, of all the old Indian fighters. William was the father of the late venerable Mrs. Jane Allen Stuart, of Owensboro, named after the oldest daughter of General Logan, and was the grandfather of Judge James Stuart of that place. A daughter of one of these pioneer McClures ran away with and married a young Irishman named Carlisle, a sprightly clerk in a country store. She was not heard of by her family for many years. The late Robert McClure Carlisle, of Kenton, was her son; the able speaker of the house of representatives in Congress, Hon. John Griffin Carlisle, is her grandson. The latter, though not himself of the Logan blood, has sought to perpetuate, in the name of his son, the recollection of the connexion of the families.

Mary, the oldest daughter of Colonel John Logan and Jane McClure, married Otho Holland Beatty, a brother of the late Judge Adam Beatty, of Mason county, and uncle of the learned Dr. Ormond Beatty, so long the president of Centre College. They lived in Frankfort; had two children—Cornelius and Sarah Ann. After the death of Mr. Beatty, Mary Logan married James Blain, and had by him three other children—John Logan Blain, Catherine, and Mary. The son married a granddaughter of Judge Innes—a daughter of John Morris, of Frankfort. Catherine married Mr. Holton, and for many years resided in Frankfort.

THE BALLENGERS.

Jane, the second daughter of Colonel John Logan and Jane McClure, married Joseph Ballenger, of Lincoln county. This Mr. Ballenger was probably the man who captured the infamous Harpes, in 1794, and lodged them in the jail at Stanford. He and Jane Logan had five children. Their son, Napoleon B., and daughter, Nancy,

never married.   Their son, John Logan Ballenger, married
a Miss Paxton.   By reference to a former page, it will be
seen that John Paxton married Martha Blair.   Their son,
Captain John Paxton, a Revolutionary soldier (he died
from a wound in the head received at Guilford), married
Phoebe Alexander, of Rockbridge.   (Captain John Paxton was a brother of the James Paxton who married
Phoebe McClung, and was the father of James A. Paxton, who married Maria Marshall.   He was a brother also
of the Isabella Paxton who márried Captain John Lyle,
and was the mother of Mary Paxton Lyle, who married
Colonel James McDowell.)   A third John Paxton, son of
Captain John and Phoebe Alexander, moved to Lincoln
county, and there married Elizabeth Logan, daughter of
John Logan (who came to Kentucky from Botetourt) and
Ann McClure; this John Logan, of Botetourt, was a
cousin of General Ben. and Colonel John Logan.   William
Paxton, son of the John who was wounded at Guilford,
and brother of the above third John, also moved to Lincoln, and there married Nancy Logan, another daughter
of John Logan, of Botetourt.   It was a daughter of
William Paxton and Nancy Logan—Mary Anne Paxton, who became the wife of John Logan Ballenger.
The latter was a lawyer by profession, a member of
the legislature from Lincoln in 1844, and a member of
the constitutional convention in 1850.   About the year
1856, he removed to Texas, and during the war he
died there, an outspoken, uncompromising Union man.
His sons, Wm. P., John L., and James Ballenger, live at
Honey Grove, Texas; Joseph Paxton Ballenger, a lawyer
of Paris, Texas, lost an arm in the Confederate service.
Jennie married Dr. Ed. Dailey, and lives at Honey Grove,
as do also Nannie and Lucy, both married.

The Davidsons.

Joseph Ballenger's daughter, Lucretia, married Colonel
Michael Davidson, of Lincoln, a son of George Davidson,
who represented the county in the legislature from 1799
to 1802—four successive terms.   Colonel Michael David-

son represented Lincoln in the house in 1816 and in 1828; and in the senate, 1836–40. He was an officer in the War of 1812—a plain, modest man, a fearless one, and a good soldier. He had six children, all of whom are dead.

Harriet Ballenger, another daughter of Joseph Ballenger and Jane Logan, married Colonel James Davidson, the twin brother of Colonel Michael. James Davidson was the senator from Lincoln from 1818 to 1826; and was for many years the state treasurer. In the War of 1812, he commanded a company at the battle of the Thames, which he led into the thickest of that blooody fight. It was his belief that a soldier of his company, named King, had really killed Tecumseh. He was an unassuming, frank, sensible, honest, and brave man. Jane, one of the daughters of Colonel James Davidson and Harriet Ballenger, married Captain Hary Innes Todd, of Frankfort. The family to which this worthy man belongs should not be confounded with that from which came the brothers, Colonel John and Generals Levi and Robert Todd. The former was seated in tide-water Virginia many years before the progenitor of the latter emigrated from Ireland to America—possibly before their more remote ancestor fled from Scotland to Ireland.

THE TODDS, OF KING AND QUEEN.

Exactly at what time the ancestor of Hary I. Todd came to Virginia, is not certainly known. He had a large grant of land direct from the crown. In the eighth volume of Henning's Statutes, page 631, may be found an act of the general assembly, of date February, 1772, docking the entail of the estate of William Todd, "*gentleman.*" It recites that one " Thomas Todd, formerly of the county of Gloucester, *gentleman*, was in his lifetime seized of a considerable estate in lands, and, among others, of a large and valuable tract lying on the Mattapony river, in the county of King and Queen, and of another tract, containing about one thousand acres, lying on the Dragon swamp, in the parish of St. Stephen, in the said county of King and Queen." In his " deed poll," dated 16th of March,

1709, this Thomas Todd granted to his son, " William Todd, and the heirs of his body, begotten of Martha Vicaris, his intended wife, five hundred acres, part of his said tract on the Mattapony river;" and by his will, of date the 4th of March, 1723, the same Thomas Todd bequeathed the tract on the Dragon Swamp to his sons, Philip and Richard Todd. By the deaths of Philip and Richard without male heirs, the whole of this estate became vested in the above William Todd, son of Thomas. From this William Todd, the elder, it descended to his grandson by Martha Vicaris—William Todd, of King and Queen—whose right therein was vested in George Brooke, William Lyne, Gregory Baylor, John Tayloe Corbin, and Richard Tunstall, as trustees, to be sold, and the proceeds re-invested as directed. From an act, on page 57 of the same volume of Henning, it is ascertained that the above William Todd, the elder, died in 1736, leaving daughters, Dorothy and Betty; grandsons, William Gordon and Richard Barbour; and sons, Richard and Thomas Todd. He left a very large estate in the parish of St. Thomas, Orange county, as well as considerable possessions in King and Queen. A large and valuable part of this property he bequeathed to his eldest son, Richard Todd, who was the father of the above William Todd, grandson of William the elder, in whom the entail docked in the first statute above mentioned had vested. This Richard Todd's wife was Elizabeth Richards, a woman of great energy and good intellect; William Todd, whose entail was docked in 1772, was their oldest son, and the noted Judge Thomas Todd, of Kentucky, their youngest. The latter is stated by Collins to have been born in King and Queen county in 1765. His father died when he was a child; his excellent mother soon followed to the grave. Thus orphaned at an early age, by his guardian he was afforded opportunities for obtaining a good English education, and the foundation of one in the classics. By the embarrassments of this guardian, he was, while still a boy, thrown upon his own resources. For a short time during the closing days of the Revolution, he was in the army. Invited to become an inmate of the family of his relative, Hary Innes, then residing in Bedford county, he became acquainted with the art of surveying, and attained that proficiency as a clerk, and those methodical habits and attention to details, which proved the foundation of future eminence. Collins asserts that he came first to Kentucky, with the family of Hary Innes, in 1786; McClung, who was not apt to have erred in such a matter, that he was at Danville in 1784, and was chosen and acted as clerk of the first convention held at that place in that year—of the convention of delegates from the militia companies, called by General Ben. Logan, which was the forerunner of all the others. From that time, he was clerk of all the succeeding conventions, until the establishment of the state in 1792. He represented Kentucky in the Virginia legislature before the separation. In 1792, he was one of the electors of the senate. He was the first clerk of the federal court in the district, and upon the establishment of the court of appeals, under the second constitution of 1799, he was appointed its first clerk. In 1801, he was appointed judge of the court of appeals, and in 1806 its chief-justice. When the Seventh United States Circuit District was formed, he was appointed by Mr. Jefferson an Associate Justice of the United States Supreme Court, which office he held until his death, in 1826. Judge Thomas Todd was an amiable, generous man, of kind heart and popular manners. That he was a man of talent and ability, and of good professional attainments, is sufficiently evidenced by the acceptable manner in which he discharged the duties imposed by those high trusts. His abilities extorted the respect, while his personal qualities won the friendship, of John Marshall. His first wife was Elizabeth Harris, a niece of the William Stewart who fell fighting at the Blue Licks. She was the mother of his sons, Colonel Charles S. and John H. Todd, and of his daughters, the first wife of the late John H. Hanna and Mrs. Edmund L. Starling. The first of these—a man of imposing manners and distinguished presence—was the confidential aide of General Harrison, by whom he was appointed minister to Russia; he married a daughter of

Governor Shelby, and their son, Thomas, commanded a company in the war with Mexico. Judge Todd married, secondly, Lucy Payne, a sister of Mrs. Madison; their mother was one of the talented Winstons. This second wife was, when she married Judge Todd, the widow of Major George Steptoe Washington, the youngest son of Colonel Samuel Washington (brother of the President) by his fourth wife. By this marriage, Judge Todd was the father of James Madison Todd, of Frankfort. John H. Todd, the other son of Judge Todd by his first wife—an amiable, sensible, and fine-looking man—represented Franklin and Owen in the legislature in 1820, '21, '22, '23. His wife was his kinswoman, the beautiful daughter of Judge Hary Innes. They had three children—Hary I. Todd; Kitty, who married General Thomas L. Crittenden; and Mrs. Wm. H. Watson. After the death of John H. Todd, his widow became the second wife of Hon. John J. Crittenden. The beauty of her face, the grace and charm of her person and manners, were but the external reflection of the loveliness of her mind and character.

Judge Innes.

In Scotland, the name of Innes is one of great antiquity. Those who bore it belonged to the gentry of the kingdom, were allied to many noble families, and, better far than that, they had brains, honesty, and pluck,—qualities that outlast titles, survive wealth, and are infinitely superior to any social position that is not built upon them. The name itself signifies an island; the barony of Innes, in Moray, is an island formed by two branches of a stream running through the estate. The hereditary knights who owned and held it with strong arms for many centuries took for their surname that of the estate. They had for their most frequent given names those of Robert, James, and Hary. The first baronet of Innes was Sir Robert; the second was also Sir Robert; the third was Sir James; the fourth was Sir Hary; the fifth was also Sir Hary; and the oldest son of the fifth Sir Hary, also named Hary, dying before his father, the fifth baronet was succeeded by Sir James Innes; who, upon becoming fifth Duke of

Roxburgh, added the name of Ker to that of Innes. Beyond the sameness of given and surnames, no fact is known to the writer which connects Judge Hary (for that is the proper way to spell it) Innes with this family, an account of whom is published in "The Scottish Nation;" and if the sensible people who have borne the name of Innes in this country preserved any record or tradition of such connexion, they have not deemed it of sufficient consequence to mention. Be this as it may, it is of record that an Episcopalian minister of high character, a man of native talent, force, and education, named Rev. Robert Innes, emigrated from Scotland to Virginia before the middle of the eighteenth century; and there married Catharine Richards, a native of the colony. They had three sons— Robert, a skillful and educated physician; Hary, who came to Kentucky; and James, the accomplished and brilliant attorney-general of Virginia, deemed by many the equal of Patrick Henry in eloquence, and assuredly his superior in acquirements. The year of Hary's birth is stated by Collins to have been 1752. That he studied law under the noted Hugh Rose is ascertained from the same source. He had successfully practiced his profession in Virginia before the Revolution. During that struggle, he was employed as the superintendent of mines to supply the patriot armies with the material of war. He came to Kentucky first as the associate of McDowell and Wallace as judges of the District Court of Kentucky. Thenceforward his name is identified with every chapter of the early history of the district and state. Among the men who figured in the movements that led to the separation from Virginia, to the establishment of the commonwealth, and who gave direction to her domestic polity, he was one of the most prominent and influential. He succeeded Walker Daniel as the attorney-general for the district; was afterward appointed judge of the United States District Court, and held the latter office until his death, in 1816. Soon after arriving at the age of manhood, Judge Innes married, in Virginia, the daughter of Colonel James

Calloway, of Bedford county. The latter was a son of
William Calloway, who was a brother of the Colonel
Richard Calloway who came to Kentucky with Boone,
helped to organize the government of Transylvania at
Boonesboro, and was killed by the Indians. William Calloway was a large land-owner in Bedford, Halifax, and
other counties. His wife was a Miss Crawford. James,
his oldest son, born in 1736, served in the French and Indian War, was colonel of Bedford county during the
Revolution, and built the first iron-works in Virginia
above Lynchburg. Colonel James was married three
times—first, in 1756, to Sarah Tate. His oldest daughter
by this marriage, Elizabeth Calloway, was the first wife of
the distinguished Judge Hary Innes. (Colonel James had in
all only twenty-one children—twelve by his first wife, and
nine by the second, Elizabeth Early.) Judge Hary Innes
and Elizabeth Calloway had four daughters. The oldest
of these, Sarah, born in 1776, was married, in May, 1792,
to Francis Thornton, of Fall Hill, near Fredericksburg,
who was the son of Francis Thornton and Ann Thompson, daughter of Rev. John Thompson by the widow oi
Governor Spottswood. This last-mentioned Francis Thornton was the son of Colonel Francis Thornton and Frances
Gregory, whose mother was Mildred Washington—the
aunt and godmother of the President. The oldest son of
Francis Thornton and Sarah Innes was the late Judge
Hary Innes Thornton, of California, whose wife was the
only sister of John J. Crittenden. Ann, the youngest
daughter of Judge Innes and Elizabeth Calloway, married
John Morris, son of William and brother of the able
Richard Morris, of Virginia. John and Ann Morris had
eleven children. The second of these, Ann, married, first,
Robert Crittenden, brother of John J., and a distinguished
congressman from Arkansas; and, second, Rev. Dr. John
Todd Edgar. Sarah, the third, married Eli Huston.
Mary, the seventh, married C. P. Bertrand, of Arkansas;
and, afterward, Captain John McDowell. Louisa, the
eighth, married John Logan Blaine, a grandson of Colonel
John Logan.

After the death of Elizabeth Calloway, Judge Innes married Mrs. Shields, and by her was the father of the beautiful woman who was first the wife of John H. Todd, and then of John J. Crittenden. As already stated, her son by her first husband, Hary Innes Todd, married Jane Davidson. They have many children.

Mary Davidson, daughter of Colonel James and Harriet Logan, married Reeves and then R. G. Samuel. Anna married Finley Hays. Harriet married Tichenor. Lucy married John N. Markham. The other children of Colonel James Davidson died single.

JUDGE CHRISTOPHER TOMPKINS.

Theodosia, the third daughter of Colonel John Logan and Jane McClure, is represented by contemporary description to have been a woman of comeliness and of sprightly mind. She married Christopher Tompkins, then a young member of the legislature from Henderson and Muhlenburg counties. He was the son of John Tompkins, a Virginian in independent circumstances, who had emigrated to Kentucky, and settled in Fayette county, in 1794; his wife, Anne Tompkins, was his first cousin. The oldest son of John and Anne Tompkins—Gwynn—a man of good mind and practical ability, represented Fayette in the legislature in 1805; while his son, Gwynn R. Tompkins,* a well-read and talented lawyer, represented that county in the same body in 1834; and Benjamin, another son of the first Gwynn, became an eminent judge in Missouri. The two daughters of John and Anne Tompkins married, respectively, a Goodloe and John Lyle, respectable farmers. John Lyle was a brother of Mary Paxton Lyle—wife of Colonel James McDowell. Judge P. W. Tompkins, of Mississippi, was the son of an elder brother of Christopher Tompkins, who was the youngest son of John and Anne. His father dying soon after coming to Kentucky, the boyhood and youth of Christopher Tompkins was passed in the home of Hon. John Breckinridge, under whom, after receiving an academical training, he was a student of

---

*The widow of Gwynn R. Tompkins is the wife of Hon. A. G. Thurman, of Ohio.

law,—the companion and friend of the oldest son of his preceptor, the amiable, handsome, and able Joseph Cabell Breckinridge. From these associations, soon after attaining maturity he removed to Henderson, where his successful professional career was commenced, and from whence he was sent to the legislature as the representative of Muhlenburg and Henderson, in 1805; and while at Frankfort met his future wife. At a very early age, he was appointed circuit judge of the Glasgow district and removed to Barren county, where he continued to reside until the end of his long and virtuous life. During his incumbency of the judicial office, it became his melancholy duty to preside at the trial of, and to pass sentence of death upon, the unfortunate John C. Hamilton for the murder of Dr. Sanderson. Hamilton belonged to a family to whom wealth had given social position. The proof against him was as conclusive as circumstantial evidence can possibly be made; not a link in the strong chain was missing. The friends of the unhappy man, who met death upon the gallows, always claimed that, however unbroken the web of testimony that pointed to his guilt and secured his conviction, he was nevertheless innocent; and a confession alleged to have been made many years afterward, and to which no publicity was given until many other years after it was alleged to have been made by the real murderer, has been asserted as a vindication of his fame. Whether the conclusions of the jury that heard the evidence or those of his family were correct, there was never a question of the fairness and freedom from prejudice of the judge who presided at the trial. In making him their confidential friend and adviser in subsequent troubles, the parents of the law's victim paid only a just tribute to his character. Judge Tompkins continued to discharge the duties of the judicial office with an ability which won plaudits from the best lawyers in the state until 1824, when he resigned to make the race for governor, in the memorable canvass of that year, as the candidate of the anti-relief party. He was opposed and overwhelmingly defeated by General Joseph Desha, who had the prestige of a well-earned military reputation, and

whose bold temper, mental vigor, and integrity in private
life, entitled him to the prominence he had won and to
the influence he had for years exerted in civil affairs.
This popular leader canvassed the state with characteristic
energy and vehemence, supplementing his zealous advocacy of the measures that had been designed to relieve the
debtor class in a time of commercial distress and monetary stringency, with the most bitter denunciation of
Judges Clarke, Blair, Boyle, Mills, and Owsley, who had, in
a case properly brought before them, decided these measures to be unconstitutional. The reader who is interested
in the details of the angry controversy that for several succeeding years convulsed the commonwealth, and had well
nigh culminated in civil war, will find them in the publications which relate to that exciting period; and from these
he will ascertain that the final judgment of the people
vindicated the views calmly urged by Judge Tompkins
and the able men who concurred with him, by majorities
as conclusive as those by which they had at first condemned them. From the conclusion of the gubernatorial
canvass, in 1824, until his election to Congress, in 1831,
Judge Tompkins diligently applied himself to the labors
of a large and lucrative practice. In Congress, he remained four years, when, upon his refusal to become a
candidate for a third term, he was appointed judge over
his former district, and held that office until his voluntary
withdrawal from all public life, at the age of sixty-seven
years. He died twelve years later, in 1854, at the venerable age of seventy-nine.

The only son of Judge Tompkins and Theodosia Logan
who lived to maturity was Christopher Tompkins, Jr.
Elected to the legislature from Barren, in 1835, when
barely eligible to the position, his talents attracted attention in a body of which some of the most gifted Kentuckians of that generation were members. He was re-elected,
but died during his second term, in his twenty-sixth year.
The oldest daughter of Judge Tompkins, Sarah Ann, married, first, Dr. R. B. Garnett, son of Richard Garnett, who
was for many years clerk of the Barren Circuit Court; by

Dr. Garnett, she was the mother of several daughters, and after his death she became the second wife of Rev. Dr. Wm. L. Breckinridge. The second daughter of Judge Tompkins married William Garnett, brother of the above-mentioned Dr. Garnett. Her son, the oldest grandson of Judge Tompkins—C. T. Garnett—was killed fighting in the front line of the Union army at Vicksburg. Another of her sons married a daughter of the late John Owsley, of Chicago. Theodosia, third daughter of Judge Tompkins, married Mr. Hall, of Barren. One of her sons, C. T. Hall, graduated with credit at West Point, was assigned to the Second Artillery, and is an officer of the regular army.

The Harrises.

Colonel John Logan's daughter, Elizabeth, married Edwin Lanier Harris, who came to Kentucky from Georgia. The mother of Mr. Harris was a Lanier; there are families of that name living in Garrard and Boyle counties; the Southern poet, Lanier, was of the same stock as Mr. Harris. On the paternal side, Isham Harris, of Tennessee, is of the same people. Harriet, daughter of Edwin L. Harris and Elizabeth Logan, married, first, Mr. Goodloe, and John Kemp Goodloe, of Louisville, is her son. The latter was a good soldier in Humphrey Marshall's regiment in the war with Mexico; from 1855 to 1861, he represented Woodford county in the legislature, and in the trying days of the early part of the latter year stood manfully by the Union; for the next four years, he was the senator from the Woodford district; was appointed United States Attorney for Louisiana, and held the place for several years. Since his return to Kentucky, Mr. Goodloe has been continuously engaged in an extensive law practice. After the death of his father, his mother married, secondly, Mr. Izett, and had by him a daughter, Harriet Izett, who married Rev. A. D. Madeira, of the Presbyterian ministry. Lucretia, the second daughter of E. L. Harris and Elizabeth Logan, married Dr. McMillen, of Lexington. Their only son, the late Henry Clay Harris, a man of naturally good and sprightly mind, represented

Floyd county in the state house of representatives in 1834, '35, '38, and in the senate from 1843 to 1847, when he removed to Covington, and there practiced law until his death. The wife of Henry Clay Harris was Rhoda Harmon Davis, daughter of James L. Davis. The wife of the latter was Louisa Harmon, a sister of the two brothers who founded Louisa, in Lawrence county, which place is said to have been named in her honor. Letitia, one of the daughters of Henry Clay Harris, married Robert Richardson, of Covington. Mr. Richardson was a boy when he volunteered as a private soldier in Cassius M. Clay's company of Marshall's cavalry regiment, with which he served in Mexico; but his youth did not prevent him from doing full duty as a soldier. At the close of hostilities, he commenced the practice of law in Covington. From 1855 to 1859, he was the representative from Covington in the legislature. During his second term, the law of 1833, prohibiting the bringing of slaves into Kentucky for purposes of traffic, was repealed, the repealing act being clothed in language that permitted even the re-opening of the slave trade with Africa. Mr. Richardson had all his life been a Democrat, then the extreme pro-slavery party of the state, but party discipline could not control his vote or voice in opposition to his judgment. Others faltered; he remained firm. The ability, the earnestness, the power with which he resisted that repeal will not be forgotten by those who heard his appeals to the sober reason of the house. In 1859, he was nominated and elected by the Democrats as superintendent of public instruction; he discharged his duties with fidelity; there was but a poor opportunity to accomplish much in the years of strife which followed. The war found him among those Democrats who stood by the flag and the government. Mr. Richardson's father, Samuel Q. Richardson, an able lawyer, was cut off in the prime of life by the hand of an assassin—John U. Waring. The wife of Sam. Q. Richardson was one of the daughters of Robert Carter Harrison, of Fayette, whose wife was a sister of the wife of the elder John Breckinridge, and a daughter of Colonel Joseph Cabell, of Virginia. The father of Robert Carter Harrison was Carter Henry Harrison, a younger brother of the signer of the Declaration of Independence, and himself a man of talent and influence in Virginia; the wife of Carter Henry Harrison was one of the daughters of Isham Randolph, of Dungeness, and sister of Jefferson's mother. No family in Virginia has been more conspicuous than the Harrisons, nor one for so long a time.

Letitia, the youngest daughter of Colonel John Logan and Jane McClure, married Mr. Mosby. Of their five children, all are dead but one. The survivor, Theodosia Mosby, married Colonel Hoskins, a true Union man, who commanded a regiment in the Federal army during the civil war, from which he came out with credit as a good soldier and officer. They live in Versailles.

Colonel John Logan had but one son to live to maturity; he was named David—a man of good sense, and of unbending integrity, with manners frank but brusque. His early manhood was passed in Frankfort, but in 1802 he returned to Lincoln county, where he continued to reside. His first wife was Mary Trigg, a daughter of Colonel Stephen Trigg. Her mother was a daughter of Israel Christian. Colonel William Christian was her brother; he was killed by Indians whom he had pursued into Indiana, in 1786. The wives of Judge Caleb Wallace, and of Colonel William Fleming, one of the heroes of Point Pleasant, were her sisters. Colonel Stephen Trigg himself was a native of Virginia, and coming to Kentucky in 1779, at once took his natural place among the leaders of the soldiers of the frontier. " His activity and courage were equal to every emergency, and brought him always to the front in the never-ceasing alarms that kept the ill-protected stations in anxious vigilance. Nature, too, had enriched him with that most rare and enviable gift, the power of winning the earnest affections of men. . . . He rose rapidly in the general esteem."—[*Brown.*] In 1780, he was made lieutenant-colonel of Lincoln county, of which Ben. Logan was colonel. (In the Virginia

Assembly of 1775, he was a delegate with Colonel Wm. Christian from Fincastle county, which then included all Kentucky. In 1780, he was a delegate with John Todd from Kentucky county, before it was subdivided.) In 1782, as lieutenant-colonel, he was in command of the fort at Harrodsburg, when he received the message from Colonel John Todd of the siege of Bryant's station; forwarding it at once to General Ben. Logan, at St. Asaphs, he marched, with Major Levi Todd and such men as could be hurriedly collected. With the Todds, Boone, McGary, Harlan, and Bulger, he pushed on from Lexington without waiting for Logan, and, at the disaster of the Blue Licks, fell in the front of the battle. By the daughter of this gifted and brave man, David Logan had but one son, Stephen Trigg Logan, born in Frankfort in 1800. His wife died soon after his return to Lincoln.

JUDGE STEPHEN TRIGG LOGAN

received his early education at Frankfort. In his boyhood, while acting as a clerk in the office of Martin D. Hardin, secretary of state, he made out the commissions for the officers of Shelby's force in the North-western campaign. His facility in learning was remarkable; at the age of seventeen he went to Glasgow to study law under Judge Christopher Tompkins. He commenced the practice in Glasgow, grew rapidly in the profession, was appointed attorney for the commonwealth, and established a reputation as a clear, animated, and incisive speaker. In 1823, he married America T. Bush, daughter of William Bush, of Glasgow. He acquired a competence, which he lost by paying security debts, and, in 1832, removed to Illinois. There he acquired a leading position, and a reputation for ability which never waned. In 1835 the legislature elected him judge of the Sangamon Circuit District; he held the office two years, when he resigned on account of the inadequacy of the salary. Elected a second time, without his consent, he declined to serve. " Thorough knowledge of the law, solidity of judgment, clearness of apprehension, promptness of decision, and a wonderful

readiness in applying legal principles to complex trans-
actions and ever-varying facts," were the qualities which
distinguished him upon the bench. Four times he was
sent to the legislature, and as a delegate to the constitutional convention of 1847 took an influential part in the
deliberations of that body. Defeated for Congress in
1848, on account of his opposition to the war with
Mexico, he withdrew altogether from political life, for
which he had neither taste nor aptitude, and so indus-
triously applied himself to his profession that he acquired
a handsome estate. When he retired from the bench in
1837, his first law partner was E. D. Baker; from 1841 to
1844, he was associated with Abraham Lincoln, to whom
he had been both friend and instructor; his next was his
son-in-law, Milton Hay. In 1860, he was a delegate for
the state at large to the convention that nominated
Abraham Lincoln, and assisted in the plans that brought
about that result. As a member of the historic peace
conference of 1861, he urged an honorable compromise of
the questions at issue; his speeches in that body have
been described as " grand and patriotic." Soon thereafter, he withdrew from the practice, as he had previously
done from politics, and passed the remainder of his life in
dignified retirement. He died in Springfield, Illinois,
July 17, 1880. In person, he was small; in dress, careless.
His forehead was high, his mouth indicated firmness, resolution; his eye, which was deep set, black, and penetra-
ting, fairly blazed when aroused. A fine judge of men,
and of the motives influencing human action, he instinctively discerned the right and wrong of a controversy, was
fearless and independent in his argumentation, and had a
wealth of concise and logical expression rarely equaled.
He was not only a bold and able advocate; he was a sound
counsellor, and an honest lawyer. Of an ardent nature,
his delivery was earnest to vehemence; his fertility in resources was remarkable; his powers of nice discrimina-
tion, of keen analysis, of critical dissection, were wonderful. With these characteristics, he was at the same time
a broad, comprehensive, compact reasoner. In the judg-

ment of his contemporaries, Judge Logan had few equals as a lawyer in Illinois, and no superior. His temper was fiery—at times, fierce; at repartee, he was very quick, pungent. In private life, he was one of the most exemplary of men. Judge Logan's oldest son, David, born in 1824, became an eminent lawyer in Oregon, and was twice the Republican candidate for Congress, both times unsuccessfully. He died in 1874. Three other sons died young. Mary, his oldest daughter, married Hon. Milton Hay, of Springfield, and left two children, Katie and Logan Hay. Katie Hay married her kinsman, Stuart Brown. Sally, the second daughter of Judge Logan, born in 1834, married Colonel Ward H. Lamon, who was United States Marshal of the District of Columbia under Lincoln. Jennie, the third daughter of Judge Logan, born February 19, 1843, married L. H. Coleman, of Springfield. They have four children. Kate, fourth daughter of Judge Logan, married Hon. David T. Littler, of Springfield. She died in 1875, leaving one child.

After the death of Mary Trigg, David Logan married his kinswoman, a sister of Judge John McKinley, by whom he had a daughter, who became the wife of Colonel L. T. Thustin, of Louisville.

GENERAL HUGH LOGAN.

Hugh, son of David and Jane Logan, was born in Augusta county, and was baptized by Rev. John Craig, March 24, 1745. It is not known whether he was the next son to General Ben. Logan, or younger than Colonel John; but it seems probable that he was the second son of his parents. It was with him that Ben. Logan left their mother on a farm on one of the forks of James river, when Ben. and John pushed out for the frontier on the Holston. He came to Kentucky a little later than either Ben. or John, but, when he did come, he acquitted himself well in the defense of the settlements, in repelling the assaults by the Indians, and in the expeditions which carried the war into the Indian territory north of the Ohio. In 1783 he was made a justice of the peace, and was added to the court of Lincoln county, of which Ben. and John were already members. The magistrates who qualified at the same time were George Adams, John Edwards, Gabriel Madison, and Alex. Robertson.—[*Collins.*] He was the representative from Lincoln in 1794, and the senator from 1800 to 1806. General Hugh Logan married Sarah Woods, by whom he had many children—Campbell, Cyrus, Green, Allen, Mary D., Sarah, and Jennie Logan. After the troubles with the Indians had ceased, he pursued the vocation of a farmer upon a large body of land he owned near the little village of Turnersville, about four miles west of Stanford, in Lincoln. All of his children married and left issue. Campbell married a Miss Hart, of Kentucky, removed to Missouri, there died, and there and in other states of the South-west his numerous respectable posterity live; of these, Dr. Birch Logan and Mrs. Sarah Hart reside in St. Louis. Green Logan married a Miss McRoberts, of Kentucky; and he, too, removed to Missouri, and his descendants live in that state. Cyrus Logan married Mahala Lewis; they lived and died in Lincoln county. Allen Logan married, first, a Miss Givens; and, second, the widow Green, whose maiden name was Barnett. He lived and died on a large farm in Lincoln. He had thirteen children—Allen, who was a merchant, and died in Missouri; Alphonzo, a merchant, who died in Texas of wounds received while fighting in the Confederate service at Murfreesboro; Hugh was a soldier in the Mexican War, is a merchant, and is living; Samuel was a fillibuster in Walker's expedition in Nicaragua, and is now a farmer in Illinois; Dr. P. W. Logan was a surgeon in the Nineteenth Kentucky Union Infantry, was afterward surgeon of Colonel Robert Johnson's (son of President Johnson) Tennessee Union regiment, was subsequently a partner of the able Dr. John Craig, in Stanford, and is now a very successful physician in Knoxville, Tennessee. General Hugh Logan's daughter, Mary D., married Robert Lewis. His daughter, Sarah, married Ezra Morrison. And his daughter, Jennie, married George Carpenter, and lived and died at Carpenter's Station, near Hustonville,

Lincoln county. One of the daughters of Mrs. Jennie Carpenter married Sowell Givens, who lives in Lincoln, near the Boyle line. The descendants of General Hugh Logan are as respectable as they are numerous. Some of them have been prominent in the professions; others have been successful as farmers and as men of business; they are all worthy, solid, substantial citizens, and their intermarriages have been with people of good character and station. In this connection it should be stated that the ground on which the First Presbyterian Church in Stanford was built was given for the purpose by General Ben. Logan, and so was the ground of the Old Buffalo Spring Church and burial-ground.

NATHANIEL LOGAN.

Of the fourth son of David and Jane Logan—Nathaniel— very little can be ascertained beyond the fact that he was one of the early pioneers, was a brave Indian fighter, and aided his brothers, the McClures, Montgomerys, Whitleys, and others, in the settlement and defense of Lincoln. One of his grandsons—a Mr. Fish—was for many years clerk of the Circuit Court of Rockcastle county.

THE BRIGGS.

Sarah, one of the daughters of David Logan—the emigrant from Ireland—and sister of General Ben., Colonel John, Hugh, and Nathaniel Logan, married Samuel Briggs, in Virginia, but whether in the neighborhood in which the family had settled, in Augusta, or on the Holston, where General Ben. and Colonel John Logan had located before coming to Kentucky, can not now be definitely asserted. Wherever they were married, it is certain that before their own migration to Lincoln county, Kentucky, they had for years resided on the Holston, and that there their children were born. The name of Samuel Briggs is found, with those of General Ben. Logan, General Wm. Campbell, Colonel Wm. Christian, the McClures, Montgomerys, Davidsons, Trimbles, Gambles, Craigs, and Alexander Breckinridge, on the list of those who called

Rev. Charles Cummings to the pastorate "of the united congregations of the Ebbing and Sinking Spring Churches, on Holston's river, Fincastle county"—the first churches ever organized in all that region.—[*Foote.*] He probably came with his family to Kentucky, together with the family of General Logan, early in 1776, and for a time lived at St. Asaphs, near Stanford. It is certain that when General Logan removed his family to the protection of the fort at Harrodsburg, his brother-in-law, Samuel Briggs, and his sister, Sarah, went with them; and that when Logan returned to brave all danger at St. Asaphs, Briggs remained at Harrodsburg; but, after Logan had built his fort, and gathered his soldiers around him, Mr. Briggs went thither with his family, and took his part in the defense of the station and in the early settlement of the country. His name, and that of his son, Benjamin Briggs, are found in the list of the ninety-nine soldiers of Logan's company. He was a good soldier and a true man—a fighting Presbyterian,—and beyond this, not much remains to be told of him or his wife. Of their children, the names of Hannah, Betsey, Benjamin, and Jane were preserved and handed down. The son, a good soldier, married, and, having issue, carried on the male line. Hannah married Hugh Logan, the son of John Logan, who removed from Botetourt county, Virginia, to Lincoln, in 1791. It is not known exactly who this John Logan, of Botetourt, was; nor how he was related, if at all, to General Ben. Logan. It is surmised that he was one of the sons of the James Logan who settled in Augusta at the same time as David, and who is believed to have been David's brother;—that John was a brother of the James Logan who married the daughter of the Presbyterian preacher, Irvine,—from which James so many Presbyterian ministers came. One of the daughters of this John Logan, of Botetourt (whose wife was also one of the Mc-Clures), married Samuel Davidson—an elder brother of Colonel James and Colonel Michael Davidson, who married Ballengers. Samuel Davidson and his wife removed to Illinois in 1824, and in that state their sons became promi-

nent politicians. Elizabeth Logan, another daughter of
John, of Botetourt, married John Paxton (son of Captain
John Paxton, who was wounded at Guilford, and a nephew
of Isabella Paxton, who married Captain John Lyle, and
was the mother of the wife of Colonel James McDowell,
of Fayette; and a first cousin of James A. Paxton, who
married Maria Marshall). Prof. James Love, of Liberty,
Missouri, is the grandson of this John Paxton and Elizabeth Logan. Another daughter of John, of Botetourt—
Nancy Logan—married William Paxton (a brother of the
above John), and their oldest daughter—Mary Ann—was
the wife of John L. Ballenger, as already stated. Elizabeth Paxton, daughter of William Paxton and Nancy
Logan, married Jackson Givens, of Lincoln county; and
Isabella Paxton, another daughter, married R. W. Givens,
of Boyle. The Hugh Logan (son of John, of Botetourt)
who married Hannah Briggs, to distinguish him from
others of the same given name was called "Tall Hugh."
They had seven children, all of whom are dead except
James, who lives in Missouri. One of the daughters of
"Tall Hugh" by a second wife was the wife of James
B. Mason, of Garrard county. Betsey Briggs, another
daughter of Sam. Briggs and Sarah Logan, is said to have
died single.

Jane Briggs married Levi Todd, in the fort of St.
Asaphs, in Lincoln county, February 25, 1779. This is
the account preserved in the family of the late Robert S.
Todd, one of her sons. The record of John T. Stuart,
one of her grandsons, says that the given name of the
Briggs who married Sarah Logan was Benjamin; that it
was their daughter Elizabeth who married Levi Todd, and
that the wedding took place at Harrodsburg. The last is
evidently erroneous, as the Briggs family, at the time of
the marriage, were residents of St. Asaphs, then a fortified station defended by strong arms and brave hearts.
Whether the wedding was at Harrod's, or at Logan's, and
whether the bride was Jane or Betsey, we may be sure
there were no engraved cards tied with silken ribbons to
bid the guests to the wedding feast, no tables decked with

silver plate emblazoned with coats-of-arms, no guest arrayed in immodest gown bought from some man mantua-
maker in Paris. There was no printing press, much less
an engraver, within hundreds of miles. Those shrewd
men and heroic women, to whom our people are indebted
for most that is either good or powerful in them, were too
seriously grappling with the stern realities of life to think
or dream of the lying vanities paraded in most American
armorial bearings. And it is the boast of the sensible
descendants of fair Jenny or Betsey Briggs, that with her
own brisk hands she spun and wove her wedding-dress
from the fiber of the wild cotton weed. The men who witnessed the exchange of vows knew that at any moment
they might be ordered to march; the women, that at
break of day they might bid their loved ones a last farewell. No shoddy nor pinchbeck was *there;* nor any shabby
imitation of the coarse profusion of an intrinsically vulgar
English squirearchy.

What is known of the antecedents of this family of

Todds,

is most honorable. Of the Covenanters captured at Bothwell
Brigg, two hundred and fifty were sentenced to be transported to America; and two hundred of these were
drowned in the shipwreck of the vessel conveying them—
off Orkney. They had been shut up below the hatches of
the ship by the orders of Paterson, the cruel merchant
who had contracted for their transportation and sale.
Fifty escaped and afterward took part in the defense of Londonderry.—[*Waddell.*] Among those who were drowned,
were Robert Todd, of Fenwick, and James Todd, of Dun-
bar. Nothing is known but the sameness of the name of
Robert Todd, of Fenwick, and the hereditary name of
Robert in the family of Levi Todd, to indicate a connexion between them. In 1679—the year in which Robert Todd, of Fenwick, was drowned—John Todd fled
from the persecutions of Claverhouse in Scotland to find
refuge in the North of Ireland. The record of Mrs. Ben.
Hardin Helm describes John Todd, the refugee, as a

" Scottish Laird," and that means simply that he owned
land in fee and was a landlord, and not at all that he belonged to or was allied with the nobility. Two of his
grandsons, Andrew and Robert Todd, came with their
families to America in 1737. Of these two, Robert Todd
was born in Ireland in 1697, died in Montgomery county,
Pennsylvania, in 1775, and was buried in the churchyard
of the Providence Presbyterian Church. His first wife,
whose name is supposed to have been Smith, died and
was buried in Ireland. In Ireland, he married, for a second wife, Isabella, sister of Major William Bodley. The
mother of Isabella and General Wm. Bodley was a Parker, a name which belongs to many families of note in
Pennsylvania. By his first wife, Robert Todd—the emigrant—had two sons, John and David. By the second
wife, he had five sons and four daughters—William, Andrew, Robert, Samuel, Levi, Elizabeth, Mary, Rebecca,
and Sarah. The last named married John Findlay, or
Finley, of whom the record says only that he " went west-
ward." He was not identical with the John Finley
who, in 1773, came to Kentucky with Thompson's surveying party, discovered the Upper Blue Lick Spring, in
Nicholas county, where, after fighting himself up to the
rank of major in the Revolution, he settled when the war
had ended. John Todd, the oldest son of Robert (the
emigrant) by his first wife, graduated at Princeton in
1749, a member of the second class admitted to a degree
by that institution; was licensed by the New Brunswick
Presbytery in the following year, and was ordained by the
same body in 1751. He then went to Virginia on the invitation of Rev. Samuel Davies, whom he assisted in min-
istering to the several congregations of which that patriotic divine was the pastor. Parson Todd for many years
taught a classical school in Virginia. Taking an active
interest in the early settlement of Kentucky, his great solicitude was to provide for the educational and religious
wants of the emigrants. He used his influence to obtain
from the Virginia Legislature the charter for Transylvania

14

Seminary, which was opened at the house of his friend, David Rice, in February, 1785, and it was he who gave to that institution the first library ever brought to Kentucky. Though it is not known that he ever came in person to Kentucky, no account of the early times in the state will be satisfactory that does not commemorate his zeal and his virtues. John Todd, son of the parson, became a Presbyterian preacher, lived for a time in Paris, and then removed to Indiana. One of the daughters of the parson married her cousin, General Robert Todd, and was the mother of the wife of General Wm. O. Butler, and of Judge Levi Todd, and General Thomas Todd, of Indiana.

Mary, the oldest daughter of Robert Todd—the emigrant—married James Parker; they had four sons and four daughters.

Elizabeth, another daughter of Robert Todd—the emigrant—married Robert Parker, brother of the above James. They had a son and a daughter. The daughter married General Andrew Porter; a daughter of General Porter married her cousin, Robert Parker, settled in Lexington, Kentucky, and was the grandmother of the wife of President Lincoln. After the death of Robert Parker, his widow, Elizabeth Todd, married Arthur McFarland, by whom she had four children.

David Todd—second son of Robert, the emigrant—was born in Ireland, April 8, 1723; when a child, was brought by his father to Pennsylvania; lived there, as a farmer, in the Providence township of Montgomery county until 1783, when he came to Kentucky. His sons—John, Robert, and Levi—had preceded him to Kentucky, and John had already been killed at the Blue Licks. His youngest son, Owen Todd (who settled in Ohio), and his daughter, Hannah (who married Elijah Smith), came with him. So, too, came his brother-in-law, James Parker, and his sister Mary. David Todd died in Fayette county, February 8, 1785. His wife, whom he married in Pennsylvania, was Hannah Owen, of Welsh descent and a Quakeress. They had four sons and two daughters—John, Robert, Levi, Owen, Elizabeth and Hannah.

The oldest son of David Todd and Hannah Owen—John—was educated in Virginia by his uncle, Parson John Todd, studied law, and became one of the deputy surveyors employed by Colonel William Preston. He is asserted by John Mason Brown to have been an aide to General Andrew Lewis in the battle of Point Pleasant. He came to Kentucky early in 1775, and was at St. Asaphs with John Floyd and General Logan in the spring of that year. He represented St. Asaphs in the abortive attempt to establish the territorial government of Transylvania. In 1777, he was one of the first two burgesses sent by Kentucky county to the Virginia General Assembly. He succeeded George Rogers Clarke in command at Kaskaskia, and was for several years civil governor and colonel of the county of Illinois. When Bryant's Station was besieged, in August, 1782, Colonel Todd was again in Kentucky. With such men as could be assembled at Lexington, and with the forces of Boonesboro and Harrodsburg, he marched, without waiting for General Logan with the well-equipped veteran fighters of Lincoln, and fell at the Blue Licks. While a burgess at Richmond he married Jane Hawkins, by whom he had a daughter. This daughter married, first, Colonel Russell, and after his death became the second wife of Robert Wickliffe, Sr. Her son by Russell dying, she made a deed of gift to her second husband by which all the large estate of Colonel John Todd passed to the family of Mr. Wickliffe, to the exclusion of those of her own blood. Mildred Hawkins, a sister of Jane, married Captain Pierce Butler of the Revolution, and was the mother of Major Thomas L., General William O., and Richard Butler, of Carrollton, and of the late Pierce Butler, of Louisville. Colonel John Todd was the best educated and most accomplished, and is represented to have been the most richly endowed by nature, of all the early pioneers and surveyors of Kentucky.

Robert, second son of David Todd and Hannah Owen, was well educated at the school of his uncle, Parson John Todd, whose daughter he married; then studied law in

Virginia, it is said in the office of General Andrew Lewis; came early to Kentucky; was sent as a burgess to the Virginia Legislature before the separation; was a member of the Danville convention of 1785; was an elector of the senate, and a senator, in 1792; was a lot-owner in Lexington in 1783; was wounded in the defense of McClellan's fort, now Georgetown, in 1776; continued to be an active and brave soldier all through the troubles with the Indians, and was often intrusted with important commands; and was, for many years after the state was established, a judge of the Circuit Court of the Fayette District.—[*Collins.*] It has been stated that one of his daughters married General Wm. O. Butler. Judge Levi and Colonel Thomas Todd, of Indiana, and the late Dr. John Todd, of Danville, were his sons.

Levi, third son of David Todd and Hannah Owen, was born in Pennsylvania in 1756; was educated with his elder brothers in Virginia, with them studied law, became a surveyor, came early to Kentucky, and at first seems to have been one of the defenders of the fort at Harrodsburg; afterward he assisted Logan to hold St. Asaphs. He was stationed at St. Asaphs when he married Jane or Betsey Briggs. Afterward, he fortified Todd's Station, in Jessamine, whence he removed to Lexington, where he was a purchaser at the first sale of lots in 1781. He was clerk of the first court of quarter sessions held in Harrodsburg, in the spring of 1777—[*McClung*]; was a member of both the Danville conventions of 1785, and of that of 1787. When Fayette county was formed, he was appointed its first clerk, and held the office until his death in 1807. He was a lieutenant under George Rogers Clarke in the successful expedition against Kaskaskia and Vincennes; was with Logan in the attack upon the Indian town when Bowman's panic thwarted the well-concerted plan; was major of Logan's Lincoln county regiment, and participated in two other expeditions against the Indians of Ohio and Indiana; and was a major in the hottest of the fight at Blue Licks, where his gallant and gifted brother fell. Afterward, he became a brigadier and then a major-general. Those military titles were won by actual service; his reputation was secured by real and hard fighting. A solid, substantial, enterprising citizen; a sensible, intelligent, well-educated man; a consistent Presbyterian; a valuable and faithful public servant; a good soldier;—of course he was respected at a time when those qualities were most useful and honored. General Levi Todd and Jane or Betsey Briggs were the parents of eleven children—Hannah, Elizabeth, John, Nancy, David, Ann Maria, Robert S., Jane, Margaret, Roger North, and Samuel. After the death of his first wife, General Todd married, secondly, Mrs. Tatum, by whom he had a son— James—the father of Dr. L. B. Todd, of Lexington.

1. Elizabeth, second child of General Levi Todd, married Charles Carr, of Fayette—son to Walter Carr, who was a member of the convention of 1799, and was several times in the legislature. They had twelve children, whose descendants live in Fayette and Missouri. Their son, Charles Carr, a lawyer, was for years judge of the Fayette County court—a Union man; his wife was a Miss Didlake. Their daughter, Mary Ellen Carr, married Alfred Young; one of her daughters is the wife of Charles S. Brent, of Lexington.

2. Dr. John, third child of General Levi Todd, married Elizabeth Smith. One of their daughters, Elizabeth Todd, is the widow of Rev. John H. Brown, of Illinois. Another daughter of Dr. John Todd—Fanny—was the first wife of Thomas H. Shelby, a grandson of the governor; and John Todd Shelby, of Lexington, is her son. This Dr. John Todd lived in Springfield, Illinois.

3. The fourth child of General Levi Todd—Nancy—married her cousin, Dr. John Todd, a son of General Robert Todd, and a brother of General Wm. O. Butler's wife. David was the only one of her sons who had issue. His wife was a Miss Hicks. Dr. Todd lived for many years in Danville, Kentucky.

4. David, fifth child of General Levi Todd, married Eliza Barr, settled in Missouri, and had eight children :— Rebecca married Samuels; Ann married Campbell; Rob-

ert married Miss Brigham; William married Miss Semmes; Letitia married her cousin, Edwin Breck; the others died single.

5. Jane Briggs Todd, eighth child of General Levi, married Judge Daniel Breck—a native of Massachusetts, the son of a Presbyterian clergyman who was a chaplain in the army of the Revolution, and was with Montgomery in the assault upon Quebec. Daniel Breck graduated at Dartmouth in 1812; settled in Richmond, Kentucky, in 1814, and by his own energy, force of character, and talents, won his way to the head of the bar of that section of the state; he was five times sent to the legislature, where he was prominent in promoting works of internal improvement; was appointed a judge of the court of appeals in 1843, and during the six years of his incumbency of the position, had the reputation of being one of the ablest of the justices of that court; resigned, in 1849, to make a successful race for Congress, and in the memorable struggle of 1850 over the compromise measures, was a staunch ally of Mr. Clay and of the Fillmore administration. He died in 1871, aged eighty-three years. He was married to Jane Briggs Todd in 1819. They had eight children—Ann Maria married Dr. Ramsey, and Daniel married Miss Ramsey; Edwin married his cousin, Letitia Todd; Elizabeth married Judge William McDowell, son of Hon. Joseph Jefferson McDowell, of Ohio, and grandson of Colonel Joseph McDowell, of the Quaker Meadows, North Carolina—" Fighting Joe;" Charles H. Breck married Miss Ford, and was county judge of Madison. Rev. Robert L. Breck is the fifth and ablest of the children of Judge Daniel Breck; a graduate of Centre College, and of the Princeton Theological Seminary, he possesses the faculty of organization, and is a preacher of more than ordinary ability. He was conspicuous, and made himself felt, in the movements that led to the establishment of the Independent Synod of Kentucky, since merged in the southern branch of the Presbyterian Church; to his zeal, efficiency, energy, and weight, more than to any other man, Central University is indebted for its establishment. His

temper and talents are both essentially aggressive—combative; by no one is he to be despised as an antagonist. A fine parliamentarian, and wielding an adroit and incisive pen, in an ecclesiastical controversy he never fails to develop the hard-hitting qualities of his sharp-shooting ancestors.

6. Roger North Todd, tenth child of General Levi, married Miss Ferguson. They had eight children. Their son, Robert L. Todd, married, first, Sallie Hall, a daughter of Rev. Nathan K. Hall, an eminent Presbyterian divine. The mother of Sallie Hall was a daughter of Colonel William Pope, one of the first settlers at the Falls of the Ohio, and a sister of General John Pope; her first husband was the Captain Trotter who charged at Mississinewa. After the death of this first wife, Mr. Todd married, secondly, Martha Edwards, daughter of Dr. Ben. Edwards, of St. Louis, whose wife was a daughter of Willis Green, of Lincoln county, Kentucky.

7. The best known of the children of General Levi Todd and Jane or Betsey Briggs was the seventh—Robert Smith Todd, who was born near Lexington, February 25, 1791, and died July 15, 1849. When about thirty years old, he was elected clerk of the Kentucky House of Representatives, and, by successive elections, held the position for twenty years; he was then three times elected representative from Fayette; in 1845, was elected to the state senate, and was a candidate for re-election when he died. He was president of the Lexington branch of the Bank of Kentucky from its establishment, in 1836, until his death.— [*Collins.*] Not a man of brilliant talents, but one of clear and strong mind, sound judgment, exemplary life and conduct, dignified and manly bearing; an influential and useful citizen. He was twice married. First, to his near relative, Eliza Ann Parker, a granddaughter of General Andrew Porter. They had eight children:—Elizabeth married Ninian W. Edwards, a leading lawyer of Springfield, Illinois, and a son of Ninian W. Edwards, who was governor of the Illinois Territory, and afterward of the state; Mary was the wife of President Abraham Lincoln, and

mother of Robert Todd Lincoln, secretary of war; Levi married Louisa Searles, of Lexington; Dr. George R. C. married Miss Curry, of Cynthiana; Frances married Dr. William Wallace, of Springfield, Illinois; Margaret married Charles H. Kellogg, of Cincinnati, Ohio. After the death of his first wife, Robert S. Todd married Elizabeth Humphreys, daughter of Dr. Alexander Humphreys, of Staunton, Virginia,—the preceptor of Dr. Ephraim McDowell, of Danville. Her mother was a daughter of Rev. John Brown, and granddaughter of John Preston. By this wife, Mr. Todd had eight children:—Samuel B. was killed in the Confederate ranks at Shiloh; David, a Confederate soldier, was shot through the lungs at the siege of Vicksburg, and died after the surrender; Alexander was killed at the battle of Baton Rouge; Catharine Bodley married W. W. Herr; Martha married C. B. White, of Alabama; and Elodie married Colonel N. H. R. Dawson, of Selma, in the same state,—now the United States Commissioner of Education, at Washington.

Emilie Todd, the fourth child of Robert S. Todd by his second wife, married the late General Ben. Hardin Helm— a son of John L. Helm. The latter was born in Hardin county in 1802; in local state affairs, he was one of the most prominent men of his generation, and in practical usefulness in the development of the material resources of Kentucky was surpassed by no other man. John L. Helm preferred to devote his attention to the material interests of the people and of the commonwealth, rather than to the discussion of national issues. Eleven times he was elected from Hardin to the house of representatives, his terms of service extending from 1826 to 1843, and five times was chosen speaker of that body. He was elected to the senate 1844–48. During the time he was in the legislature, the system of internal improvements was commenced and prosecuted; the turnpikes built, which preceded the railroads, and the slackwater navigation pushed forward; the Louisville and Lexington railroad constructed;—all by the aid of the state. Of all these measures, which added greatly to the wealth of Kentucky, Mr.

Helm was an earnest, an influential, and a sagacious advocate. His services to the state in shaping the laws and devising the means for meeting the large expenditures incurred, in creating the board of commissioners of the sinking fund, and providing for the extinguishment of the large debt entailed by this wise policy, were highly important. In 1849 Mr. Helm was elected lieutenant-governor of the state, in which capacity he presided over the senate. He opposed the system of an elective judiciary incorporated into the constitution of 1850. When Mr. Crittenden resigned the governorship, in 1850, to accept a place in Mr. Fillmore's cabinet as attorney-general, Mr. Helm succeeded him and filled out his term. He built the Louisville and Nashville railroad. At a time of great monetary stringency, when all similar enterprises in the state had failed or had been sacrificed to the mortgagees, and when a similar fate seemed awaiting the corporation of which he was the president, it was his invincible will, his unquailing grit, his indomitable energy, his signal capacity for affairs, and the public confidence in his ability and integrity, that averted the disaster, pushed the road through to completion, and saved it to the stockholders. Others reaped the benefit of his labors, but simple justice to a capable and bold man demands that it be stated, that to John L. Helm, and not to James Guthrie, belongs the credit of triumphant success in the initial step in the material development of Southern Kentucky—the construction of the railway which renders so much of the South tributary to Louisville. He was indeed a useful, vigorous, clear-headed man, with a natural turn for practical affairs. In 1865, Mr. Helm was again elected to the state senate, and served until 1867. In the latter year, he was the candidate for governor chosen by the re-organized Democracy, and after a canvass of the state in which he exhibited mental faculties unimpaired by advancing years, was elected by a very large majority. The strain upon his physical strength produced by his exertions, brought on a spell of sickness which prevented him from going to Frankfort to be inaugurated. Consequently, that ceremony was performed at his residence, in Elizabethtown. In a few days thereafter, he died.

The wife of Governor Helm was Lucinda Barbour Hardin, one of the daughters of Ben. Hardin—a most trenchant public speaker, a master of the keenest satire and powerful invective, and, as a lawyer, not inferior to any man in Kentucky of his day. The father of Mr. Hardin had the same given name as his celebrated son; his mother was Sarah, sister of Colonel John Hardin; his father and mother were full first cousins. When Magoffin sent in his first message to the legislature of 1859–60, much of its space was given to statistics by which it was attempted to show that the marriage of blood relatives was productive of insanity and idiocy in their offspring, and urging the general assembly to enact laws prohibitory of such marriages. Immediately thereafter, a communication appeared in the "Frankfort Commonwealth," denouncing the proposed attempt to cast such a slur upon the thousands of reputable people of the state who were children of blood relatives, ridiculing the arguments of the governor, and offering to produce two instances of the marriages of first cousins belonging to two of the most intellectual families in the state, in which the offspring were the very most intellectual members of those families; and asserting the ability of the writer to find children of first cousins in Kentucky whom the public would readily pronounce, one for one, superior to the governor, and to every one who defended his position. One of the persons referred to, was Ben. Hardin—the "Old Kitchen Knife," as John Randolph styled him. The communication created an uproar of laughter at Magoffin and defeated the measure. It was written by Rev. Dr. Robt. J. Breckinridge.

Ben. Hardin's wife was the sister of Major James Barbour, of Danville—an officer in the War of 1812—and a daughter of Ambrose Barbour, a Virginian who emigrated at an early day to Kentucky. Ambrose was a son of James Barbour, one of the first vestrymen in St. Mark's Parish, Culpepper county, Virginia. James—a member of the Burgesses of 1764, son of the above

James, and brother of Ambrose—was the ancestor of the late John S. Barbour, the brilliant congressman, and of the present John S. Barbour, president of the Virginia Midland Railroad. Thomas—another son of James, the vestryman, and brother of Ambrose—represented Orange in the Burgesses in 1775. This Thomas Barbour married Isabella Thomas, daughter of Richard Thomas and Isabella Pendleton; the latter was the daughter of Philip Pendleton, the ancestor of the distinguished families in Virginia, Ohio, and the South, of that name. This Thomas Barbour and Isabella Thomas were the parents of Hon. Philip Pendleton Barbour, speaker of Congress and of the Virginia convention of 1829–30, and an associate justice of the United States Supreme Court; and of James Barbour, the able and distinguished governor of Virginia, United States senator, minister to England, and secretary of war. The latter was the father of the late Ben. Johnson Barbour. Ambrose Barbour, who came to Kentucky, married Catherine Thomas, sister of the above Isabella, and they were the parents of Major James Barbour, of Danville, and of Ben. Hardin's wife. Major Barbour and Mrs. Hardin were double first cousins of Judge and Governor Barbour. Major Barbour married the daughter of Willis Green, of Lincoln; they were the parents of James Barbour, of Maysville, and Rev. Dr. Lewis Green Barbour, of Central University.

General Ben. Hardin Helm—grandson of Ben. Hardin and Miss Barbour, and son of Governor John L. Helm and Lucinda Barbour Hardin—was born in Hardin county, June 2, 1831; was for a time a pupil at the military school near Frankfort, but, after a brief stay there, entered West Point, from which institution he graduated in 1851; then served several months on the frontier as a second lieutenant in the regular army. Resigning his commission, he graduated at the Louisville Law School, in 1853, and was for several months a student in the law department of Harvard. He was elected to the state legislature from Hardin in 1855, and during the session met with Emilie Todd, whom he married shortly after the adjournment, in

1856. In August of the latter year, he was elected commonwealth attorney for the Hardin district. Having tendered his services to the Confederate government, in September, 1861, he was commissioned as colonel of the First Kentucky Confederate Cavalry, and covered the retreat from Bowling Green. In February, 1862, he was brigaded with the Kentucky infantry, at Murfreesboro, under General Breckinridge. About that time he " was assigned to the Third Brigade of the Reserve Corps; in July, 1862, took command of the Second Brigade of that corps; was wounded in an engagement, August 5th; after recovery, commanded the post at Chattanooga; subsequently, was placed in command of the Eastern District of the Gulf Department; in February, 1863, took charge of the Kentucky brigade in Breckinridge's division; was actively engaged in the arduous campaign soon after passed through by his brigade; and, in the battle of Chickamauga, fell mortally wounded, September 20, 1863; and, at midnight of that day, breathed his last."—[*Biographical Encyclopedia of Kentucky.*] General Helm was tall and symmetrically formed; his countenance was pleasing; his address winning. He was not an orator, but was a fluent, an interesting and forcible speaker. A fine specimen of a Kentuckian, his record as a soldier was highly honorable; his death one that a soldier who feels his cause to be just right willingly meets. General Helm and Emilie Todd had a son and several daughters. Mrs. Emilie Helm is living in Elizabethtown, and to her the writer is indebted for the facts concerning her Todd ancestors.

THE STUARTS.

Hannah, the oldest daughter of General Levi Todd and Jane (or Betsey) Briggs, was born in the fort at Harrodsburg; the precise date of her birth is unknown to the writer, but it was probably in the year 1780. Contemporary description represents her to have been of unusual beauty of face and person in her youth, and, in maturer years, as a woman of uncommon force of character. In the early bloom of womanhood, she became the wife of Rev. Robert Stuart, a native of Virginia.

The name of Stuart supports the family tradition that their ancestor emigrated from Scotland to Ireland; it is not improbable that he was one of the colonists induced to locate in the latter country by Montgomery and Hamilton. His descendant, Archibald Stuart, married, in Ireland, Janet Brown, sister of Rev. John Brown, who was the father of the first United States Senator from Kentucky. Archibald Stuart emigrated to Pennsylvania in 1727, and thence to Augusta county in 1738. Major Alexander Stuart (who was captured, unwounded, at Guilford) was his son. Judge Archibald Stuart was the son of Major Alexander Stuart by his first wife, Mary Patterson; and Hon. A. H. H. Stuart was one of the sons of Judge Archibald. It has already been stated that Major Alexander Stuart married, for a second wife, the widow Paxton, whose maiden name was Mary Moore, and who belonged to the Rutherford-Alliene-Walker breed from which came Dr. John P. Campbell, the McPheeters, the Browns (sons of Rev. Samuel Brown), the wife of Rev. Robert Logan, and so many other Presbyterian ministers. It has been stated also that Judge Alexander Stuart was the son of Major Alexander Stuart by this second wife; that Hon. Archibald Stuart, of Patrick—an officer of the War of 1812, an able lawyer, and eloquent orator—was a son of Judge Archibald Stuart; and that General James Ewell Brown Stuart—the Murat of the Confederacy—was the son of Hon. Archibald Stuart, of Patrick. The history of this branch of the Stuarts is stated at greater detail in Peyton's " History of Augusta County."

Some time after 1740, Archibald Stuart (husband of Janet Brown) was followed to the Valley by two younger brothers—John and David. The latter was the ancestor of the Stuarts of South Carolina. The former—John Stuart—must not be confounded with the John Stuart who came over with Dinwiddie, married the widow Paul (Jane Linn), and was the father of Colonel John Stuart, of Greenbrier. The men were different, the families in this country distinct. The John Stuart to whom reference is now made settled in Augusta county, in what is now Rockbridge, was a member of the Timber Ridge congregation, and married a Miss Walker, of the Rutherford-Alliene-Walker family—the family of preaching talents—of Walker's creek. Many of his descendants still live in that vicinity. One of the sons of this John Stuart and Miss Walker—Robert Stuart—was born on Walker's creek, August 14, 1772. The Stuarts were fighters. The Walkers were fighters with preaching tendencies; when their descendants were not taking a lively hand in a fight, they were generally preaching or marrying preachers. Robert Stuart's talents sent him to the pulpit. He was well educated at Liberty Hall, under Dr. Graham, where he was a fellow-student with Dr. George A. Baxter, who succeeded Graham as principal of that academy, and succeeded John Holt Rice in the Union Theological Seminary. His theological training was received at Hampden Sidney. After preaching in Virginia several years, he came to Kentucky before the beginning of the nineteenth century. On the amalgamation of the Transylvania Seminary with the Kentucky Academy, under the title of Transylvania University, in 1798, he was selected as one of the first three professors of the latter institution, and held the position of professor of languages a number of years. For more than half a century, he filled the pulpits of the churches at Walnut Hill, in Fayette county, and at Salem, Clarke county. The degree of doctor of divinity that was conferred upon him was merited by his learning and long service. He died at the age of eighty-four years. His wife, Hannah Todd, died in 1832. They had seven children: 1. Mary Jane Stuart married Daniel B. Price, long the clerk of the Circuit Court of Jessamine. She is still living with her son, Dan. B. Price, in Versailles. Her son, Robert S. Price, resides in Jessamine. Her daughter, Eliza, married Mr. Hemphill, and lives in the same county. Louisa Price married Mr. Berryman. 2. Eliza A. Stuart married Dr. Steele, the Presbyterian minister of Hillsboro, Ohio; she died in 1884, aged seventy-nine years.

3. David Stuart was a Presbyterian minister, and long the principal of a female academy in Shelbyville, Kentucky. He married a Miss Winchester. His son, Winchester H. Stuart, married his kinswoman, Nettie Chinn; they live in Shelbyville. The other children of Rev. Robert Stuart were: 4, Hon. John Todd; 5, Robert; 6, Samuel; and 7, Margaret.

HON. JOHN TODD STUART.

John Todd Stuart was born near Lexington, Kentucky, November 10, 1807; was educated at Centre College and Transylvania; studied law under Judge Daniel Breck, who had married his aunt; was licensed by judges of the court of appeals. In October, 1828, he removed to Springfield, Illinois, there entered upon the practice of his profession, and there continued to reside until his death, on the 28th of November, 1885. In 1832, he was elected to the legislature of that state. "He had so grown in the confidence and attachment of the people that there was a pressing demand for his services, although he had only attained the age of twenty-five years. . . . Mr. Stuart soon took high rank with his associates, and challenged their esteem and admiration."—[*Judge David Davis.*] He was re-elected to that body, 1834–35; it was largely owing to his advocacy that the aid of the state was extended to the construction of the Illinois and Michigan canal, which gave the first great impulse to the growth of Chicago. "I do not believe there was any other man in the state who could have successfully overcome the combined and opposing obstacles arrayed against the measure."—[*Judge Goodrich.*] Abraham Lincoln was a member of the lower house of the legislature of 1834–36. Said Judge Davis, in his address before the Illinois Bar Association:

"The part which Stuart took in shaping Lincoln's destiny is not generally known outside of the circle of their immediate friends. They lodged at the same house, and occupied the same bed, during the session of the legislature. Both were Whigs in politics, and trusted friends, and each estimated aright the abilities of the other. Both were honest men with deep convictions, and appreciated by their fellow-members. The one was liberally educated and a lawyer; the other, uneducated, and engaged in the humble occupation of a land surveyor. Stuart saw at once that there must be a change of occupation to give Lincoln a fair start in life, and that the study and practice of the law were necessary to stimulate his ambition, and develop his faculties. When the subject was introduced, it appeared that Lincoln had never entertained the idea of becoming a lawyer, and stated difficulties which he deemed insurmountable. These Stuart overcame, and Lincoln agreed to give the matter a thoughtful consideration. The result was that he yielded to Stuart's solicitations, and read law at his country home, some distance from Springfield, under the directions of Stuart, and with books loaned by him for the purpose. On Lincoln's admission to the bar, Stuart formed a partnership with him, which continued, I think, until Stuart went to Congress. Every lawyer, and indeed every thoughtful and intelligent person, can readily see the influence which the choice of the legal profession had on Lincoln's life."

In 1836, Mr. Stuart was defeated for Congress by Colonel May, the Democratic candidate. Two years later, he defeated Stephen A. Douglas for a seat in the National House of Representatives. The campaign, which lasted five months, was arduous and exciting, the parties were thoroughly aroused, the heat of debate put the candidates on their metal and elicited their best powers. They were equally matched; Stuart won. In 1840, he achieved an easy victory over Judge Ralston, and in 1842 declined to run a third time. His successors were John J. Hardin, E. D. Baker, and Abraham Lincoln. From 1848 to 1852, Mr. Stuart was a member of the state senate, where his services were of the greatest importance, "placing him in the category of statesmen."—[*Davis.*] He was devoted to the Whig party while it lived. In the formation of the Republican party, Stuart thought he saw a standing menace to the peace and quiet of the country. In the contest of 1860, Mr. Stuart supported John Bell for President; after that, he acted with the Democratic party, but never considered himself a member of it. During the war, he did not approve the measures of the administration, and seemed to lose all hope, but his love of country did not diminish. In a letter to Governor Campbell, of Tennessee, a Union man, of date 14th February, 1863, he says: "I am for maintaining the Union without conditions, and at all hazards, and for preserving the integrity of our entire territory under the constitution, as our fathers made it." Again he says: "If we cease fighting in the present condition of the contest, it would be virtually a dissolution of the Union." This result, which he feared, he dreaded above all things. He deplored the war "as a mistake and crime on the part of the South." "The battle," in his opinion, "should have been fought at the ballot-box, under the Union and constitution." The whole letter breathes a spirit of fervent patriotism, but it is very despondent. Mr. Stuart re-entered Congress in 1862, defeating Leonard Swett, the Republican candidate. He did not take this step because he had any greater love than formerly for politics, but in the hope, as he tells Campbell, that he might "be instrumental in restoring the country to union, peace, and prosperity."

As a lawyer, it is sufficient to say of Hon. John Todd Stuart that he held his own with Davis, Lincoln, Douglas, Logan, Hardin, Baker, and men of like caliber. As a man, he was the personification of generosity. In the early days of Bloomington, when the Presbyterians of that place desired a lot he owned in that city upon which to erect a church, and were too poor to purchase it, he donated the lot, worth five hundred dollars, to the congregation, though he owned no other property there, and his own circumstances were limited. He was a brave man. While solicitous to give offense to no one, he allowed no person to infringe upon his rights, either as a lawyer or as a man—charming in the social circle, and devoted to his family and their comfort. His friendship was strong and enduring, and was equal to all demands made upon it. Besides, he was an honest and conscientious man, and discharged with fidelity every duty which the opportunities of life afforded him. Uniformly courteous in his intercourse with his fellow-men, of polished manners and com-

15

manding presence, he impressed all with whom he associated as one of nature's noblemen.

In October, 1837, John T. Stuart married Mary Virginia, daughter of General Francis Nash, a Virginian who had settled in St. Louis county, Missouri; her mother was a Miss Bland, of Eastern Virginia. General Nash was a great-nephew of the General Francis Nash who was killed in the battle of Germantown. Hon. Abner Nash and Judge Frederick Nash, of North Carolina, were his near kinsmen; the mother of Rev. Nash Legrand, and of Lucy Legrand—the wife of Major John McDowell—was his kinswoman. Mr. Stuart and Mary Virginia Nash were the parents of six children: 1. Betty, who was the first wife of C. C. Brown, of Springfield, Illinois. Their son, Stuart Brown, is a lawyer of that city. 2, John T.; 3, Frank; 4, Robert L.; 5, Virginia; and 6, Hannah Stuart.

THE McKINLEYS.

The other daughter of David and Jane Logan—sister of General Ben. and Colonel John—married Dr. Andrew McKinley, of Culpepper county, Virginia. She came with her husband to Lincoln county at an early day, and, like the others, found a refuge in St. Asaphs. Dr. McKinley died in Lincoln in 1786; his wife survived him. One of their daughters was the second wife of her cousin, David Logan, son of Colonel John and father of Hon. Stephen T. Logan; and the wife of Colonel L. T. Thurston, of Louisville, was the offspring of that marriage. Judge John McKinley, son of Dr. Andrew McKinley and Mary Logan, was born in Culpepper county in 1780. During the first year of the present century, he was admitted to the bar in Frankfort; he continued to practice law successfully in Kentucky until 1818. He then removed to Alabama. From that state he was elected, in 1826, to fill a vacancy in the United States Senate; at the end of the term was re-elected and served another. In 1833 he was elected a representative in Congress, and in 1837 was appointed associate justice of the United States Supreme Court. He discharged the responsible duties of the latter

position with fidelity and ability until his death, in 1852, in
the city of Louisville.—[*Biographical Encyclopedia of Kentucky.*] In person, Judge McKinley was tall, his figure robust, and presence commanding. In Alabama he married
Juliana Bryan. Their daughter married Alexander Pope
Churchill, who represented Jefferson in the legislature,
1839–50, and was colonel of a Kentucky regiment in the war
with Mexico. Colonel Churchill's daughter, Julia, married
D. A. January, of St. Louis. His second daughter, Mary
Moss, is the wife of her kinsman, Alexander Pope Humphrey, son of the eloquent divine and elegant scholar,
the late Dr. E. P. Humphrey, of Louisville; the son has
an enviable position at the Louisville bar, is a man of
scholarly attainments and brilliant talents. Andrew Mc-
Kinley, son of the judge, was register of the Kentucky
Land Office, 1855–59, and now resides in St. Louis. His
wife was a Miss Wilcox—daughter of Senator Crittenden's
third wife by her first husband. Mrs. Crittenden was a
daughter of Dr. James Moss. Her mother was a Miss
Woodson, granddaughter of Colonel John Woodson, of
Albemarle county, Virginia, whose wife was Dorothea,
daughter of Isham Randolph, of Dungeness, and sister of
President Jefferson's mother. One of Andrew McKinley's
daughters is the wife of St. John Boyle, of Louisville—
son of General J. T., and grandson of Judge John Boyle,
of the Kentucky Court of Appeals.

JOHN LOGAN, OF BOTETOURT.

Traditions preserved among various branches of the
Logan family represent the John Logan who came from
Botetourt to Lincoln county to have been a first cousin of
General Ben. Logan and his brothers; and, although there
is no known record evidence to sustain those traditions,
the personal resemblance of their descendants, the sameness of given names among them, and other circumstances,
contribute to verify their correctness. It is believed that
this John Logan was a son of the James Logan who was
a soldier from Augusta in the French and Indian War,
and a brother of the James Logan who married Hannah

Irvine, and was the ancestor of so many ministers; and
that the first-named James was a brother of David, the
father of General Ben. Logan.   Yet it may be, that this
John was a son of the John Logan who was a contribu-
ting member of Rev. John Brown's New Providence congregation in 1754, who was also a brother of David Logan.
This John Logan came to Lincoln after his kinsmen had
made their settlement in that county, was for many years
a ruling elder in the first Presbyterian Church in Stanford, and was buried in the Old Buffalo Presbyterian Cem-
etery.   His wife was Ann McClure, who was probably a
sister of Jane McClure, who married Colonel John Logan.
They had seven children : 1. William married Sally Hoskins.   2. Elizabeth married John Paxton; and Prof. James
Love, of Liberty, Missouri, is their grandson.   3. John
married Miss McKinley, probably a sister of Judge John
McKinley.   4. Mary married James Logan, of whom
hereafter.   5. Sarah married Samuel Davidson, an elder
brother of Colonel James Davidson.   6. Nancy married
William Paxton; and several families of Paxtons in Lincoln and in Missouri, as well as the families of R. W. and
Jackson Givens, of Lincoln, are her descendants.   7. Hugh
married his kinswoman, Hannah Briggs, and left many
descendants in Garrard, Lincoln, and Missouri; Miss Sa-
mantha Logan, of Louisville, is his granddaughter.

The James Logan who married John Logan's daughter,
Mary, was a native of Ireland, and if related to his wife
at all, they certainly had no common ancestor in America.
They had a number of children.   The late Gordon Logan,
of Shelbyville, was one of their sons, and Emmitt G.
Logan, the editor of the "Louisville Times," is one of
their grandsons.   The wife of Gordon Logan—Mary E.
Ballou—was a great-granddaughter of Rev. William Marshall, one of the most eloquent of the pioneer Baptist
ministers of Kentucky, and a younger brother of Colonel
Thomas Marshall; the wife of Rev. Wm. Marshall was
Mary Ann Pickett.   Emmitt G. Logan, and the sons of
his brother Ben., who died at Hopkinsville some months

since, are said to be the only descendants of James and
Mary Logan who bear the name.

What has been here written relates to a Presbyterian
family of plain people; not to the rich, nor to the fashion-
able, still less to the aristocratic,—as a grotesque combination of pretension, innate coarseness, opaque dullness and
illiteracy, is sometimes called by those in this country who
do not exactly understand the terms they employ. None
of them lived in a "palatial residence;" not one of them
was ever "in the swim," nor sought to be in it; they had
not that peculiar and indefinable sort of "social position"
which the weak ascribe to mere wealth, and which rarely
survives a second generation. The standing they had
among their neighbors, and wherever any of them lived,
was theirs by birthright, and came without scuffling; it
was of the kind that people of sense all over the world
concede to mental vigor and moral worth, and was only
the natural recognition by others of their possession of
these qualities and of their public services. The progenitors of these people in Virginia and in Kentucky were
eminently respectable and intelligent, types of the race by
which the Valley of Virginia was peopled, and of the
early Kentucky pioneers;—high types, it is true, but not
the less surely types of the Scotch-Irish Presbyterians who
settled that Valley, who were the leading, aggressive spirits in the earliest colonization of Kentucky, and who impressed their mental characteristics and martial ardor
upon the generations which followed them. The facts
show how, in this blessed land, unaided save by their own
talents and energies, the most unassuming may rise to the
highest offices of the state; and that, when the descendants of such a race stand firmly by the sound principles of
morality and religion transmitted to them by those who
have gone before, the gifts of God follow them in all their
branches.

THE ALLENS.

Most happily there are in this republican country but few large inherited fortunes, and no hereditary rank. The Shakespeares, Bacons, Miltons, Fredericks, and Napoleons have failed to transmit their transcendent genius. Yet talents of a very high order are often hereditable, and marked moral qualities are frequently transmitted through the generations, here and elsewhere over the world, wherever the waters run. It was a favorite sentiment of Carlyle, the apostle of heroism, that when a hardy, good stock of humanity once takes root in a land it never dies out, remaining always, sometime obscured it may be, yet always capable of bearing good and sound fruit.

Among other Scotch who left their native land to escape religious persecution, and found homes in the North of Ireland, was a family of Allens. One of the descendants of this family, named James Allen, and of the Presbyterian faith, lost his life in one of the numerous political agitations which distracted Ireland during the first half of the last century. There was no tradition, however vague, that the ancestors of this James Allen had ever been connected with or allied to the nobility or gentry of either Scotland or Ireland. The station of the family was with the respectable middle class; they disported no coat-of-arms, nor laid claim to any aristocratic descent, whether near or distant. The Allen who fell was as reputable in character as he was respectable in station, and was the owner of a small freehold estate. After his death, his widow determined to emigrate to the American colonies, sold the small property belonging to the family in Ireland, transmitted the proceeds by an agent to be invested in a new home in Pennsylvania near the Virginia line, and in time followed, with her younger children, to find, upon her arrival, that no deed had been taken for the land she had bought, and that she and her offspring were without

home or money among strangers. Fortunately the sur-
soundings of their lives had made them self-reliant and
accustomed them to the idea of making their own way.
They still possessed that rugged personal independence
which proceeds from proud self-respect and a conscious-
ness of capacity to "hold one's own" with one's fellows.
With their own money they had paid for their passage,
and had bought the land on which they expected to live,
and which they had lost through the carelessness or
treachery of the agent the widow had trusted. Refusing
to succumb to adverse fortune, with brave hearts and
stout arms they all set in to win a new home and to wrest
success from the hands of chance. In time they found
their way to the Valley of Virginia, where so many of
their countrymen had settled, and where they prospered,
took root, and put forth branches. Some of their descendants yet remain in Augusta and Rockbridge, while
others emancipated their slaves, and removed at an early
day to Ohio and Indiana. There are numerous other families of Allens that trace their origin to ancestors who
emigrated from Ireland to the Valley, who have the same
given names, and physical attributes similar to those of
the descendants of this Irish widow; but no connection is
known to have existed between them, nor does their history concern the reader.

One of the sons of the energetic widow Allen bore his
father's given name of James. Born in Ireland, and early
bereaved of his paternal protector, he came, when a lad,
with his mother to Virginia, was educated in the best
schools of the Valley, and having remained with his
mother and the family until they had secured comfortable
homes and were thriving, he then struck out for himself
to the West Indies in quest of fortune. There the years
of his early manhood were passed. Meeting rapidly with
greater success than his hopes had led him to anticipate,
he returned to his kindred in the Old Dominion and settled among them in what is now Rockbridge county.
There he met, wooed, and wedded Mary Kelsey, or Kelsoe,
as the name is variously spelled by different members of

the same general family. She, too, was of the Scotch-Irish race. Little is known by the writer of this latter family except that its material was sound, good, and durable; in proof of which, it need only be stated that Dr. David Nelson, the great preacher and author of the able 'and widely-read work on infidelity, and Dr. Samuel K. Nelson, at one time connected with Centre College, and pastor of the Danville Presbyterian Church—two of the foremost of the Presbyterian ministry more than half a century ago—were descendants of one of the sisters of the wife of James Allen. Attracted by the fame of the richer lands and wider field for enterprise afforded by Kentucky, and with the hope of quicker and larger fortune to be won in the dark and bloody ground, all that he had accumulated in Virginia was converted into money; and in the year 1779, with his family in a wagon, he set out across the mountains, braving the perils of the wilderness, for the land of the blue grass and the canebrake, following the old road over which the earlier hunters and settlers from the Holston had preceded him, remaining a few days with Benjamin Logan, at St. Asaphs, and ending his toilsome journey at Daugherty's Station, on Clark's Run, about one and a half miles from Danville. There he remained several months, forming the acquaintance of and a warm friendship for Joseph and Jean Daviess, the former a Virginian of Irish extraction, the latter a Virginian-born woman of Scotch descent. Tiring of the confinement of the station, and anxious to remove their young families from contact with the rude associations incident to border life in a fort, James Allen and Joseph Daviess determined to hazard the perils of an exposed and isolated location further down Clark's Run, where they built two cabins, with a block-house between;—the first cabins built in that section of Kentucky outside a fort or station. There the stout-hearted friends lived for three years, remote from neighbors, and in the midst of constant dangers from savage warfare. Seldom, if ever, have there sprung from two adjoining log cabins six more remarkable men than the three sons of Joseph and Jean Daviess—

Joseph Hamilton, Samuel, and Judge James Daviess—and the sons of James Allen and Mary Kelsey—John, Joseph, and James Allen. About the year 1784, James Allen bought a large body of land near the present town of Bloomfield, in Nelson county, and, after building upon it a comfortable dwelling, returned to his cabin in Lincoln for his family; but, when he had conveyed his wife and children to his new possessions, he found their intended home in ashes, the Indians, during his absence, having burned it and the sheltering fort near which it was built. With indomitable energy and unyielding will, another home soon occupied the site of the one destroyed—a commodious residence which stands to this day, and was, until recently, owned by his great-grandson, who bears his name. Here he lived to an extreme old age, in the midst of broad acres his rifle had helped to redeem from the Indians, and which had been converted by his labor from a wild canebrake into a blooming and fruitful garden; blessed with abundance far beyond the rosiest dreams of the Irish lad who had crossed the ocean with his widowed mother nearly a century before, respected by all for the courage, strong sense, and incorruptible integrity which were his distinguishing characteristics, and with the public praise of his offspring making sweet music for his ears.

Colonel John Allen.

John, the first son of James Allen and Mary Kelsey, was born in Rockbridge county, Virginia, on the 30th day of December, 1771, and before he had attained the age of eight years, accompanied his parents to Kentucky, walking most of the way over the mountains. His opportunities for attending school during the six following years were limited by the exigencies of the situation of the family, in constant peril from Indian forays; yet, under the direction of his intelligent parents, with such assistance as the neighborhood afforded, he had, at the age of fourteen, laid the foundation of an excellent English education. In 1786, he attended the school of Mr. Skackelford—an educated Virginian—in Bardstown, under whose instruction he obtained a

thorough knowledge of the rudiments of both Greek and
Latin, becoming an excellent grammarian in those languages. Afterward, he had the advantage of several years
instruction by the celebrated Dr. Priestley, the most
noted scholar of his day in the West. There his classmates were John Rowan, John Pope, Felix Grundy, Archibald Cameron, the able Presbyterian divine, and his former
playmate—the gifted Joseph Hamilton Daviess. Seldom
has a galaxy of intellectual stars of such magnitude assembled themselves in the same class beneath the roof of a
log-cabin school-house; and able as all of them were, and
conspicuous as all became, not one of the group exhibited
greater capacity for the acquisition of knowledge, possessed more shining talents, or became more illustrious
than John Allen. After completing his classical education with Dr. Priestly, he visited relatives in Virginia, and
there attracted the attention and formed the acquaintance
of the distinguished Colonel Archibald Stuart—the father
of General A. H. H. Stuart, secretary of the interior under
Mr. Fillmore. Colonel Stuart was commissary of Colonel
Sam. McDowell's regiment, but in the battle of Guilford
fought as a private soldier; in the same engagement, his
father, Major Alexander Stuart, was captured. Afterward,
Colonel Stuart distinguished himself as an aide of General Greene. After the Revolution, he studied law under
Mr. Jefferson, and soon rose to eminent distinction in his
profession, was a member of the Virginia convention
which ratified the Constitution of the United States, enjoyed the friendship and esteem of most of the great leaders, statesmen, and patriots of his day, and afterward became one of the most able and learned jurists of his state.
Engaged in the trial of an important land suit in Rockbridge, he was struck with the extraordinary intelligence,
quick perceptions, and sound judgment displayed by a
youth of about twenty years of age, who had been introduced as a witness, and who had gained a knowledge of
the matters in issue by having assisted in the survey of
the land in litigation while on a visit from Kentucky.
Seeking an acquaintance with the youth, he ascertained

that his name was John Allen, the son of a former citizen of Rockbridge, then living in Kentucky; and the interview confirming all the prepossessions in his favor made by the intelligence exhibited as a witness, Colonel Stuart proposed to him to become a lawyer, which he ascertained to be the dearest wish of the young man's heart, and which he was prevented from indulging by the want of ready money to defray the expenses during the time that must be passed in the study of the profession;—all he had being not more than sufficient to supply him with clothing for about three years. High-spirited, and unwilling to accept favors or benefits from a stranger, he at first rejected the proposition of Colonel Stuart to go home with him, become a member of his family, and to study law under his instruction; but finally yielded to it, upon the representation that the benefits accruing would be reciprocal, and that he could more than pay for his board and instruction by the assistance he could render the generous gentleman who sought to befriend him, and to give an opening for the splendid talents he discerned beneath a manner that was as modest as it was engaging. The friendship thus auspiciously begun rapidly warmed and ripened, and ceased only with the life of Allen, who continued an inmate of Colonel Stuart's family for several years; in the meantime he devoted himself to his studies with remarkable assiduity and concentration. These being completed, he was persuaded by Colonel Stuart to accompany him upon the circuit, in order to familiarize himself with the practice and usages of the courts;—at one of which he was induced to participate in a trial of a cause in which Colonel Stuart was the sole counsel for the plaintiff, in whose behalf it was arranged that Allen should make the opening speech, to be followed by the counsel for the defendant, Colonel Stuart to make the closing argument. What Allen said was sensible enough; but it was awkwardly delivered and with the most painful hesitation; and, overwhelmed with embarrassment as he was, his "maiden" effort was a performance unsatisfactory to his auditors, and most dampening to his own ambition.

Stuart, knowing the latent power that was within his protege, resolved at once to give him a second chance, and changed his tactics. Going to the defendant's counsel, who was a friend, and explaining his purpose, he urged him, in his reply to Allen, to do so with such sharpness as would arouse the fire that needed only the stroke of the flint to make it sparkle, and to "put him on his metal." Assenting to this, the opposing counsel assailed Allen's speech with unusual asperity and biting sarcasm. Seeing Allen nettled and stung by the unexpected severity of the criticism of his speech, Stuart told him he must reply, and explained that, in order that Allen might do so, he would surrender to his young associate the right to conclude for the plaintiff. No sooner had the opposing counsel closed than Allen once more took the floor, completely transformed in appearance as in manner; every trace of bashfulness or embarrassment had disappeared, the hesitancy of speech had vanished; his clear blue eye sparkled and lightened with intelligence and ardor; his tall, slender person, drawn to its full height, seemed instinct with animation and intellect; his gesticulation became as graceful as it was impetuous; his voice rang out like the clear tones of a bell; his utterances were rapid, clear cut, eloquent, and elegant, while his logic was irresistible. The ruse had succeeded admirably; the electrified audience gave him the most rapt attention; and, when he closed, the most enthusiastic commendations from every quarter greeted the orator just awakened to a sense of his own genius. A speedy explanation from Stuart that he had stimulated the assault upon him removed every trace of resentment from his amiable temper, and the three had a hearty laugh over the ruse and its happy results. The partnership between Colonel Stuart and John Allen was dissolved, 1795, by the return of the latter to Kentucky. In 1799, Stuart went upon the bench, where he illustrated the highest qualities of the jurist, and in his life the most amiable characteristics of the gentleman.

Upon his return to Kentucky, Mr. Allen located in Shelby county; there first entered upon the practice of his profession in this state, outstripped all competition and almost immediately placed himself in the very first rank of the brilliant generation which then gave the commonwealth a fame which still clings to her in tradition. In Shelby he met and married Jane, the oldest daughter of General Benjamin Logan and Ann Montgomery, an admirable woman, possessed of personal comeliness and rare mental endowments—a worthy mate for such a man. In 1800, he was elected to represent Shelby in the state legislature; and at a time when there was no beaten road, but the whole future policy of the yet infant commonwealth had to be formed; when new questions of finance had to be decided, and the relations of the state to her sisters and to the general government had to be determined; he exhibited the highest qualities of the thoughtful, patriotic statesman. Removing to Frankfort, in order to be nearer the court of appeals and the federal courts, he was elected to the house of representatives from the county in 1803, and was re-elected in 1804, '05, '06. At the bar, in the legislative councils of the state, his highest powers and most shining talents were put to the severest tests by ever-recurring collisions with Joseph H. Daviess, Henry Clay, Felix Grundy, John Rowan, Jesse Bledsoe, Isham Talbott, John Boyle, old Humphrey Marshall, John Brown, John Breckinridge, John Pope, and the Hardins;— any one of whom would have been recognized as a great ruler of men in any age and in any country; their equals have not since been found among the sons of Kentucky; and very seldom, if ever, has any land over which the free sun flings his radiant smile contained an equal number of men of the same generation who were their superiors. At the bar, on the hustings, in the legislative halls, as an eloquent advocate, an impassioned and magnetic popular orator, and a thoroughly-equipped debater, among all these able and brilliant men, John Allen had but two rivals—his old friend and playmate of the log-cabin days, Joseph Hamilton Daviess, and the " Mill Boy of the Hanover Slashes," Henry Clay. Nor was he the inferior of either in that knightly courage that always compelled re-

spect, nor in any grace or gift that wins or leads the minds
or moves the hearts of men.   In the judgment of all who
knew him, had he lived, his reputation and fame would
not have been dimmed even by those of Henry Clay.
Such was the success attending his forensic efforts, there
was scarcely a case of importance for hundreds of miles
around in which he was not retained; every-where in
requisition, his services readily commanded the largest
fees.   In 1806, he was associated with Mr. Clay in the defense of Aaron Burr, and in the memorable scene in the
federal court-room at Frankfort it was he who first clashed
with the fiery Daviess, then the able and distinguished
United States Attorney for Kentucky.

Elected Vice-President in 1801, Burr had lost the confidence of the Republican Democrats, of which party he
had been a member; and had quarrelled with President
Jefferson.   Becoming a candidate for governor of New
York in opposition to the regular Republican-Democratic
candidate in order to retrieve his falling fortunes, he was
defeated mainly by the influence of the statesman, Alexander Hamilton.   The latter had spoken and written of
Burr in injurious terms, which aggravated the hatred of a
man already goaded to desperation by his loss of power
and popularity; unquestionably the language used by
Hamilton justified the challenge that was sent by his
enemy, if the so-called code of honor be accepted as a
guide.   Conscious of this, and that his own lapses from
morality in other respects precluded him from assigning his
well-matured convictions against the practice of duelling
as a reason for declining the combat, Hamilton accepted
the challenge, and fell before Burr's unerring aim.   Burr
found himself abandoned by the mass of the Democrats,
regarded with abhorrence by the Federalists, and banished
from all the legitimate and honorable walks of ambition.
In this desperate state of his political fortunes, he sought
the West, and became deeply involved in schemes as desperate and daring as any which the annals of ill-regulated
ambition can furnish.   The groundwork of his plan, undoubtedly, was to organize a military force upon the western

waters, descend the Mississippi, and wrest from Spain an indefinite portion of her territory adjoining the Gulf of Mexico. The South-western portion of the United States, embracing New Orleans and the adjacent territory, was, either by force or persuasion, to become a part of the new empire, of which New Orleans was to become the capital, and Burr the chief, under some one of the many names which, in modern times, disguise despotic power under a republican guise. These were the essential and indispensable features of the plan. But, if circumstances were favorable, the project was to extend much farther, and the whole country west of the Alleghenies was to be wrested from the American Union, and to become a portion of this new and magnificent empire.—[*McClung.*] The attention of the reader will not be occupied with the details of the plans, nor by the movements by which Burr sought to accomplish his schemes. The idea of separation from the eastern states had been much agitated in Kentucky, and that agitation had left material for the accomplished conspirator to work upon to advantage. John Adair heartily indorsed and stood ready to co-operate with his project, so far as it meditated an attack upon the Spanish provinces; and General Wilkinson gave Burr every reason to believe that he would be assisted by that restless intriguer. The motion made by Daviess, the United States Attorney, on November 3, 1806, for process to compel the attendance of Burr before the Federal District Court at Frankfort, presided over by Judge Hary Innes, to answer to a charge of a high misdemeanor, in organizing a military expedition against a friendly power, from within the jurisdiction and territory of the United States, was supported by the affidavit of Daviess himself, setting forth, with great accuracy, the preparations which were then being made by Burr. After considering the motion two days, it was overruled by Judge Innes. Shortly after this action had been taken by the judge, Burr, who had been at Lexington, entered the court-house, and, after insinuating that Daviess had taken advantage of his absence to make it, requested the judge to entertain the motion *then*, and declared that he had voluntarily attended, so that the prosecutor might have an opportunity to prove his charges. Daviess accepted the challenge, and, after conferring with the marshal of the court, announced his opinion that he could have his witnesses in attendance on the following Wednesday. On that day Daviess discovered that one of his most important witnesses, Davis Floyd, was absent—conveniently absent—and, with manifest reluctance, asked a postponement of the case. Judge Innes refused to grant the postponement, and immediately discharged the grand jury. Accompanied by Henry Clay and John Allen as his counsel, Burr entered the court-room, expressed his regret that the grand jury had been discharged, and inquired the reason; which Daviess stated, adding that Floyd was attending a meeting of the territorial legislature of Indiana. Burr repudiated the purposes attributed to him by Daviess, and at his instance another day was set for the appearance of the witnesses before the grand jury. Upon the 25th of November, Daviess informed the court that Floyd would attend on the 2d of December following; another grand jury was summoned for that day. When it came, Burr, attended by Clay and Allen, again came into court, and sat as if indifferently awaiting an expected attack. But Daviess was compelled to announce his inability to proceed on account of the absence of John Adair, whose evidence was indispensable, who had been properly summoned, and had absented himself; and asked another postponement, and an attachment for Adair to compel his attendance. Burr remained silent. Allen opened the discussion in opposition to the motion of Daviess with all the fire and zeal of his nature. Allen confined himself to the legal questions and technicalities involved; in which he had the advantage of Daviess, as a sufficient time had not elapsed to have given him the legal right to the rule he had asked for against Adair. The entrance of Clay into this discussion was the signal for the commencement of the most passionate and bitter personalities between him and Daviess, in which Clay had the audience, with whom the Federal principles of Daviess

were most odious, entirely on his side. Judge Innes refused to retain the grand jury unless some business was
brought before them. To gain time, Daviess sent up to
the grand jury an indictment against Adair, which was
returned "not a true bill." His motion for an attachment
against Adair was refused by the court.. Daviess asked an
adjournment until the next day. In a private interview in
the interval, Daviess obtained from the judge an expression of opinion that it would be allowable for him to attend the grand jury in their room, and examine the witnesses. When the court convened the next morning, he
made a motion accordingly; it was resisted by Allen and
Clay, and refused by the court. The grand jury retired;
such witnesses as had attended were sworn and examined;
and, in the absence of those by whom alone Daviess could
have sustained his charge, the jury returned: "Not a true
bill:" as Daviess expected. Going further than this, the
grand jury returned into court a written paper, signed by
all of them, completely exonerating Burr from the accu-
sation preferred against him. Allen moved that a copy of
this report should be taken and published in the newspapers, which was granted; and the acquittal of Burr was
celebrated by a grand ball, in which the accomplished conspirator was the hero and lion of the night—[*McClung.*]
Clay and Allen had satisfied the public, already captured
by the graceful address, elegant manners and easy effront-
ery of Burr, that their client was the victim of the personal and political hatred of the Federalists, of whom Daviess and the family of his wife were the most obnoxious
because the more conspicuous, the boldest, and the most
open and candid in their speech. Subsequent events vindicated the motives, the judgment, and actions of Daviess,
incontestably demonstrated that he had thoroughly understood the designs of Burr and his associates, and had,
with surprising accuracy, set forth and described the preparations then being made by him, and cleared the fame of
that brilliant genius and most ardent and unselfish of pa-
16

triots from the unmerited obloquy with which for a time
he was overwhelmed.

It has been urged that Daviess was premature in his mo-
tions. His preparation of his case; his carefulness of details in a matter of such magnitude; and even his capacity
as a lawyer have been made the subject of invidious criticism. Yet it is certain that neither forethought nor care
on his part could have secured the attendance of witnesses
whose interest and determination were to be absent; and
it may well be doubted if any evidence whatever could
have secured the conviction of Burr in the state of public
sentiment in Kentucky. Though foiled in his immediate
purpose, the action of Daviess was not without results the
most important. By directing public attention to and
boldly denouncing the designs of Burr as treasonable in
their nature, it aroused the reflecting to a realization of
their real character, placed the unwary on their guard,
by compelling Burr and his coadjutors to disavow the
purposes attributed to them it estopped them from
openly defending and maintaining their schemes, and compelled them to refrain from what might soon have culminated not only in a most formidable filibustering expedition against Spain, but in a widespread and dangerous
revolt against the Union. To his counsel, Burr gave written assurances of the injustice of the accusations. And
even old Humphrey Marshall so far relented from his in-
tense hostility as to place on record his own conviction,
that Allen had neither complicity in nor knowledge of the
schemes of the wily plotter, whose ambitious dreams had
led him to aspire to becoming the Cæsar in an empire comprising Mexico, the Louisiana territory, and, ultimately, the
whole of the Ohio and Mississippi valleys. The hostility
between Clay and Daviess, engendered by the acrimonious
personalities that passed between them, came near resulting in a duel, in which one or the other of those gifted
and gallant men would probably have fallen; and, accompanied by Dr. Louis Marshall, whose sister he had married, Daviess, in anticipation of the meeting, went to the
residence of Col. Richard C. Anderson, in Jefferson county,

to prepare for it. (Col. Anderson's wife was a second cousin of Dr. Marshall and of Mrs. Daviess). The interposition of friends prevented the catastrophe. Daviess was reserved for a glorious death at Tippecanoe, when leading a charge he had himself advised against the Indians, while Clay lived to earn an enduring fame as orator, patriot, and statesman. Between Daviess and Allen there was no interruption of the personal friendship which began in the rude log cabins on Clarke's Run, and which survived all collisions at the bar and all political differences. In domestic life John Allen was one of the most exemplary of men. His morals were pure; his disposition affectionate and amiable. Still he was not free from the influence of that pernicious public sentiment that sanctioned, perhaps stimulated duelling. In the duel on the Kentucky river, between John Rowan and Dr. Chambers, in which the latter fell with a bullet through his heart, Allen and Daviess were the seconds of their former classmate. For an insult offered in the court room, Allen called Isham Talbott to the field; a fight was prevented by an ample apology made by Talbott, on the ground, where Allen awaited him.

In 1807, Allen was elected to the Kentucky Senate from Franklin, and held that place until 1810. In 1808, he became a candidate for governor against the veteran General Charles Scott, whose heroic and distinguished military record extended from Braddock's defeat to Wayne's victory at the Fallen Timbers. Allen's canvass was one of remarkable brilliancy and power. The old soldier, shrewd as he was blunt, did not attempt to answer his young and splendidly-gifted competitor; but, assenting to all of his positions, complimented him upon the eloquence that was made the more charming by scholarly attainments; and expressed pride in the part he had himself taken in the glorious struggles by which the country had been won from the British, wrested from the savage, and redeemed from the wilderness, so that the rose and expectancy of the fair state, like Allen, might be educated and given a field in which their talents could win wealth, honor, and renown. He urged the people to transfer the gifted orator to Congress, or to the federal senate, where he would reflect lustre upon the state, and achieve for himself laurels that time could not wither, rather than bury his talents in the office of Governor;—a position, he argued, which afforded no opportunities for Allen's powers, required only corn-field sense, firmness, and an honest purpose to do right, and was a fitting reward for a rough-riding, untutored old soldier like himself, whose life had been too much occupied with hard fighting to have enabled him to learn much from books. Such an appeal from one of Scott's prestige for unselfish gallantry was not to be resisted by Kentuckians, who went in crowds to hear Allen, and turned out by thousands to vote for Scott. Humphrey Marshall intimates, too, that in the reaction which set in upon the full disclosure of Burr's plans the popular indignation extended to his counsel, and helped to swell Scott's majority. In 1810 Allen was re-elected to the senate from Shelby. The generations that succeeded him have cause to regret that none of his speeches were ever reported. His greatest achievements, and most brilliant efforts, were at the bar; there he had no superior in the commonwealth.

When the War of 1812 commenced, all the surroundings of John Allen prompted him to yield to a spirit of patriotic elation which impelled him to the front. It was not for such as he to remain in inglorious safety in peaceful Kentucky while calls for help were borne on every breeze that swept from Ohio, Indiana, and Illinois. His experience with Scott in the campaign for governor was well calculated to arouse within him an honorable ambition for military distinction. His playmate and friend, his antagonist in a generous rivalry—Daviess—on the fatal 7th of November, 1811, had already fallen. On the 5th of June, 1812, John Allen was commissioned as colonel of the First Regiment of Kentucky Riflemen—the first regiment raised for service against the British, in Kentucky, in that war. The commission was issued by Governor Charles Scott, was countersigned by Jesse Bledsoe as sec-

retary of state, and the written part of it is in the hand-
writing of Judge Stephen Trigg Logan, afterward of
Illinois. That it was immediately accepted is evidenced
by the indorsement on its back by Martin D. Hardin.
His military career was brief; it had a glorious ending at
the disaster of the melancholy Raisin. The hardships of
the memorable campaign in the dead of the ensuing
winter, are pictured in his private letters to his wife.
Those letters tell of the departure and results of the expedition against Mississinewa, or " Turtlestown," as Colonel Allen called the principal Indian town. Frequent
mention is made in them of " Little Bland " Ballard, son
of the old Indian fighter of the same name; and of the
gallant Simpson, an attached friend whom he had induced
to study law, and in whose early distinction in that profession he had a pardonable pride. They give details concerning George Madison, the second major of the command, and afterward governor; of Martin D. Hardin, the
first major, who had married his wife's sister; and of her
young brothers, Dr. Ben. and Robert Logan. One of the
letters informs Mrs. Allen of the death of Lawba, son of
the Chief Moluntha, whose life had been saved by Lytle,
who had been adopted and reared by Mrs. Allen's father,
General Logan, and who ever afterward called himself
" Captain Logan." In the War of 1812, Captain Logan
rendered valuable services to General Harrison. Wounded
by unjust imputations upon his fidelity, he determined to
vindicate it by some deed of daring, and for that purpose
left the camp in company with the Indian braves, Captain
Johnny and Bright Horn. At noon of the same day—November 22, 1812—they were surprised by the Potawatamie
chief, Winnemac; Elliott, a half-breed; and five other
Indians. They were disarmed by their captors, but Captain Logan so won upon the confidence of Winnemac that
their arms were restored. Logan, having communicated
his purpose to Captain Johnny and Bright Horn, seized
the first opportunity of attacking the party of Winnemac,
who, with four of his party, was killed in the fight that
followed, while the other two saved themselves by flight.

Logan was shot through the body and mortally wounded, but rode on horseback to General Winchester's camp, which he reached the next morning. After lingering in great pain three days, he died, and was buried with the honors of war. In the midst of his agony, he was seen to smile, and, on being questioned, explained that when he recalled to mind the manner in which he had seen Captain Johnny scalp Winnemac, while at the same time watching the movements of the others of Winnemac's party to prevent them from shooting him, he could not keep from laughing. Logan left a dying request that Major Hardin would convey his children to Kentucky, and rear them with the whites; Hardin endeavored to comply with the request, but the Indians of the village in which they lived, and their mother, a bad woman, would not permit it.

The last letter ever written by Colonel Allen was on the night of the 21st of January, 1813—the night before the battle—was addressed to his old preceptor and friend, Judge Archibald Stuart, and is still in the possession of Hon. A. H. H. Stuart, of Staunton. After describing in detail the relative positions of the opposing forces, and dwelling upon the certainty of an engagement the ensuing day, he concluded: "We meet the enemy to-morrow. I trust we will render a good account of ourselves, or that I will never live to bear the tale of our disgrace." He was not disappointed in the fate he craved in case of defeat— a disaster which clothed all Kentucky in mourning for the flower of the state there stricken down. Though grievously wounded in the thigh, Colonel Allen several times attempted to rally his men, entreating them to halt and sell their lives as dearly as possible. He had fallen back about two miles toward the fort, when, wearied and exhausted, and probably disdaining to survive defeat, he sat down upon a log, determined to await his fate. An Indian chief observing him to be an officer of distinction, and anxious to take him prisoner, as soon as he came near Allen threw his rifle across his lap, and told him to surrender and he should be safe. But another savage having at the same time advanced with hostile demonstrations, Colonel Allen, with one stroke of his sword, laid him dead at his feet. A third Indian, who was near, immediately shot him through the heart. The body was never recovered. Thus fell one of Kentucky's first, greatest, and purest citizens. The blood of young Robert Logan also mingled itself with the swift current of the Raisin. The only portrait of Colonel Allen known to be in existence is in the possession of Judge Wm. M. Dickson, of Avondale, who married his granddaughter. He was more than six feet in height, was slenderly but compactly and gracefully built; his hair was sandy, complexion florid, and skin thin; his eyes were large, clear, and bright, and of a very deep blue;—his whole appearance plainly indicated his Scoto-Celtic extraction.

THE CRITTENDENS.

Four daughters of Colonel John Allen and Jane Logan transmitted to their children the rich heritage of his fame. The oldest daughter, Anna Maria Allen, was probably born about the year 1802. On the 14th of May, 1818, she married Henry, one of the four talented sons of Major John Crittenden. The latter was a native of Virginia, of English descent. In the Revolution he was a lieutenant of one of the Virginia regiments of the Continental army, and afterward a major of the Virginia state line. After the close of that struggle, he came to Kentucky, and in 1783 and 1784, when there were but three counties in the District of Kentucky, was the representative from Fayette in the Virginia House of Burgesses. His reputation among his contemporaries, as handed down by them, was that of a brave soldier and efficient officer, a public-spirited and patriotic citizen, and a candid, honorable, and intelligent man. If a tree may be judged by its fruit, it will be unnecessary to add to this contemporary estimate of his virtues further than to say, that he was the father of John J., Thomas T., Henry, and Robert Crittenden, and of the wife of Judge Hary Innes Thornton. The sons were gallant men, of strong intellects and brilliant gifts, cultivated in mind and of captivating address, high types of gentlemen and of Kentuckians. The elder brother, John Jordan, was twelve times elected to the state house of representatives, and was six times chosen speaker of that body; he was secretary of state under James T. Morehead; governor of the state; a representative, and three times a senator in Congress; and was twice attorney-general of the United States. His courage in battle was made as conspicuous at the Thames, where he acted as aide to Shelby, as his patriotism was made on every occasion when it was tested. Thomas T. Crittenden, the next brother, was frequently in the legislature, was secretary of state under Metcalfe, and a distinguished judge. Robert was governor of the Arkansas Territory, and a brilliant member of Congress from that state. Of Henry, Collins says that he "devoted himself to agricultural pursuits, was nevertheless so conspicuous for talent that his countrymen insisted on their right occasionally to withdraw him from the labors of the farm to those of the public councils." The wife of Major John Crittenden—mother of these brothers—was Judith Harris. On the paternal side, she was of Scotch blood. Her mother, a Miss Jordan, was a member of an intellectual and educated family of French Huguenots. Henry Crittenden was born in Woodford county, May 24, 1792. Receiving a good classical education, he did not study a profession, but added the pursuit of a manufacturer to that of a farmer. In these were buried talents that would have won him fame in any profession. His was an amiable temper, a handsome person, and a most winning manner. As a public speaker, it is said he was the equal of his oldest brother. He had been subpenaed as a witness in a case in which John U. Waring was a party. The desperado sent him word that, if he gave his testimony, he (Waring) would kill him. Despising the menace, Mr. Crittenden testified to the facts; and the murderer embraced the first opportunity presented, when Crittenden was not on guard, by stabbing him in the abdomen. Of fever resulting from this wound, Henry Crittenden died, about two years after receiving it, on the 21st of December, 1834. John Allen, the oldest son of Henry Crittenden and Anna Maria Allen, was at one time marshal of the Louisville Chancery Court, and afterward for years was a clerk in the auditor's office. He married a daughter of Richard Jackson, of Franklin county, and had issue. William Logan, the second son of Henry Crittenden, graduated with credit at West Point, served as an officer in the regular army in the war with Mexico; resigned to embark in the Lopez expedition against Cuba; was captured at Cardenas; was sentenced to death by the Spaniards, refused to kneel or to have his eyes bandaged, and with his own hand gave the signal for the volley of musketry which pierced his breast with many wounds. The third son, named Henry—a talented and lovable man—died unmarried in 1860. The fourth and youngest son of Henry Crittenden, and Anna Maria Allen—Thomas T. Crittenden—graduated at Centre College in 1855; married Carrie Jackson, in Frankfort, in November, 1856; commenced the practice of law in Missouri; was lieutenant-colonel of the Seventh Missouri Federal Cavalry during the civil war; was twice a representative in Congress from the Lexington, Missouri, District, and was four years governor of that state. Governor Crittenden is now a resident of Kansas City, where he is a successful lawyer, and the president of a national bank.

THE MURRAYS.

After the death of Henry Crittenden, his widow married Colonel David R. Murray, of Cloverport, Kentucky. This gentleman was the son of Scotch-Irish parents who emigrated, in 1790, from Virginia to Washington county, Kentucky, where he was born, in 1793. At the age of nineteen years, he volunteered as a soldier in the War of 1812. At the close of hostilities, he engaged in mercantile business in Springfield, Kentucky; afterward removing to Hardinsburg, Breckinridge county, he continued in commercial pursuits until his death, in May, 1871. Colonel Murray was three times sent to the legislature from

Breckinridge. He was a man of sense, integrity, high character, and a consistent Presbyterian. His first wife was a Miss Huston, cousin to his second wife; they had several children. Colonel Murray and Anna Maria Allen had four sons—John Allen, Eli Huston, Logan C., and David R. Murray. Of these, John Allen Murray represented Breckinridge in the legislature, 1867–69. Afterward, he was judge of the criminal court of his judicial district. He married twice, and has issue. Judge Murray is a successful lawyer of Cloverport. Eli H. Murray, the second son, was born at Cloverport, February 10, 1843, and was well educated under private tutors. In 1861, at the age of eighteen, he recruited a company for the Third Kentucky Union Cavalry (Colonel James S. Jackson), and was elected its captain. For good conduct, he was promoted major in November of that year, and, August 13, 1862, was promoted colonel, continuing in the service until the close of the war. He was engaged in all the campaigns under Buell, Rosecrans, and Thomas; and commanded half of the cavalry force in Sherman's march to the sea. At Corinth, he commanded his own regiment; at Chattanooga, he commanded a brigade; he fought gallantly in the battles of Dalton, Resaca, Iuka, and Shiloh. For good conduct in these campaigns, and in that of Sherman's march, he was commissioned a brigadier-general before he was twenty-two years old. Placed in command of the South-western District of Kentucky, his activity in military affairs commanded the most favorable notice of the government; while his integrity, good sense, and conservatism in civil matters won the respect of the people of all parties. When the war closed, he studied law, graduating with honor in the Louisville Law School in 1866. By General Grant he was appointed United States Marshal for Kentucky in 1869, and held the place seven years. By President Hayes, in 1880, he was appointed governor of Utah, and held the place until 1885. His administration in that territory was distinguished by the fearlessness and vigor with which he enforced the laws and maintained the authority of the government. He now resides in Salt

Lake City. January 18, 1876, General Murray married, in Louisville, Evelyn Neale; they have several children. He is over six feet high, his presence commanding, his countenance handsome, his manners dignified and winning. The third son of Colonel D. R. Murray and Anna Maria Allen—Logan Crittenden—was born August 15, 1845; was educated at home, and at Princeton College, New Jersey, where he graduated, in 1866. In 1870, he was appointed cashier of the Kentucky National Bank of Louisville, and established for himself a valuable reputation as a financier. He held that position for twelve years, and until, on the organization of the United States National Bank of New York, he resigned his position in Louisville to accept that of vice-president of the latter bank. He is now its president, and for several years has been president of the National Bankers' Association of the United States. On the 6th of November, 1866, Mr. Murray married Hattie, daughter of A. A. Gordon, of Louisville. Her father was a descendant of a brother of the wife of the "Blind Preacher" pictured by Wirt—Rev. Mr. Waddell. Her mother was a granddaughter of Alexander Scott Bullitt. They have four children. David R., the fourth and youngest son of Colonel Murray, was a senator from Breckinridge, 1877–81, and is now a practicing lawyer of that county. He is married, and has issue.

Mrs. Murray (Anna Maria Allen), was an earnest, yes, an aggressive Presbyterian. Her home was, for many years, the hospitable resting-place of every minister of the gospel who entered the town in which she lived. She was uncommonly intelligent and well informed; careless of forms and mere conventionalities, she grasped and easily comprehended that which was real and valuable. Her mind was masculine in its breadth and strength. With these endowments she had the comeliness which attracts, and the sympathetic tenderness which adorns true womanhood. She died in 1877.

The Butlers.

Eliza Sarah, second daughter of Col. John Allen and Jane Logan, was born in Shelby county, Kentucky, in September, 1806. Losing her father in childhood, and her mother in a few years following him to the grave, a part of her girlhood was passed in the family of Martin D. Hardin, her uncle by marriage. At the early age of sixteen years, in 1822, she married Pierce Butler, the youngest son of Pierce Butler and Mildred Hawkins. If, in this country, there are any families which can properly be called "historic," surely the "Butlers of the Pennsylvania line," or "the fighting Butlers," as they are sometimes called, may well be regarded as constituting one of those families.

The record in the family Bible of the progenitor of this family in America states, that Mr. Thomas Butler "was born in the Parish of Kilkenny, City of Wicklow, Ireland, April 6th, 1720; married Eleanor Parker (daughter of Anthony Parker, of county of Wexford), October 26, 1741." Their oldest son, Richard Butler, was born in St. Bridget's parish, Dublin, April 1, 1743. The uniform family tradition is, that Thomas Butler was an officer of ordnance in the British army, engaged in some act of rebellion against the crown, and for a considerable time concealed himself in London. There he was joined by his devoted wife, and there, in St. Andrews, January 6, 1745, their second son, William, was born. Several years passed before a suitable opportunity occurred of escaping to America. But, in the year 1748, the family left Britain, and the third son, Thomas, was born at sea, on shipboard, May 28, 1748. They settled in Pennsylvania, and Mary, their oldest daughter, was born in that province, Nov. 3, 1749; Rebecca, the second daughter, was born in Lancaster, Pennsylvania, September 19, 1751; Pierce, the fourth son, was born in Carlisle, Pennsylvania, April 4, 1760; Edward, the fifth son, at Mt. Pleasant, Pennsylvania, March 20, 1762; and Eleanor, the third daughter, was born at Carlisle, December 31, 1763. The vague, almost intangible tradition, or alleged tradition, that Thomas Butler, of Kilkenny, was related to the families of the same surname, who have for centuries borne the titles of Ormonde, Dunboyne, Carrick, and others, was treated by his descendants in Kentucky with an indifference that amounted to actual contempt. It was sufficient for those staunch and consistent republicans, that he was in station a gentleman, a man of education and of honor; that his was a sterling character, and that in the Revolution he was an active patriot;—those were all the titles of nobility to which they attached any value. While all of his sons were in the army, Thomas Butler put to use the knowledge he had obtained in the ordnance department of the British army, by establishing and operating a manufactory of arms for the Americans. When those sons were absent on duty a threatened outbreak of the western Indians, in 1781, made their father volunteer for the defense of the frontier. His neighbors protesting against the action of the old man, Eleanor, his brave wife, responded: "Let him go; I can get along without him, and raise a little to help feed the army besides; and the country needs every man who can shoulder a musket." Thomas and Eleanor Butler were Episcopalians. This was the family, and not one of Connecticut, as has been erroneously stated, to whom Washington referred, when, seated at his table and surrounded by officers, he gave the toast: "The Butlers and their five sons." The family was in some way related to the Colonel John Butler, of New York, the son-in-law of Sir William Johnson, and a British officer. When bidding farewell to his sons, the parting injunction of Thomas was, that if they ever met John Butler, they must "bring him his head."—[*Pennsylvania Magazine.*]

The two oldest sons of this pair, Richard and William Butler, some years before the Revolution, were Indian traders, at Old Chillicothe. The Indians rose against them; William escaped; Richard was captured by the Indians, who put out one of his eyes, then adopted him into their tribe, and married him to a squaw. In a few months Richard made his way back to Pennsylvania, where, years afterward, his son by the Indian woman visited his family at Pittsburg. About the year 1770, Richard and William Butler resumed their partnership as Indian traders, established their headquarters at Pittsburg, and pushed their ventures not only through Ohio, Indiana and Illinois, but even among the tribes beyond the Mississippi. During the few years of peace that elapsed, they were signally successful, cultivated friendly relations with the red men, and gained an acquaintance with their languages, customs and modes of warfare, which was of service in the period of strife that followed. At Pittsburg, these two brothers were living and carrying on their trade, when, in the spring of 1774, Dr. John Connolly, the nephew of Lord Dunmore, in the name and by the authority of that functionary, seized upon and dismantled Fort Pitt, which Dunmore claimed to be on territory belonging to Virginia, and built another which he called Fort Dunmore. Among the Pennsylvanians whom Connolly arbitrarily arrested was William Butler. The conduct of some of the Virginians, under Connolly's orders, excited the suspicions and fears of the Indians, on whose peaceful settlement opposite Fort Pitt they had fired. On the 16th of April, 1774, a canoe, laden with peltries belonging to the Butler brothers, was fired upon by the Indians, and a white man, one of their employes, was killed. Five days after this occurrence, Connolly wrote to the settlers along the Ohio that the Shawanese were not to be trusted, and urging them to prepare to avenge any wrong the Indians might do them. When his first canoe had been attacked, William Butler had sent other agents to attend to his peltries further down the Ohio, in the Shawanese country. Connolly's letter had fallen into the hands of Michael Cresap, who attacked one of the canoes dispatched by William Butler, containing two friendly Indians and two white men, and inhumanly butchered the red men. Continuing their murders, Cresap and Daniel Greathouse massacred the friendly and unsuspecting Indians at Captina and Yellow creek, including the family of Logan—the celebrated Mingo chief. These were the atrocities that led to the war of 1774, known as Dunmore's. The letters of the

Butlers, protesting against these proceedings, are preserved in the American Archives and in the Colonial Records of Pennsylvania.

Richard Butler warmly espoused the cause of Pennsylvania in the dispute with Connolly, and raised a company of one hundred men to sustain that colony. At the outbreak of the Revolution, he was appointed one of the agents of the commissioners for the middle department of Indians, for which service his experience and knowledge of the red men peculiarly fitted him. His energy and activity in this capacity received the especial thanks of the Continental Congress, which, on the 16th of May, 1776, expressed, by formal resolution, their regret that, by accepting the position, he had lost his opportunity of securing a commission in the Continental service, and promised to promote him as soon as possible. On July 20, 1776, upon the especial recommendation of the convention of Pennsylvania, he was elected by Congress a major of one of the battalions raised for the defense of the Western frontier. From that date he continued in active service until the close of the war. September 28, 1776, he was commissioned by Congress a lieutenant-colonel of the Pennsylvania line; on the 7th of June, 1777, he was commissioned colonel of the Fifth Pennsylvania regiment. In the latter year, Daniel Morgan's celebrated rifle corps was organized, and Richard Butler was made its lieutenant-colonel. He was in the sharpest of the actions in New Jersey, in the battles of Bemiss Heights and Stillwater; in the latter severe engagement he led the rifle corps against the right wing of the British army. He helped to force Burgoyne to surrender, and was present when the army of that commander capitulated; after which he had a separate command of riflemen in New Jersey. He commanded the left column of the American army at the storming of Stony Point. It was mainly through his exertions, and because of the love borne him by the soldiers, that the revolt against Wayne was quelled. To his skill in training, and to his example in leading them to victory, the rifle corps was indebted for much of its celebrity and efficiency. He was at the side of Arnold when the latter was wounded in the attack on the Brunswicker's camp at Saratoga. After the surrender of Cornwallis, he was with Wayne in Georgia, and did not return until the echo of the last gun had died away forever. According to the terms of an act of Congress passed September 30, 1783, he was made a brevet brigadier-general. Congress elected him one of the commissioners to negotiate treaties with the Six Nations and other Indian tribes. The other commissioners were George Rogers Clarke and General Samuel Parsons. In publications designed to celebrate Clarke, that adventurous and gallant officer has been styled the commissioner-general on the occasion of the council with the Indians at the mouth of the Miami, in 1786. General Clarke had no such office, bore no such title; he was a fellow-commissioner with the others—nothing more. In the publications referred to, Clarke is represented to have pushed off a table with his cane the Indian wampum of black and white, which an impudent and truculent chief had presented to signify that his braves were ready for either peace or war, as the whites chose; and, when the incensed warriors rose in their wrath at the insult, "to have stamped with his foot upon the insulted symbol," and, ordering them to "begone, dogs," to have driven them from his presence and cowed them into submission by a glance of his flashing eye. The needless misrepresentation could not add to the fame of the hero who won Illinois. This statement was not made public until 1830, many years after General Clarke's death; it can not be shown to have had his sanction or authority. He was present when a scene somewhat similar did take place, but he was not the actor therein. Richard Butler kept a diary of the events of each day's journey, and of the council itself, which was published in the "Olden Time." That journal was written at the time of the occurrences narrated; is plain, direct, unpretending, and in style is worthy of the gallant soldier whom "Light Horse Harry Lee" described as "the renowned second and rival of Morgan at Saratoga." In this diary, Colonel Butler re-

cords the speech made by Kekewepellethe, a Shawanee
captain; then that made by John Harris; and states that
when the latter had concluded, he "produced a large belt
and a road belt." This was on Sunday, January 29th.
The next day, the commissioners met again with the chiefs
of the Shawanese, who expressed dissatisfaction with the
boundaries allotted to that tribe, as designated in the articles of the treaty which had been presented. The chiefs
of all the tribes were then sent for, and the commissioners
went into council. The articles were presented to the
formal council of all the tribes. Kekewepellethe addressed the commissioners in angry tones, and laid down
a *black string.* Colonel Butler replied, giving the Indians
their choice of peace or war, telling them shortly that
neither the black string nor any other given in such a
manner would be received from them. Butler then took
up their black string, and contemptuously dashed it upon
the table; he threw down a black and white string; and
the commissioners left the council. In the afternoon,
the Shawanese sent a message to the commissioners, re-
questing their presence in the council. Upon their attendance, Kekewepellethe expressed regret that there should
have been a misunderstanding, and, at the conclusion of
his humble remarks, presented a *white string*, and asked
for peace. The commissioners responded in appropriate
terms, and laid down a *white string*, signifying their will-
ingness to grant peace. Colonel Butler adds: " The council then broke up. It was worthy of observation to see
the different degrees of agitation which appeared in the
young Indians; at the delivery of Kekewepellethe's speech,
they appeared raised and ready for war; on the speech I
spoke, they appeared rather distressed and chagrined by
the contrast of the speeches, and convinced of the futility
of their arguments."—[*Olden Time.*]

Having thus discharged this duty, Colonel Richard Butler was chosen superintendent of Indian affairs for the
Northern district. In 1788, he was lieutenant of the
county of Alleghany, and held the office until his appoint-

17

ment as judge of the court of common pleas for that county. In 1790, he was chosen state senator. In 1791, he was made major-general, and second in command under St. Clair, in the expedition against the Western Indians; and he commanded the right wing of the army in the disastrous battle of November 4, 1791. His advice having been rejected by St. Clair, General Butler anticipated the surprise that followed. The night before the battle, he opened a bottle of wine at his mess-table, saying to his companions: "Let us eat, drink and be merry, for to-morrow we die." "In the battle of the next morning, the intrepid Butler closed his military career in death—his coolness preserved and courage remaining unshaken till the last moment of existence. While enabled to keep the field, his exertions were truly heroic. He repeatedly led his men to the charge, and, with slaughter, drove the enemy before him; but being at length compelled to retire to his tent, from the number and severity of his wounds, he was receiving surgical aid, when a ferocious warrior, rushing into his presence, gave him a mortal blow with his tomahawk. But even then the gallant soldier died not unrevenged. He had anticipated the catastrophe, and discharging a pistol he held in his hand, lodged its contents in the breast of his enemy, who, uttering a hideous yell, fell by his side and expired."—[*Garden's Revolutionary Anecdotes.*] Years after this battle, Cornplanter returned to the widow of General Butler his sword and medal as a member of the Order of the Cincinnati. General Butler married Maria, daughter of General James Smith, of Pennsylvania. They had two sons and a daughter—William, James and Mary. The first was a lieutenant in the navy, and died in the service, and on duty, in the early part of the War of 1812. The second was the gallant captain of the famous "Pittsburg Blues," a company which fought well and received complimentary mention for gallantry at Mississinewa and on other bloody fields of that war. Captain James Butler married a sister of Charles Wilkins, of Kentucky; they left three children—John, Richard and Mary—of whom Richard married Miss Black, and left several children in California, where he died. Mary, the daughter of General Richard Butler, married Isaac Meason, a wealthy citizen of Pennsylvania. She is represented to have been a woman of rich mental endowments, and of high character. She died at Uniontown, Pennsylvania, a few years since, at the age of ninety-six years. Her grandson, Isaac Meason, resides in Nashville, Tennessee.

William, the second son of Thomas Butler, the emigrant, and Eleanor Parker, entered the Revolutionary army, January 6, 1776, as captain in Colonel Arthur St. Clair's battalion; October 7th of that year, was promoted major; he served during the campaign in Canada; was promoted lieutenant-colonel of the Fourth Pennsylvania Regiment, for gallantry in the field. All through the war, in the hardest-fought battles, he was conspicuous for courage and good conduct. In 1783 he retired from the army, and died in Pittsburg in 1789. His wife was Jane Carmichael, of Pittsburg. They had four children—William, Richard, Rebecca, and Harriet. The first was a lieutenant-commandant in the navy, and died in the service, unmarried. The second—Richard—was a lieutenant in the Second, Infantry of the regular army, commanded by his uncle, Colonel Thomas Butler; was in the fight at St. Clair's defeat, and was for some time in command at Fort Laramie, which was erected on the site of the store burned by General Logan, in Clarke's expedition. He was with Wayne at the victory of the Fallen Timbers, and for a time was assistant adjutant-general of Mad Anthony's staff. With his regiment he went south, and was stationed at Fort Adams. While in Louisiana, he was appointed lieutenant-colonel of the Forty-fourth United States Infantry; was then stationed at New Orleans, and commanded his regiment in the battles at that place. In the South he married a Miss Farrar, an heiress of Louisiana, resigned from the army, and became a wealthy sugar planter. He and his wife, and his wife's brother, Captain Farrar, died at Pass Christian, in 1820, of yellow fever. Colonel William Butler's daughter, Harriet, married Captain Moses Hook; and his daughter, Rebecca Butler, married James McCutcheon, of New Orleans. Mrs. Mc-Cutcheon's grandchildren now reside at Pass Christian, Louisiana.

Thomas Butler, third son of the emigrant, was a student of law in the office of Judge Wilson, when, January 5, 1776, he was commissioned first lieutenant in his brother William's company, St. Clair's battalion; October 4th of that year, for good conduct, he was promoted to be captain in the Third Pennsylvania. At the battle of Brandywine, Alexander Hamilton, then an aide on the staff of Washington, brought to him, upon the field, the thanks of the commander-in-chief, "for his intrepid conduct in rallying some retreating troops, and checking the enemy by a severe fire; and at Monmouth, General Wayne thanked him for defending a defile, in the face of a severe fire from the enemy, while Colonel Richard Butler's regiment made good its retreat." He remained in the army until the close of the war, taking part in many of the severest of its battles; then became a farmer in Pennsylvania. In 1791, before the outbreak of hostilities with the Indians, he re-entered the army, and led his men to the front; his rank was that of major. At St. Clair's defeat his leg was broken by a ball; but he kept his horse after receiving the wound, and, on horseback, led a charge against the savage warriors. With great difficulty, he was finally removed from the field by Edward, his surviving and youngest brother. In 1794, he was lieutenant-colonel commandant of the Fourth Sub-Legion, at Fort Lafayette, Pittsburg, and, more by the influence of his name, and by his threats, than by the force under his command, prevented the insurgents in Shay's rebellion from seizing that post. Not long after this he was ordered to the South. The State of Georgia claimed to own what was known as the Natchez district, and had enacted a statute for the establishment of a land office therein. Among other large sales of land Georgia had made, was one of 3,500,000 acres, embracing the present northern counties of Alabama, to the "Tennessee Company." Spain claimed to own most of this territory, under her treaties with France and Great Britain, and a diplomatic correspondence was in progress between the United States and that power in regard to their respective rights. In the meantime, the Choctaws, Creeks, Cherokees and Chickasaws regarded with jealousy and bitter anger the projected seizure of their domain. The prompt action of Colonel Butler prevented an outbreak by the Indians. Zachariah Coxe had built a boat to transport an armed colony for the seizure of the Muscle Shoals, on the Tennessee river, in behalf of the "Tennessee Company," but Colonel Butler prevented this by issuing an order to his troops at South-West Point to keep a sharp lookout for the boat, and, if necessary, to fire upon and sink it. A complication with Spain was thus avoided. Colonel Thomas Butler was the gallant officer who won the ill-will of General Wilkinson, and was, by that conspirator, hounded to death. He died September 7, 1805, and was then colonel of the Second Infantry. His wife was Sarah Semple, of Pittsburg. They had three sons and a daughter—Thomas, Robert, William Edward and Lydia. The first was the able and distinguished Judge Butler, of Louisiana; he married Anna Ellis, of Mississippi; they had four sons and four daughters—Pierce, Richard, Thomas, Edward, Margaret, Sarah, Anna and Mary—all of whom, except Thomas, were living in Louisiana in 1881. Robert, the second son of Colonel Thomas Butler and Sarah Semple, an officer of the regular army, was the adjutant-general of Jackson's army at New Orleans, and of the Southern division, with the rank of colonel. For his gallant and meritorious services he was made a brevet brigadier-general. In 1821, he resigned his commission in the army, and was appointed surveyor-general of public lands in Florida; he died at Tullahoma, in that state. General Robert Butler married Rachel, daughter of Colonel Robert Hays and Jane Donelson; her mother was a sister of the wife of General Andrew Jackson. They had four children—Thomas, Robert, Jane and Ellen. The daughters married, respectively, Mr. Patton and Mr. Hawkins. Robert Patton, of Tullahoma, is a son of the former. Wm. Edward, third son of Colonel Thomas Butler, a surgeon in the United States army, was also at the battle of New Orleans. At a ball given in that city, after the victory, a wag, who had stepped upon his toes, apologized by saying, that "it was impossible for any one to move in New Orleans without jostling or treading upon the toes of a Butler"—alluding to the number of the name and family who had been in the fight. He, too, married a niece of Mrs. Jackson, Patsey Hays; and his sister, Lydia, married Colonel Stokely Hays, a nephew of "Old Hickory's" wife. Dr. Wm. E. Butler lived at Jackson, Tennessee. He had one son—William. Mrs. Lydia Butler Hays lived at Nashville; she left a son and a daughter.

Edward Butler, the fifth son of the emigrant, was too young to enter the army at the beginning of the Revolution, but, while still a mere boy, was made an ensign in the Ninth Pennsylvania, commanded by his brother Richard. January 28, 1779, he was promoted lieutenant for meritorious service in the field, and continued in the active service until 1783. At that time, he was a lieutenant in the Second Pennsylvania. He was a captain at St. Clair's defeat, was with Wayne in his successful campaign, and was adjutant-general in Wayne's army in 1796;—a handsome, gallant soldier, and an accomplished gentleman, who died at Springfield, Tennessee, May 6, 1803. His wife was Isabella, daughter of Captain George Fowler, of the British Grenadiers. The latter, three times led the British "forlorn hope" against the American lines, and, on entering their works, was presented by General Sir Robert Pigott with a grenadier's cap, "for his desperate gallantry." Captain Edward Butler had three sons and two daughters; two of the sons died young; Caroline, one of the daughters, married Robert Bell, of Louisiana; Eliza Eleanor, the other, married John Donelson, of Alabama, a nephew of Mrs. Jackson. The surviving son, Edward George Washington Butler, was born in 1801, and, on the death of his father, was consigned to the guardianship of General Andrew Jackson, in whose family the years of his boyhood were passed. He graduated from West Point, in

1820, in the artillery corps; served for a time on topo-
graphical and ordnance duty; in 1823, was assigned to
the staff of General E. P. Gaines, as aide; resigned, 28th
of May, 1831; was major-general of Louisiana militia in
1845; re-entered the regular army, as colonel of the Third
United States Dragoons, in 1847, and commanded the department of the Upper Rio Grande, Mexico, in that year
and the next; then was a planter until the civil war. Colonel E. G. W. Butler married, April 4, 1826, Frances
Parke, the oldest daughter of Colonel Lawrence Lewis
and "Nelly" Custis; her father was the nephew of Washington; her mother, the granddaughter of Washington's
wife. They had two sons and two daughters—Edward G.
W., Lawrence Lewis, Mrs. Williamson, and Mrs. Turnbull,
of Louisiana. The first graduated at the University of
Virginia, at Harvard, and at the New Orleans Law School;
was secretary of legation at Berlin for six years; at the
beginning of the civil war, entered the Confederate army
as major of the Eleventh Louisiana Infantry; and died
gloriously in battle at Belmont, in 1861, desiring General
Polk to tell his father that he "had died like a Butler—in
the discharge of his duty." In delivering the message,
with his dead body, General Polk remarked to his father:
"You have reason to be proud of such a son, and to be
reconciled to such a death;" and General R. E. Lee wrote:
"I still grieve over the death of your gallant son. His
message to you, through General Polk, proves him a
hero." Lawrence Lewis, second son of Colonel E. G. W.
Butler and Frances Parke Lewis, graduated at the University of Virginia, and in the law schools of New Orleans,
and Paris, France, and commenced the practice in New
Orleans. Soon afterward, on the outbreak of civil war, he
went with Dewees' battalion to the Virginia peninsula;
then joined the Eleventh Louisiana Regiment at Columbus, Kentucky, and served on the staffs of Generals Polk
and Wright until the termination of the conflict. He
married the daughter of Mr. Gay, a congressman from
Louisiana, and is successfully engaged in mercantile pursuits in St. Louis. In that city, Colonel E. G. W. Butler,

a few months ago, passed away. Much of the account here given of this historic family is taken from his letters.

Pierce, the fourth son of Thomas Butler and Eleanor Parker, was commissioned first lieutenant in the Third Pennsylvania, Colonel Thomas Craig's regiment, September 1, 1777, being then eighteen years old. He endured the winter at Valley Forge, fought in the battle of Monmouth, and in various other engagements, and took part in the capture of Cornwallis, at Yorktown. He went with Wayne to the South, and there remained until 1783. He came out of the war with the rank of captain. The next year, he came to Kentucky in a military capacity, and not long after married Mildred Hawkins, who was then living with her sister, the widow of Colonel John Todd. He had part in several of the campaigns against the Indians, before the separation of Kentucky from Virginia. By Shelby he was appointed, in 1792, the first adjutant-general of Kentucky, and continued to hold that office through successive administrations, until the close of Shelby's second term, in 1816. In that capacity, he organized the Kentucky contingent which fought under Wayne, and was with it at the Fallen Timbers. A writer in the *Pennsylvania Magazine* asserts that he accompanied one of the detachments of Kentuckians to the field, in 1812. On all occasions, he acquitted himself in a manner worthy of one of the five brothers, of whom Lafayette, who knew them all, wrote, in a letter still preserved and in the possession of a connexion of the family: "When I wished a thing well done, I ordered a Butler to do it." Captain Pierce Butler and Mildred Hawkins first settled in what is now Jessamine county, where Hickman creek empties itself into the Kentucky. There their oldest son, Thomas Langford Butler, was born, on the 10th of April, 1789. He went into the War of 1812 at its beginning, and remained in active service until its close. At New Orleans, he was a captain and aide to " Old Hickory," from whom he received the most complimentary mention. For gallantry, he was brevetted major. It would have been impossible for a man who united the blood of Butler and of

Hawkins to have been otherwise than gallant. He represented Carroll county in the legislature, 1824–48. He died
in Louisville in 1881, aged ninety-two years. His wife
was his cousin—a Miss Hawkins. Their only daughter
married the late Philip O. Turpin, whose descendants live
in Texas and Kentucky; the only son of Mr. Turpin who
was old enough to bear arms—Butler Turpin—entered the
Confederate army in 1862, at the age of sixteen, and remained in that service until Lee's surrender. Mr. Turpin
had two daughters;—Fannie married Evan Southgate, a
soldier of the Confederate army, who died in that service;
and Sallie, who married Edward Southgate, a brother of
Evan, and who, when a boy, enlisted in the Confederate
army, remained with it until the close of the war, and is now
a prominent minister of the Methodist Church. From the
mouth of Hickman, Captain Pierce Butler removed to
Carrollton, Kentucky, and there his second and most distinguished son—William Orlando—was born, 19th of April,
1791. In the War of 1812 he was among the first to volunteer as a private in Hart's company, and went immediately to the front to the relief of Fort Wayne. In that
second struggle for independence, he was greatly distinguished. He was soon promoted to ensign in the Seventeenth Regular Infantry. In both battles of the Raisin,
his daring and self-devotion were pre-eminently conspicuous; in the fight on the 22d of January, 1813, he was
wounded and captured. In the attack at Pensacola, he
was captain of the Forty-fourth Infantry. He was at the
battle of New Orleans on December 13, 1814, as well as in
that of January 8, 1815. There a number of British
sharpshooters were covered by a large sugar-house, and
Captain Butler volunteered to go alone and burn it. He
had succeeded in his mission when a number of British
soldiers sprang from their places of concealment with their
rifles leveled at his head. He laughed, threw his sword
among the sugar-stalks, crying out, " I will be prisoner to
the man who gets my sword;" and, while the men were
scrambling for the weapon, he jumped from the blazing
building and effected his escape. Of his conduct in these

battles, General Jackson reported that " he displayed the heroic chivalry and calmness of judgment in the midst of danger which distinguished the valuable officer in the hour of battle." For his gallantry in the field, he was brevetted major. In 1816, '17, he was Jackson's aide; then resigned, and commenced the practice of the law at Carrollton, and was immediately sent to the legislature from Gallatin county, 1817–18. He represented his district in Congress, 1839–43, and refused to be a candidate for a third term. In 1844, he was the Democratic candidate against Owsley for governor, and cut down the Whig majority from 20,000 to 4,624. June, 1846, he was appointed major-general of volunteers, and went to the assistance of Taylor in Mexico. At Monterey, he was second in command, and acted an important part in the capture of that stronghold. It was he who gave the order for the charge which was led by Aleck McClung with the Mississippi company of the brave Captain Willis. In the storming of the ramparts, General Butler was severely wounded. He succeeded General Scott as commander-in-chief of the army, which position he retained until the treaty of peace. In 1848, he was the Democratic candidate for vice-president on the ticket with Cass. In 1861, he was a member of the peace conference. He died in 1881, in his ninety-first year. General Butler married Eliza, daughter of General Robert Todd; they had no issue. Richard Parker, third son of Captain Pierce Butler, was a lawyer by profession, but never practiced; for many years he was clerk of the Carroll Circuit Court. His first wife was a daughter of Rice Bullock, who was a member from the Kentucky district of the Virginia convention which adopted the federal constitution, and who, with Humphrey Marshall and Robert Breckinridge, voted for that adoption. The oldest daughter of Richard Butler and Miss Bullock married John W. Menzies—a member of Congress from the Covington district, 1861–63, and now judge of the chancery court of that judicial district; their only daughter, Fanny Menzies—married her relative, Xenophon Hawkins, one of Morgan's Confederate soldiers. The other daughter of Richard Butler, Carrie, married Charles Powell, a Confederate soldier. After the death of his first wife, Richard Butler married a daughter of the learned Dr. Blythe, president of Hanover College. Captain Pierce Butler's daughter, Caroline, was the second wife of Judge James Pryor. The second wife of Dr. U. E. Ewing, a successful physician of Louisville, and a man of sense and force of character, was Captain Pierce Butler's daughter Jane. Their oldest daughter, Mildred Ewing, in 1859, married George B. Anderson, then a captain in the regular army. He resigned, in 1861, to enter the Confederate army; was in the first battle of Manassas, and all through the campaigns of 1862 on the Virginia peninsula, and when he died from wounds received at Antietam, he was a brigadier-general; the Southern army contained no braver soldier. His widow married, secondly, James M. Carlisle, a distinguished lawyer of Washington city. Dr. Ewing's second daughter, Eleanor Butler, married J. M. Wright, who left the military academy at West Point, before graduating, to enter the Federal army; he was the son of Major-General Wright, of the regular army, who, during the war, was in command on the Pacific coast. J. M. Wright was made a captain on the staff of General Buell, and was with that officer at Shiloh, and in all of his subsequent campaigns. He was on the staff of Gen. Boyle, was Adjutant-General of Kentucky under Gov. McCreary, and is now marshal of the United States Supreme Court. The third daughter of Dr. Ewing and Jane Butler—Jane—married George K. Speed, of Louisville, whose mother was the niece of the poet Keats, and who was himself a Federal soldier.

The fourth son of Captain Pierce Butler and Mildred Hawkins was named Pierce; he was born at Carrollton, October 4, 1794; graduated in the collegiate and law departments of Transylvania University; commenced the practice in Lexington; represented Fayette in the legislature, 1820; removed to Versailles, and represented Woodford in the legislature, 1821–22. In the latter year, Pierce Butler married Eliza Sarah, daughter of Colonel John

Allen and Jane Logan, and not long after moved to Shelby county, where he continued to practice his profession with eminent success. The people of Shelby sent him to the legislature, 1829, '30, '32. Having removed to Louisville as a larger field for practice, he represented that city in the legislature, 1838–39, and in the senate, 1845–47. Probably no other man was ever sent to the general assembly from four different counties of this state. Unlike his brothers, he was a staunch Whig in politics. As a lawyer, he was able and thorough; and as an advocate and public speaker at once ardent and brilliant. His eyes were large and dark; his hair, a dark brown; his countenance handsome, noble, and animated; his person rather smaller than the average, but symmetrical and elegant in its proportions; his manners, which were graceful, had about them a dignified reserved which invited confidence while they enforced respect and repelled familiarity; his spirit was bold and high; and, on points of integrity and honor, he was scrupulous, punctilious, and immovable. In every community in which he lived, Pierce Butler was respected and honored as one of its leading and most upright citizens. He died in Louisville, of cholera, in 1851. His widow survived him until July 28, 1867, when she died, in Maysville, Kentucky. This daughter of a " man whose triumphs in the forum and conduct in the field had added dignity and luster to the annals of the state, exhibited in a remarkable degree that strength and acuteness of intellect, that intrepidity of spirit, and that calm persistency of purpose which in stormier times had achieved the triumphs of her illustrious sire. And yet, with all this masculine force of intellect, there was nothing to awe or repel; she presented a combination of attractions as rare as it is exquisite. Solidity of attainment with grace of expression, depth of cultivation with refinement of manner, dignity of thought with delicacy of tone—all these combined not only to impress upon her the stamp of intellectual superiority, but to render her the central charm and attraction of the circle in which she moved." The oldest son of Pierce Butler and Eliza Sarah Allen—John Russell But-

ler—was born in Shelby county in 1823; graduated at
Centre College, and in the Louisville Medical College;
volunteered as a private soldier in the Mexican War, but
was soon transferred to the regulars, and promoted to lieutenant; continued in the service some time after the close
of that war, and left it with the rank of captain. In
1862, he raised a regiment of cavalry for the Confederate
service, and commanded it until the fall of 1864, when he
went to Canada to organize a force for the release of Confederate prisoners. Colonel J. Russ. Butler married Jane,
one of the daughters of that learned physician and cultivated gentleman, Dr. Charles W. Short. The father of
the latter, Peyton Short, was a native of Virginia, a member of an influential family long seated in that colony, and
a younger brother of William Short, a distinguished diplomatist, who served the republic in its earlier years as minister to Spain and other countries. Peyton Short came to
Kentucky while it was yet a district of Virginia, and in
1792 was chosen one of the first senators of the new commonwealth. His wife was a daughter of Hon. John Cleves
Symmes, of North Bend, who, after having been a soldier
in the Revolution, and a distinguished judge in New
Jersey, bought many thousands of acres in the North-
western Territory, and made his home on the banks of the
Ohio, at the spot which was subsequently made historic as
the site of the " log-cabin " of one of his sons-in-law, General Wm. Henry Harrison. The wife of Judge Symmes
was one of the Livingstons, of New Jersey and New
York—a name which has been made illustrious by the attainments, talents, and public services of its many members. Peyton Short and Miss Symmes had many children.
One of their daughters was the wife of Dr. Ben. Dudley, the eminent physician and surgeon, of Lexington.
Another daughter married Edward Green, of Hopkinsville; and a third, the elder James Weir, of Greenville.
The sons of Peyton Short—Judge William Short, of Ohio,
and Dr. Charles W. Short, of Louisville—inherited the
large estate of their uncle, the diplomatist, who died a
bachelor. Colonel J. Russ. Butler and Jane Short had
many children, who live in Louisville. Their oldest son,

Pierce, married a daughter of General Jere T. Boyle, and granddaughter of the able Judge John Boyle. Colonel Butler is dead; his widow resides in Louisville. The second son of Pierce Butler and Eliza S. Allen was named for his uncle—Wm. O. Butler. When the war broke out, he was a cotton-planter in Mississippi; he entered the Confederate army in 1862, and remained in it until the surrender of Lee at Appomattox. At first, he was a private, then a lieutenant in Morgan's cavalry. Having been transferred to the command of General Wheeler, he was made inspector-general on the staff of General Kelly, with the rank of captain, was at the side of his chief when Kelly was killed, and had his own horse shot from under him by the same volley. Captain Wm. O. Butler married Ella Coburn, a great-granddaughter of Judge John Coburn and Mary Moss. Judge Coburn was first a district judge of Mason county, then circuit judge, then judge of the territory of Orleans under Jefferson. Collins describes him as "one of the most indefatigable, efficient, and accomplished political writers of his day." Captain Wm. O. Butler and Ella Coburn have several children, and reside at Carrollton, Kentucky. The only daughter of Pierce Butler and Eliza S. Allen—Nannie—was born in Louisville, July 21, 1840; married Thos. M. Green, in Louisville, April 24, 1860; died in Maysville, June 11, 1881. Mr. Green is the son of John Green, of Lincoln, and Mary Keith Marshall; they had nine children—all living.

By some it will be regarded as noteworthy that of this Butler family all the male members were officers in the Revolution; the five sons of that generation all had sons, and of these all but one were in the War of 1812, and that one was then only nine years old; the *Pennsylvania Magazine* states that at least nine were officers in the war with Mexico; and in the civil war every male descendant of Captain Pierce Butler (who settled in Kentucky) who was capable of bearing arms was in the Confederate army, while the husbands of all his female descendants who were capable of bearing arms were either in the Confederate or Federal army—with one exception, the writer of these lines.

THE PARKERS.

Jane Logan Allen, third daughter of Colonel John Allen and Jane Logan, was born in Shelby county about the year 1808, and there married Dr. John Todd Parker, then of Woodford county.

It will be remembered that Mary and Elizabeth Todd, daughters of Robert Todd, the emigrant (who was the grandfather of Colonel John and Generals Levi and Robert Todd) and Isabella Bodley, married, respectively, two brothers—James and William Parker. James Parker and Mary Todd had four sons and four daughters; one of the sons was Robert Parker, a major in the Revolution. William Parker and Elizabeth Todd had one son, who was also a major, and a daughter; the latter became the the second wife of

GENERAL ANDREW PORTER,

of Pennsylvania. This able and celebrated man was the son of Robert Porter, who emigrated from near Londonderry, Ireland, to America, in 1720, and settled on a farm near Norristown, Pennsylvania. He was a Presbyterian elder. He had nine sons, eight of whom became farmers or tradesmen. His son, Andrew, was born on the 24th of September, 1743. The *Pennsylvania Magazine* states that from childhood Andrew exhibited an extraordinary appetite for books, reading and mastering the contents of all he could procure. The effort of his father to force him, at the age of eighteen, to learn a trade met with a signal failure; it was soon discovered that he was too intent on the acquisition of knowledge, and too little disposed to manual labor, to be useful in any handicraft. He had already mastered, without aid, some of the higher branches of mathematics, for which he had disclosed a taste and remarkable talent; and it is related that he spoiled all the tools in the shop in which he was employed in constructing a sun dial from a suitable stone he had selected from an adjacent soap-stone quarry. Attempts to confine him to the labors of the farm proving equally futile, his father, in despair, determined to fit him for the calling of a country schoolmaster. He was accordingly sent, for a short time, to the school of a Mr. Mennon, where he made wonderful progress in his mathematical studies; and then opened a small school in the vicinity of his home. In a conversation with Dr. David Rittenhouse, upon whom he had called to borrow some work on conic sections, that gentleman was so impressed by the extent of the information and unusual capacity of the boy, that he urged him to leave the country, proceed to Philadelphia, and there establish a school. Acting upon this counsel, he removed to Philadelphia, in 1767, and there opened an English and mathematical school, which he conducted with great reputation for nine years, during which time he had become an accurate astronomer. His success as a teacher was such that, in 1776, his pupils numbered more than one hundred, the fees affording him an abundant living for his family of five children, who had recently lost their mother. Abandoning all selfish considerations, he responded to his country's call in the spring of 1776; in June, was made a captain of marines, which position he soon exchanged for the same rank in the artillery; and in this corps continued to serve until the close of the war. He was successively promoted major, lieutenant-colonel, lieutenant-colonel commandant, and colonel of the Fourth Regiment of Artillery, which latter rank and command he had at the disbanding of the army. In the cannonade at Trenton he was personally engaged, as well as in the battles of Princeton, Brandywine, and Germantown; in the first, he received on the field in person the thanks and praise of Washington; and in the last he stood by his guns while nearly his whole command were killed or captured. In 1779, he was detached for duty under General Clinton in Sullivan's operations against the Indians, and was in the battle at Tioga Point. When the siege of Yorktown was determined upon, he protested against the order which deprived him of the opportunity to further participate in active field operations by directing him to Philadelphia to superintend the laboratory at which the various kinds of ammunition used in the siege were prepared; but his objections were silenced by a letter written to him by Washington, in which the commander-in-chief said: "Our success depends much on the manner in which our cartridges, bombs, and matches are prepared. The eye of science is required to superintend their preparation. . . . There is not an officer in the army better qualified than yourself for the station I have assigned you." After the Revolution, General Porter was for years employed as the commissary of the commission which determined the boundary lines between Virginia and Pennsylvania and what is now Ohio. He was made brigadier-general, and then major-general, of the Pennsylvania militia, and then surveyor-general of that state. In the war of 1812 he was appointed by President Madison brigadier-general in the regular army, and secretary of war, but declined both positions on the ground that a younger man might serve the country more efficiently. When a captain in the army, General Porter had a misunderstanding with Major Eustace in regard to a question of rank, which was at first deemed trifling. Not long after, Porter, on entering the dining-room of a hotel, heard Major Eustace say: "He is nothing but a d——d schoolmaster." On asking Eustace whether the words had been applied to him, and receiving an affirmative response, Porter rejoined: "I have been a schoolmaster, sir, and have not forgotten my vocation;" and, drawing his sword, struck Eustace with the back of it on the shoulders. In the duel which was at once ar-arranged, Major Eustace was shot through the heart at the first fire. A court-martial acquitted Porter, and the colonial council promoted him to the place which had been filled by Eustace.—[*Pennsylvania Magazine.*]

General Andrew Porter was twice married;—first, to Elizabeth McDowell, on the 10th of March, 1767; and, secondly, to Elizabeth, daughter of William Parker and Elizabeth Todd, on the 20th of May, 1777; the brother of his second wife was the gallant Major Parker, of the Revolution. By the first wife, he had five children: Robert, who was an eminent lawyer and judge in Pennsylvania;

18

Elizabeth Rittenhouse, of whom hereafter; Mary, who married her cousin, Robert Porter, and settled in Kentucky; and Andrew and William, who respectively became wealthy merchants in New Orleans and Baltimore. By his second wife—Elizabeth Parker—General Porter had eight children : Charlotte married Robert Brooke, and had sons who were distinguished as lawyers and successful as merchants in Philadelphia; John Ewing changed his name to Parker, and became an eminent physician in North Carolina; Harriet was the wife of Colonel Thomas McKeen; David Rittenhouse was the distinguished governor of Pennsylvania, and General Horace Porter was *his* son; George Bryan, an eminent lawyer, was governor of Michigan territory under Jackson, and *his* son, Andrew, fought at Vera Cruz, Cerro Gordo, Contreras, Cherubusco, and Chapultepec, was brevetted lieutenant-colonel for gallant and meritorious conduct, as a brigadier-general in the civil war, fought all through McClellan's peninsula campaign, and died in Europe from disease contracted in the service; and James Madison Porter, who, after having attained distinction at the bar, in the deliberative bodies of Pennsylvania, and on the bench, was secretary of war under Tyler. Andrew Parker, son of James Madison Porter, graduated at West Point, entered the regular army, and was commissary-general under McClellan and Thomas.— [*Pennsylvania Magazine.*]

Elizabeth Rittenhouse Porter, the oldest daughter of General Andrew Porter by his first wife, married Robert Parker, son of James Parker and Mary Todd, and first cousin of General Porter's second wife. He was a major in the Revolution. This marriage took place in 1790, and the newly-wedded pair made their bridal trip from Pennsylvania to Lexington, Kentucky, on horseback. In Lexington Major Robert Parker is said to have built the first brick house erected in that city. Major Robert Parker and Elizabeth R. Porter had four sons and two daughters. Their oldest daughter married Major Richardson, whose son by her—John C. Richardson—became an eminent lawyer in St. Louis. The other daughter married Robert S. Todd, of Lexington, and was the mother of the wife of

President Lincoln. The oldest son—Dr. James P. Parker—married the daughter of General Milliken, who gave his name to the historic "bend" above Vicksburg; and their son, John, is a man of wealth in New Orleans. Another son of Major Robert Parker—Andrew—was the father of Carilla Parker, who is the wife of Mr. William Irvine, of Boyle county; they are the parents of many children—among them, Rev. Alexander Irvine, a worthy Presbyterian minister.

The fourth son of Major Robert Parker—Dr. John Todd—married Jane Logan Allen, as already stated. Dr. Parker was a well-educated, skillful, and successful physician; his wife was a woman of mental and personal attractions. They had six children who grew to maturity: Betty, a woman of strong mind and fluent speech, married Samuel Boyd; she died November 6, 1888, leaving two married daughters, who reside in Cass county, Missouri. Annie Marie Parker married Wm. M. Dickson, in Lexington, October 19, 1852. She was a woman of talent. Her husband graduated at Miami University, built up a large law practice in Cincinnati, was for years judge of one of the principal courts of that city, and enjoys an enviable reputation as a man of integrity, as a well-equipped lawyer and an able judge, and as a vigorous contributor to the press and to historical and literary magazines.* Mrs. Dickson is dead. Three of her children live: Parker, William Lowry, and Jennie. Colonel Robert Henry, third child of Dr. John Todd Parker, has a large family, and lives in Abilene, Texas. Dr. John Allen Parker, the fourth child, died soon after the war. Mary Eliza, fifth child, married John J. Dickson, a brother of Judge Dickson; they live in Iowa. The sixth child of Dr. John Parker and Jane Logan Allen—James Porter Parker—graduated with credit at West Point, was a colonel of artillery in the Confederate army, and is now a civil engineer in New Mexico.

---

* The paternal grandfather of Judge Dickson was Scotch and for fifty years a Presbyterian minister. His mother was a Lowry, and descended from the Campbells and Ochiltrees of the Valley.

Mary Kelsey, fourth daughter of Colonel John Allen and Jane Logan, married General Thomas Newton, of Little Rock, Arkansas. Their daughter, Anna, is the wife of Colonel Richard Johnson, an editor and lawyer of Little Rock, and a brother of the former senator from Arkansas. Colonel Johnson was a Confederate soldier, and is a man of reputation as a political writer and in the legal profession. Thomas and Robert Newton—sons of General Newton and Mary K. Allen—were gallant officers in the Confederate service, and are not less distinguished in civil life.

Sarah Allen—daughter of the pioneer, James Allen, and Mary Kelsey—first married Mr. Singleton, and then Andrew Rowan. The latter was a brother of Judge John Rowan, and was himself a man of marked intellect and great force of character. The descendants of Sarah Allen are scattered over the Green river country, and are highly respectable in character, attainments, mental attributes, and standing. The men acquitted themselves well as officers in the Federal service. Her sons were Allen and Stanley, and her daughter was Mary Singleton. Allen had a son, Dr. William Singleton, who was a successful physician and surgeon of the Third Kentucky Union Cavalry. He continued in the service until forced to leave it by disease, contracted in the line of duty, from which he died. One of his daughters married a son of Hon. Wm. N. Sweeney, of Owensboro. Stanley Singleton left several daughters, one of whom married General A. M. Stout, of the Federal army; another married John Johnston, of McLean; a third married Dr. Davis, of Muhlenberg; and the fourth, Mr. Newman, of Henderson. By Andrew Rowan, Sarah Allen had a daughter, Eliza Rowan, who married Mr. Harwood; and a son, Joseph Allen Rowan, who graduated at West Point, and died early and childless.

Joe Allen,

the second son of James Allen and Mary Kelsey, was as remarkable for the persistence with which he resisted every effort to draw him into public life, for which he was well adapted by education and a vigorous intellect, as he was for his uncommon strong practical sense, his benevolence, his rich and racy humor, his integrity and utter fearlessness. With his brother-in-law, Joseph Huston, he removed to what was afterward Breckinridge county some years before the beginning of this century, and while it was still almost unpeopled. Indian raids had not ceased, and in repelling them, and carrying the war into their own territory north of the Ohio, the deliberate courage and herculean frame and strength of the young Allen enabled him to do good service and effective fighting. In two of the campaigns of the War of 1812, he was captain of the advance-guard, or, as it was called, "the company of spies." Twice was he offered, and as often refused, the colonelcy of a regiment, alleging as his reason "that he knew how to command his company, but did not know that he could command a larger body," which, he contended, should always be placed under the orders of trained and educated officers. At that early period, horse thieves had collected in large numbers in Indiana, from whence they made excursions into Kentucky. It was Joe Allen who organized and led the band of Kentuckians against the marauders, broke up and burned their settlements, killed many of them, and dispersed their whole body. Upon his return, he was asked what had become of the leader of the gang; and replied that the last he had seen of him was through the sights of his rifle. The governor of Indiana sent a body of soldiers to Hardinsburg to capture Allen, who rallied his men, and made prisoners of the soldiers, who then fraternized with their captors. On the organization of Breckinridge county, in 1800, Joseph Allen was appointed clerk of the circuit court, held the office until 1852 under that appointment, and was then elected for six additional years; this was the single instance of his ever being a candidate for any place. Albeit, a leader in all public enterprises, a good lawyer, an electrical speaker, personally greatly beloved, and in every way singularly well qualified for public affairs, Joe Allen resolutely turned his back upon every proposition to enter public life. In 1803 he married Margaret Crawford, the daughter of a highly-respectable farmer who had recently removed to Breckinridge from Botetourt county, Virginia. They had five children. Jane Allen, their oldest daughter, married John McClarty, a merchant of Hardinsburg, by whom she had nine children; one of these, Clinton McClarty, was elected clerk of the house of representatives in 1859, was a candidate for clerk of the court of appeals in 1860, was a soldier in the Confederate army, and is now a bank officer in Louisiana. Horace, the second child of Joe Allen, married Elizabeth Larue, of the county of that name; their son, Joseph Allen, is a merchant in Louisville, and their daughter, Mary L., married Wm. Piatt, now of Barren county. Mary, the third child of Joseph Allen, married Francis Peyton, a prominent lawyer. They had six children—Joseph A. Peyton; Cornelia, who married D. C. Gannaway; Margaret, who first married Jas. D. Morton, and then George Chick, of Breckinridge; Alfred H. and Ellen Peyton. Ellen, fourth child of Joe Allen, married Dr. Wathen, of Breckinridge county.

ALFRED ALLEN,

the fifth child of Joe Allen and Margaret Crawford, represented Breckinridge county in the legislature in 1838–39; was then appointed by Governor Clark commonwealth attorney for that district, in which position he was continued, by successive appointments and an election, until 1856; in 1859, was the Whig candidate for lieutenant-governor; was re-elected to the legislature in 1861, and continued in that capacity until 1866, when he resigned in order to accept the consulship to Foochoo, China, where he remained until recalled at his own request. Mr. Allen, in 1853, married Mary E. Jennings, by whom he has two children—Horace and Mary Allen.

THE HUSTONS.

Margaret, the second daughter of James Allen and Mary Kelsey, in the dawn of her womanhood married Joseph Huston, and before the beginning of the century settled in Breckinridge county. Her husband was a member of the legislature in 1813, and died about that time. Margaret remained a widow, and until her death success- fully conducted her own business affairs, which her sound judgment, independent character, and a mind of masculine clearness and vigor, enabled her to do with ease. She had three children—Eli, Eliza, and Felix Huston. Eliza was the first wife of Colonel David R. Murray, of Cloverport. Eli Huston received an excellent academical and legal education, but in his early manhood was disqualified from the practice in Kentucky because of a duel in which he was the challenging party, and which resulted unhappily for both parties. Thus driven to other pursuits, he pros- ecuted them with such diligence and success as soon ren- dered him independent. His younger brother, Felix, who had been involved on his account in the same duel, and had like him suffered disqualification from the practice of law, had wandered off into Mississippi, then the refuge of adventurous spirits, and had there risen rapidly into prom- inence in a profession which had been closed to them in Kentucky. At the instance and upon the invitation of the younger brother, Eli Huston joined him in Mississippi, and soon gained high rank as a lawyer at the bar of Natchez. After a very few years of practice, he was made a circuit judge of the Natchez district, and died while an incumbent of the office. Before the duel referred to, Eli Huston had married, in Frankfort, a daughter of John Morris, and granddaughter of Judge Hary Innes. Their children are all dead, their only living descendant being a granddaughter, Mrs. Durell, of Arkansas. Felix, the other son of Joseph Huston and Margaret Allen, had at- tained his majority a short time before he forfeited his law practice, and went to Mississippi. There the peculiar quality called "pluck" was as essential to success at the bar, at that time, as either brains or learning, and the man was fortunate whose quality in that particular was not subjected to the severest test at some point of his career. Felix Huston, at the very outset of his residence in Missis- sippi, demonstrated that his professional attainments were in every way respectable, that his mental caliber was superior, and he embraced the very first occasion that presented itself in the course of his law practice to satisfy all who were curious on the subject that he had no prejudice against the smell of gunpowder. Possessed of a good legal mind, of attractive oratorical gifts, high spirit, and a commanding presence, he won reputation as an advocate, an honorable standing as a lawyer and counsellor, and pecuniary prosperity. He was the second of S. S. Prentiss in his duel with Henry S. Foote, and of General Allen in the duel with Alex. McClung in which Allen lost his life. In the midst of this career, he was offered by Sam. Houston, then president of Texas, the supreme command of the Texan army, on condition that he would recruit in the states and equip two regiments for service in Texas. Ambitious for military distinction, he accepted the offer, complied with the conditions, transported his men to Texas, was appointed a major-general by Houston, and was placed in temporary command of the Texan forces. Houston refused to permit the invasion of Mexico, which had been one of the stipulations of the contract. The quarrel that resulted between General Huston and the Texan President culminated in the former being superseded in command by General Albert Sidney Johnston. Smarting under a sense of ill-usage, and precluded by their relative positions from seeking redress at the hands of the president, General Huston, instead of maneuvering to undermine General Johnston, or, by abuse, to draw a challenge from him, went straight to the end he sought by sending him immediately a respectful but peremptory demand for a meeting. The challenge was promptly accepted by Johnston, who fell with a wound in the thigh that well-nigh proved fatal. Huston, bitterly regretting his act, was unremitting in his attentions to his antagonist. They became friends, and continued so through life. There was much in common between the two men; though of different breeds, they came from the same Scotch Irish race. General Johnston derived his strong, well-marked features, his every valuable mental and moral characteristic, and all that he had in him that was good or heroic, or capable of

becoming great, from his mother, the pious daughter of
Edward Harris—a plain Presbyterian elder. There was
precious little of the "cavalier" about *him*. General Felix
Huston fought several good battles with the Indians while
in the Texan service, the most important of which was
that of Plumb creek. Finding himself much embarrassed
by his large expenditures for Texas, he resumed the practice of law in Louisiana, and died about the time of the
beginning of the civil war. General Felix Huston married a Miss Dangerfield, a member of the Virginia family
of that name, and a descendant of Colonel Charles Mynn
Thruston, of the Revolution. They left several children,
who reside in Mississippi and Louisiana.

James Allen, of Nelson.

The third and youngest son of James Allen, the pioneer,
and Mary Kelsey, bore the christian name of his father,
and remained upon the farm near Bloomfield, in Nelson
county, which that father had redeemed from the wilderness. He represented Nelson in the legislature of 1825,
but his tastes inclined him to agricultural rather than to
professional pursuits, and rendered him averse to public
life. He was a man of strong mind, of high personal
character, and of undeviating integrity—qualities that
marked all his conduct, and entitled him to the influence
he exerted in the community in which he lived. James
Allen married Mary Read, of Woodford county. Their
only son, John Allen, accumulated a handsome fortune as
a merchant in Louisville, and died unmarried. Their
daughter, Mary Allen, married H. E. Rowland, and had one
son, James A. Rowland, who married Ada, daughter of
Hon. Simeon C. Anderson, formerly a member of Congress
from the Garrard district, and whose wife was a daughter
of Governor Owsley. He married secondly Ellen W. Suter,
by whom he had two children, both living. Mrs. Rowland
is still living near Bloomfield. Another daughter of James
Allen, Nancy, married a Mr. Allen, who was not related to
her; they are both dead. The third daughter of James Allen and Mary Read—Amanda—married Charles Q. Arm-

strong, a merchant of Louisville. They had five children. Their only son, John Allen Armstrong, resides in Louisville. Kate, the oldest daughter, is the wife of Captain John H. Leathers, who was distinguished for gallantry in the Confederate army, and is now the cashier of a bank in Louisville. Annie E. Armstrong married Rev. E. H. Pearce, an educated gentleman, who, in his early manhood, was a successful teacher, and is now a prominent minister of the Methodist Church. The other daughters of Mrs. Amanda F. Armstrong—Mrs. Lottie A. Offutt and Mrs. Mattie Wilkinson—reside in Nelson county.

In what has been written in the foregoing pages, the purpose was to present the men and the families, an imperfect account of whom has been given, as fair types of those who wrested Kentucky from the savage, redeemed her waste places, carried the torch of learning into the wilderness, founded the state, and left the impress of their own characteristics upon her people. General Ben. Logan and his brothers, Colonel John Hardin, the Todds, Colonel Stephen Trigg, and others, were selected as types of the fearless men of iron nerve who were among the earliest and most successful of the stern warriors who won the land, helped to extend the boundaries of our country, afterward had an active part in the civil affairs of the district, and molded political opinion in the commonwealth. Men like these, with capacity for military combination, and imbued with the ambition of empire, proved themselves in time of peace as competent in civic councils as they had been efficient in the field, and their descendants have ever since been useful and influential in all public affairs; while the mere guides and scouts, whose instincts, passions, and rude aspirations were those of the hunter only, passed away, leaving scarce a trace of their existence upon the body politic. Judge Samuel McDowell and his sons, Judge Innes, Judge Caleb Wallace, Major John Crittenden, and others like them, were chosen as types of the men who, after having been conspicuous for years before and during the Revolution in the civil and military affairs of Virginia, came to Kentucky after the close of hostilities with the British, participated in the subsequent organization, movements, and achievements of the expeditions against the Indians, in the political deliberations which led to the separation from Virginia and to the establishment of the commonwealth, and directed popular sentiment in the infancy of our state. In the personal character of Judge McDowell, there were embodied those qualities of judicious forbearance, patient endurance, fixed purpose, calm but resolute persistence, obedience to law, and undying love of liberty and country, which were so splendidly illustrated by Kentuckians in the long-protracted throes of parturition through which the district passed before statehood was achieved; and which acted as an effective foil to the allurements of the Spaniard and the machinations of his emissaries. The letter of the younger Samuel McDowell—the first United States Marshal—expresses concisely and forcibly the principles transmitted to the Union men of the present generation by the patriots of that early day, discloses the forces that were arrayed against national life from the very dawn of the republic, emphasizes the unshrinking determination with which those principles of disintegration were from the first combated, and without alteration or addition might have served as a platform for the Union men of Kentucky in 1861;—as the watchword and countersign for the brave men who went to the field. The gifted and heroic Allen; the brilliant and gallant Daviess—the prosecutor of Burr and hero of Tippecanoe; the scholarly, talented, and brave Rowan; the able, profound, learned, and soldierly Martin D. Hardin; the accomplished, eloquent, graceful, and well-equipped William Logan; the strong-minded and thoroughly-trained Alexander K. Marshall, and others like them, were chosen as types of the generation which closely followed the pioneers—whose professional attainments, whose triumphs at the bar, on the bench, in the forum, and on the hustings, and whose knightly bearing and gallantry in battle, rivaling the achievements of the men of the Elizabethan era, rendered our state honorable in the eyes of their countrymen. Immediately following them, and partly contemporary with them, were John J. Crittenden—a man who was inferior to no other of his day in the mental strength that addresses itself to the judgment, in the shining talents that captivate and lead the minds of men, in the manly virtues that attract and win their enduring affections, nor in any of the graces which fascinate and charm,— a man who was made even more illustrious by unselfish patriotism in the hour of national peril than by his courage in battle or his forensic victories; the other Crittenden brothers; John J. Marshall, by many regarded as the most intellectual of his name; the able William T. Barry; the Butlers, gallant scions of a line of soldiers, whose civil talents were only less conspicuous than their military careers; rare Ben. Hardin, who was the equal of any and superior to most of his contemporaries as a lawyer, and not inferior to any of them in the acuteness nor in the robustness of his understanding; the courtly and richly-gifted Richard Clough Anderson, Jr.; John Boyle, the son of one of the earliest and bravest of the pioneers, and perhaps the most acute metaphysician of all our jurists; the Wickliffes, men of attainments and unquestioned vigor; the amiable, accomplished, and handsome Joseph Cabell Breckinridge, who transmitted to his only son, General John C. Breckinridge, the talents, the noble presence, and the intrepidity he had himself inherited from his mother, Mary Hopkins Cabell, and from his father, the elder John Breckinridge; James C. Pickett, the graceful writer and scholarly diplomatist; and John Green, of Lincoln, one of the earliest, and firmest, and boldest of the anti-slavery Presbyterian laity, and one of the very ablest of the unflinching leaders of the "Old Court" and Whig parties. Next in the order of this remarkable succession of brilliant galaxies came Robert J. Breckinridge, an accomplished master of the Anglo-Saxon tongue, possessed of unsurpassed powers of sarcasm, and who, when aroused by a fitting occasion, was wonderfully eloquent,—who was for a time a shining light at the bar and in politics, and

who, flitting from these like a meteor, became, with a
single exception, incomparably the greatest of our theologians; John A. McClung, noted as a lawyer and statesman, and distinguished as a publicist, as an orator and as
a divine; their kinsman, the scholarly and graceful orator,
Thomas F. Marshall, whose greatest faculty was that of
an inexorable logician; Richard H. Menifee, whose perfect
dignity and remarkable force of character, whose indomitable pride which never descended into vanity, whose admirable poise, untiring industry, unbending will, fixed
purpose, and vaulting ambition, combined with an ardent
and earnest nature, electrical eloquence, and mental
strength, rendered him superior to Marshall, by whom he
was excelled in grace and in the culture of the schools;
and Christopher Tompkins, Jr.,—the grandson of Colonel
John Logan,—who was, in the estimation of many, the
most gifted and promising of them all. Among these native and adopted sons of Kentucky, there was not one
who was intellectually the superior of John Poage Campbell, nor one who was his equal in the extent, variety, depth,
thoroughness, and elegance of his culture. Dr. Campbell's
detection of "the character and tendency" of the Darwinian system of philosophy (Lexington, 1812) is peculiarly interesting as "an illustration of the intellectual life
of the pioneer period, as well as suggestive and valuable
by reason of its singular pertinence to present issues in
the world of scientific and religious thought." It was
certainly no small feat of scholarship at that early period
to trace the germs of the Darwinian "theory" to the old
pagan philosophers of Greece and Rome, and at the same
time to anticipate the inevitable effects of the developed
hypothesis upon the orthodox faiths of modern times.
When we remember that these "Letters" were addressed
to Colonel Daviess, the able and dauntless prosecutor of
Aaron Burr, we can readily understand that the "learned
professions" were ably represented in Kentucky in pioneer
times. Dr. Campbell, Dr. Cameron, Drs. John and Robert
J. Breckinridge, Dr. John A. McClung, and Dr. Lewis
Warner Green (the old president of Hampden Sidney),

may be accepted as fair examples of the classical and theological training imparted by the early schools of Virginia and Kentucky; and we may doubt if it will be seriously maintained by the most skeptical inquirer that the type of *theologian and scholar* is appreciably higher at the present day. In medicine and surgery, it is only necessary to mention Dr. Ephraim McDowell, the originator of abdominal surgery; Dr. Benjamin Dudley, the famous lithotomist; and Dr. Brashear, one of the most distinguished of that remarkable group of surgeons which seems to have sprung up spontaneously in the young commonwealth of the West. Nor must the professional *educators* of these days be overlooked. Dr. James Priestley, Dr. Louis Marshall (youngest brother of the Chief-Justice), Joshua Fry, " Dominie " Thompson, and other learned Scotchmen, Dr. John C. Young, Dr. Lewis W. Green, Dr. Wm. L. Breckinridge, and others, were men admirably fitted by character and accomplishments to train the young men of an ambitious and advancing commonwealth, and it is still esteemed a distinction in Kentucky to have been an alumnus of those pioneer schools. Let the *men* they produced speak for the thoroughness of the training and for the erudition and capacity of the instructors.

The sources of the extraordinary development of intellectual life in the early days of Kentucky, the martial character of her people in the formative period, and the characteristics which distinguish the better class of her population of the present generation, must be sought for in the character, antecedents, history, and surroundings of those from whom they sprung. The earliest explorers of Kentucky were not the hunters like Findlay, Boone, Kenton, and Stover; they were Dr. Thomas Walker, Captain Charles Campbell, and other educated Virginians, whose descendants and kindred have since been prominent among her people for an hundred years. Among the very earliest of the surveyors were Hancock and Willis Lee—a name which has been historic in America for two centuries,— who were the lineal descendants of William Brewster—the Presbyterian elder who became the leader of the Leyden

Pilgrims,—and who combined with those strains of vigorous blood that which flowed in the veins of Washington. They were the elder brothers of John Lee, who won his title of major by gallantry in the Revolution, who settled in Woodford county, and who was the ancestor of Senator Call, of Florida, of Generals George B. and Thomas L. Crittenden, and of their nephew, Dr. Young, now the president of Centre College. With them came their young kinsman, John W. Willis, who, upon the killing of some and the dispersion of the rest of the party by the Indians, with three companions descended the Kentucky river to its mouth, and then went down the Ohio and Mississippi to New Orleans, in an Indian pirogue;—the first white men speaking English who ever made the voyage. After this, he fought from the beginning to the close of the Revolution, and came out of it with the rank and command of a major. He had been educated in the best schools of Scotland; and was lineally descended from Colonel Francis Willis, a burgess in 1652, from Colonel Augustine Warner, speaker of the Burgesses in 1676, and from the aunt and god-mother of Washington. Many of his kindred live in Kentucky to-day, where some of them have been prominent in all the professions. The earliest of the hardy pioneers who made permanent lodgments, took root, and put forth branches in Kentucky, were not the illiterate, half-civilized men of rude and exaggerated speech some historians have represented them to have been. While some of them may have been of this class and character, they were comparatively few in number, and they were speedily lost sight of in the advancing waves of immigration, leaving scarcely a ripple upon the surface to tell that they were ever here. Among these pioneers were men from the best of the English, Welsh, and Scotch stocks of tide-water Virginia; but the mass of them came from the Scotch-Irish Calvinistic people of the Valley, of the Holston, and of North Carolina—than whom the sun never shone upon a more vigorous or a more enduring race. These people were not sprung from a dissolute, a self-indulgent, an idle, or an effete gentry;

they had none of these nor any of the other characteristics which are vulgarly attributed to the " cavalier." Nor
were they ever intermingled with that pauper or semi-
criminal class who were sold into temporary servitude to
pay their fines and the expenses of their transportation to
the colony. For men like them to have been evolved
from such antecedents, from such worthless surroundings,
would have been a violation of nature's immutable law.
These men were not only singularly cool and fearless in
danger, intrepid in action, and daring in enterprise; they
were, as a class, a sober, earnest, independent, law-abiding,
liberty-loving, church-going, bible-reading, devil-defying,
God-fearing people;—the equals morally and intellectually
of the Puritans of New England, or of the best of those
from whom they sprung—the " Puritans of the South," as
the Scotch-Irish Presbyterians and Huguenots of Virginia
and the Carolinas have been appropriately described,—or
of any other breed or race of men the world ever saw.
That the pioneers came mainly from this people, their
very names sufficiently prove; and that they were what
they were was the result of the operation for years of natural causes and inevitable laws. Their ancestors had endured all hardships, made every sacrifice, and fought in
Scotland for their religious convictions. Thence they had
gone to the North of Ireland—with whose aboriginal people they did not mingle,—where they converted Ulster,
Down, and Antrim from a scene of desolation into a
blooming garden. There they fought for civil and religious liberty as represented by the princes of Nassau and
Hanover, and then were betrayed, proscribed, and perse-
cuted by the dynasties whose thrones they had secured,
and whose battles they had won. To secure the liberty of
conscience denied to them at home, many thousands of
this peculiar and indomitable people crossed the Atlantic
to build new homes in Connecticut, New Jersey, Pennsylvania, Virginia, and North Carolina, where their thrift,
energy, industry, and intelligence produced fruits as the
same qualities had previously produced them in Ireland.
The very poverty of the soil of Scotland had forced their

ancestors to seek compensation in education; the descendants in America manifested their inherited aspirations for moral and religious advancement and intellectual culture by building schools, colleges, and churches. They had brought with them from Ireland the germs of republican principles; they were the first and boldest to speak for independence; they filled the ranks, and were the best soldiers, of the patriot armies. In Virginia they had been conspicuous in the French and Indian wars; their names are found among the most heroic on every battle-field of the Revolution. Their sons who came to Kentucky exhibited the qualities that came to them as their most valuable inheritance from the ages: In confronting the forces of nature, in their warfare with the Indians and British, in the deeds of heroism and self-devotion which extort the admiration of every reader. These qualities were elicited, tested, strengthened, and made resplendent by the circumstances of their situation. That their descendants have been generous, hospitable, self-reliant, brave, and martial, was only their birthright. At Tippecanoe, on the Raisin, on the Thames, on the waters of Erie, at New Orleans, at the Alamo, before the battlements of Monterey, on the plains of Mexico, at Cardenas, and on every hard-fought field of the civil war, the hereditary characteristics of the Scotch-Irish race were splendidly illustrated. As in Scotland, Ireland, the Middle States, in Virginia, and in the Carolinas, their ambition for cultivation and intellectual life was early manifested in Kentucky. Many of them had been well educated; those whose limited advantages had denied them a liberal or elegant culture were the more emulous to obtain it for their offspring. With the Indian war-whoop ringing in their ears, they gave to and obtained for their children the very best instruction possible to be had, and planned and provided for the erection of schools and colleges. They founded Transylvania; they established Centre College; and they inaugurated the common-school system. At Danville, among them, and by them, began the revolt against slavery; in their midst

19

the first candidate of the Liberty party, James G. Birney, was born, was reared, and was educated, and among them he was married. Their surroundings forced them to be self-reliant, developed every latent energy, and stimulated every manly and intellectual quality. They were compelled to rely on their own manhood and mental vigor for their influence on others, for their standing among their fellows, and even for existence; and they judged all other men by their possession of or deficiency in qualities that were valuable, solid, staying, and useful. Wealth was soon created among them by their own energies, but the possession of wealth did not fix any man's caste or social position. Family influence was potential only so far as the public discerned in the individual the valuable characteristics common to his kindred. Even now the men who lead in the commonwealth, and who are really respected, are not the men of wealth, but the men of brains, of moral worth and manly virtues; and where this sincere deference is paid to the wealthy, it is not to nor because of his riches, but for some admirable personal quality the individual himself possesses. Cut off as her people were by mountains and long distances from the coasts before the age of steam, in the formative period the commercial instinct was more tardily developed in Kentucky than in communities more favorably situated; the vigorous, the gifted, the enterprising, the ambitious, turned to the liberal professions, or to that of arms, as fitting fields for their talents and energies, and sought to win fame and honor by deeds of valor and by forensic display. The contents of the few newspapers were meager; the books that were read were by the best authors; their contents were mastered and assimilated, and furnished suggestions to their readers for new trains of thought. Neither in law nor in politics was there a beaten track; the necessity for mastering principles rather than memorizing precedents promoted originality of thought, and developed the constructive faculty. The pioneers at first lived in rude log-cabins built by their own hands; but in those modest domiciles were frequently found proud spirits, culti-

vated minds, kindly and gentle manners, the masculine
and delicate feminine virtues, and an unfailing hospitality.
As the years passed on, those rude log structures gave
way to others of substantial brick or stone, whose walls
were decorated with quaint wood-carvings, and in many
instances were adorned with portraits which, in coloring,
in expression, and in accurate and vivid delineation, were
no mean specimens of the painter's art. Those houses
were the abodes of a hearty and genuine hospitality, as
generous as it was unaffected and unassuming. Could
what has been writen be enforced with engravings of
these portraits, the reader would cheerfully admit that
the originals they represented were men of a high order
of intellectuality, among the first of the English-speaking
races. They were not only strong themselves, but they
impressed themselves upon others. The greatest of all
Kentuckians, he whose eloquence and patriotism gave
most renown to the state, Henry Clay, while he was not
one of these men, nor of this race, was never greater than
when he gave voice to their sentiments, and acted in har-
mony with their views.

Wherever these people have gone, their places have been
in front, and those places were taken without other aid
than the brain and worth of the men to whom they were
conceded. In Ohio were the McDowells, Trimbles, and
others of the same race, and allied one with the other. In
Illinois were the kinsmen, John T. Stuart, John J. Hardin and Stephen Trigg Logan. They were all Whigs; all
opposed the extension of slavery; all were the friends and
encouragers of Lincoln; one was his instructor and law
partner; another was largely instrumental in securing his
nomination; he married their kinswoman; the influence the
association may have exerted in molding his opinions, if
any, may be left to conjecture. Whether you go with John
McKinley to Alabama, with the Hustons to Mississippi,
with the Campbells to Nebraska, or with others to Tennessee, Missouri, Arkansas, Utah and California, it is a repetition of the same story. If the indulgent reader is struck

with the monotony of the descriptions given of these men, he will generously remember that, when not of the same immediate family, they are nearly all of the same race and of kindred qualities. Believing that distinguishing characteristics of mind and body appear in families and different breeds, as well as in races of men and women, and continue in them for many generations, for centuries,—for good or for evil, for honor or disgrace,—the writer offers no apology for the genealogical features of these pages. Nor does he deem it necessary to dwell upon the influence of Calvinism upon the character of these people, upon Kentucky, and upon the country. Secure, beyond all contradiction, *its* history stands fast. Exalting God, it abases man in His presence. Making all men lowly before Him, it renders them high and strong before kings. Extinguishing fear, making final triumph certain, inspiring with enthusiasm, it gives strength alike to the heart and arm of those whose faith is built upon its firm foundation. From the first moment their ranks were formed, the armies marching under its banners always began the swelling chorus of victory. The history of the faith is the story of its leaders and of the people imbued with its doctrines. Of these, none shed a more imperishable luster upon their race, than did the Scotch followers of John Knox, from whom the Virginians of the Valley have sprung. The latter were men whom Washington trusted in times that tried men's souls; they were men upon whom Lee, and the Confederacy, whose foremost military chieftain he was, leaned as upon a "strong right arm." Among them, both Lee and Washington found their most capable advisers in war and in peace. The names of these peerless Virginians are permanently linked with the history of that gallant race, and, in inseparable association, reflect luster upon the greatest of their schools. The distinctive qualities which exalt these fine, historic figures above the shabbiness, assumption, frivolity, indolence and coarse debauchery or superfine gentility of a "cavalier" environment, were precisely those mental and moral characteristics, which, by a natural affinity, brought them *en rapport* with the McDowells, Lewises, Campbells, Prestons, Jacksons and Stuarts of the Valley;—all of whom were " clansmen of an antique type, Calvinists of the strictest sect, and, in their social characteristics, Virginians to the manner born."

INDEX.

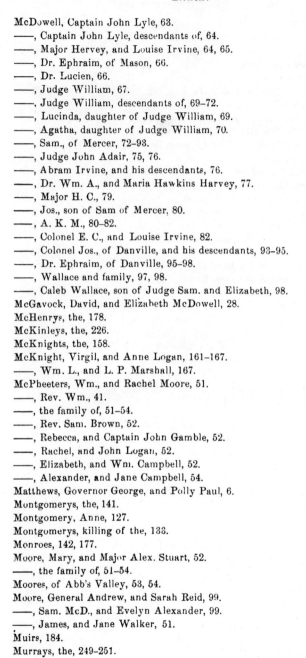